S0-BII-468

THE ENGLISH LITERARY JOURNAL TO 1900

AMERICAN LITERATURE, ENGLISH LITERATURE, AND WORLD LITERATURES IN ENGLISH: AN INFORMATION GUIDE SERIES

Series Editor: Theodore Grieder, Curator, Division of Special Collections, Fales Library, New York University, New York, New York

Associate Editor: Duane DeVries, Assistant Professor, Polytechnic Institute of New York, Brooklyn, New York

Other books on American and English literature in this series:

THE ENGLISH LITERARY JOURNAL, 1900-1950—*Edited by Michael N. Stanton**

THE LITERARY JOURNAL IN AMERICA TO 1900—*Edited by Edward Chielens*

THE LITERARY JOURNAL IN AMERICA, 1900-1950—*Edited by Edward Chielens**

ENGLISH DRAMA TO 1660—*Edited by Frieda Elaine Penninger*

ENGLISH DRAMA, 1660-1800—*Edited by Frederick M. Link*

ENGLISH DRAMA AND THEATRE, 1880-1900—*Edited by L. W. Conolly and J. P. Wearing*

ENGLISH DRAMA, 1900-1950—*Edited by E. H. Mikhail*

CONTEMPORARY DRAMA IN AMERICA AND ENGLAND, 1950-1970—*Edited by Richard H. Harris**

ENGLISH-CANADIAN LITERATURE TO 1900—*Edited by R. G. Moyles*

ENGLISH PROSE, PROSE FICTION, AND CRITICISM TO 1600—*Edited by S. K. Heninger, Jr.*

OLD AND MIDDLE ENGLISH POETRY TO 1500—*Edited by Walter H. Beale*

ENGLISH POETRY, 1500-1660—*Edited by S. K. Heninger, Jr.**

ENGLISH POETRY, 1660-1800—*Edited by Christopher Cohane**

ENGLISH POETRY IN THE NINETEENTH CENTURY—*Edited by Donald Reiman**

ENGLISH POETRY, 1900-1950—*Edited by Emily Ann Anderson**

CONTEMPORARY POETRY IN AMERICA AND ENGLAND, 1950-1970—*Edited by Calvin Skaggs**

*in preparation

The above series is part of the

GALE INFORMATION GUIDE LIBRARY

The Library consists of a number of separate series of guides covering major areas in the social sciences, humanities, and current affairs.

General Editor: Paul Wasserman, Professor and former Dean, School of Library and Information Services, University of Maryland

THE ENGLISH LITERARY JOURNAL TO 1900

A GUIDE TO INFORMATION SOURCES

Volume 8 in the American Literature, English Literature, and World Literatures in English Information Guide Series

Robert B. White, Jr.

Professor of English
North Carolina State University

Gale Research Company
Book Tower, Detroit, Michigan 48226

Library of Congress Cataloging in Publication Data

White, Robert B 1930-
The English literary journal to 1900.

(American literature, English literature, and world literatures in English information guide series ; v. 8) (Gale information guide library)
Includes index.
1. English periodicals--History--Bibliography. 2. English literature--Periodicals--History--Bibliography. I. Title.
Z6956.G6W47 [PN5114] 016.81'05 73-16998
ISBN 0-8103-1228-X

VITA

Robert B. White, Jr. is currently professor and assistant head of the department of English at North Carolina State University where he has taught for eighteen years. He received his A.B., his M.A., and his Ph.D. from the University of North Carolina at Chapel Hill. He has published a number of articles on a variety of subjects including British periodicals, Shakespeare, PARADISE LOST, Ben Jonson's poetry, Chaucer's CANTERBURY TALES, and SIR GAWAIN AND THE GREEN KNIGHT.

CONTENTS

PREFACE

I have endeavored--and, I hasten to add, without hope of completeness--to compile a bibliography of what has been written since about 1890 and what is now accessible to the general reader concerning pre-1900 British literary periodicals. Several categories of material have been excluded. At the request of my publisher I have not included any foreign language publications, a category easily enough identified, or any "obscure" and "rare" materials not generally available, a category not so easily identified. Not all of the items included here are generally available, but all are important for the serious researcher; some items which have been omitted would certainly have been judged differently by other bibliographers. At my own determination, for example, the materials pertaining to the Junius letters have been excluded. What follows, then, is a bibliography of secondary materials and modern critical editions of primary materials. It constitutes, I believe, more than the general user will need or, for that matter, have available. For those researchers who wish to pursue their subjects beyond the resources listed here, guides for their tasks are listed in chapter 1: "Bibliographies and Bibliographical Aids." The bibliographies by Weed and Bond (No. 118) and by Ward (Nos. 112 and 113) will be particularly useful, and may be augmented by many other bibliographies. Students of the periodical have good reason to be profoundly grateful to Professors Bond and Ward, for each has devoted a lifetime to careful study of the periodic press, and each has shared generously the fruits of his research with others.

Since my concern has been for the literary periodical before 1900, this is by no means a definitive bibliography of studies of the newspaper and its development, though much appears here which pertains to both newspapers and literary periodicals. In their early history, at least, the two are virtually indistinguishable. Further, the sections here on Swift, Dickens, Johnson, Burke, Coleridge, Gaskell, or even Addison should not be considered definitive, since only his or her relationship to the literary periodic press is relevant to the bibliography. Many of my entries cite references to reviews, but I have not attempted completeness here. Neither have I hoped for completeness in the listing of dissertations, though many are included. The pressure of time and space has prevented more extensive annotation of entries. Under each main heading, authors are listed alphabetically; however, if several entries by the same author are listed together, they are arranged in chronological order to prevent an item containing "Further comments on . . ." from preceding the item it should follow.

In format, I have listed first a group of useful bibliographies and bibliographical aids and then a section of general studies of the periodic press. Chapter 3, the largest, is an alphabetical list of titles of periodicals with relevant studies. All books and articles have been listed under periodical titles where possible. The fourth and fifth chapters are concerned with persons and places respectively. At the risk of redundancy I have made cross-references wherever I have seen even the slightest need for such an aid. The latest year of attempted comprehensive coverage was 1972, though some items published since then do appear.

Finally, I would like to express my appreciation to several people. My general editor, Theodore Grieder, has been generous with both encouragement and tolerance as has Dedria Bryfonski of the Gale Research Co. My debt to Professor Richmond P. Bond is extensive. He has been teacher, adviser, critic, and friend for many years. It was upon his recommendation that I was invited to take up this project; and with his kind permission and encouragement, I have adapted the format and a portion of the content of this work from the bibliography compiled by him and Katherine Kirtley Weed published in 1946 (see chapter 1, No. 118). Whatever merits the present work may have are owing to him; its defects, of course, are my own. Also I would like to thank my wife, Barbara, for her enthusiastic support and encouragement.

A last word, one of sincere apology, is due those critics and scholars whose works, great and small, I have inadvertently overlooked.

ABBREVIATIONS

ABC AMERICAN BOOK COLLECTOR

AH AMERICAN HERITAGE

AHR AMERICAN HISTORICAL REVIEW

AL AMERICAN LITERATURE

AQ AMERICAN QUARTERLY

AS AMERICAN SPEECH

ATQ AMERICAN TRANSCENDENTAL QUARTERLY

AULLA Australasian Universities Language and Literature Association (PROCEEDINGS)

BC BOOK COLLECTOR

BIHR BULLETIN OF THE INSTITUTE OF HISTORICAL RESEARCH

BNYPL BULLETIN OF THE NEW YORK PUBLIC LIBRARY

BSUF BALL STATE UNIVERSITY FORUM

BUSE BOSTON UNIVERSITY STUDIES IN ENGLISH

CLSB CHARLES LAMB SOCIETY BULLETIN

CompLit COMPARATIVE LITERATURE

ConR CONTEMPORARY REVIEW

CR CRITICAL REVIEW

DA DISSERTATION ABSTRACTS

DAI DISSERTATION ABSTRACTS INTERNATIONAL

DownR DOWNSIDE REVIEW

EA ETUDES ANGLAISES

EC ESSAYS IN CRITICISM

ECS EIGHTEENTH-CENTURY STUDIES

EHR ENGLISH HISTORICAL REVIEW

ELH ELH: A JOURNAL OF ENGLISH LITERARY HISTORY

ELN ENGLISH LANGUAGE NOTES

ES ENGLISH STUDIES

ESQ EMERSON SOCIETY QUARTERLY

EUQ EMORY UNIVERSITY QUARTERLY

Abbreviations

FR — FORTNIGHTLY REVIEW

HLB — HUNTINGTON LIBRARY BULLETIN

HLQ — HUNTINGTON LIBRARY QUARTERLY

JEGP — JOURNAL OF ENGLISH AND GERMANIC PHILOLOGY

JGE — JOURNAL OF GENERAL EDUCATION

JHI — JOURNAL OF THE HISTORY OF IDEAS

JMH — JOURNAL OF MODERN HISTORY

JNT — JOURNAL OF NARRATIVE TECHNIQUE

JPC — JOURNAL OF POPULAR CULTURE

JPE — JOURNAL OF POLITICAL ECONOMY

JQ — JOURNALISM QUARTERLY

JRLB — JOHN RYLANDS LIBRARY BULLETIN

JRUL — JOURNAL OF THE RUTGERS UNIVERSITY LIBRARY

KSJ — KEATS-SHELLEY JOURNAL

KSMB — KEATS-SHELLEY MEMORIAL BULLETIN

ManR — MANCHESTER REVIEW

MLN — MODERN LANGUAGE NOTES

MLQ — MODERN LANGUAGE QUARTERLY

MLR — MODERN LANGUAGE REVIEW

MMR — MONTHLY MUSICAL REVIEW

MP — MODERN PHILOLOGY

N&Q — NOTES & QUERIES

NC — NINETEENTH CENTURY

NCF — NINETEENTH-CENTURY FICTION

NEMLA — Northeast Modern Language Association (NEWSLETTER)

NR — NATIONAL REVIEW

PBSA — PAPERS OF THE BIBLIOGRAPHICAL SOCIETY OF AMERICA

PELL — PAPERS ON ENGLISH LANGUAGE AND LITERATURE

PLL — PAPERS ON LANGUAGE AND LITERATURE

PLPLS-LHS — PROCEEDINGS OF THE LEEDS PHILOSOPHICAL AND LITERARY SOCIETY, LITERARY AND HISTORICAL SECTION

PMLA — PMLA: PUBLICATIONS OF THE MODERN LANGUAGE ASSOCIATION

PQ — PHILOLOGICAL QUARTERLY

PULC — PRINCETON UNIVERSITY LIBRARY CHRONICLE

QJS — QUARTERLY JOURNAL OF SPEECH

QR — QUARTERLY REVIEW

RECTR — RESTORATION AND EIGHTEENTH-CENTURY THEATRE RESEARCH

REL	REVIEW OF ENGLISH LITERATURE (Leeds)
RES	REVIEW OF ENGLISH STUDIES
RS	RESEARCH STUDIES (Washington State University)
SAMLA	South Atlantic Modern Language Association
SAQ	SOUTH ATLANTIC QUARTERLY
SB	STUDIES IN BIBLIOGRAPHY
SBHT	STUDIES IN BURKE AND HIS TIME
SEL	STUDIES IN ENGLISH LITERATURE
SGG	STUDIA GERMANICA GANDENSIA
SIR	STUDIES IN ROMANTICISM
SN&Q	SCOTTISH NOTES & QUERIES
SNL	SATIRE NEWSLETTER
SP	STUDIES IN PHILOLOGY
SR	SEWANEE REVIEW
SRAZ	STUDIA ROMANICA ET ANGLICA ZAGRABIENSIA
SSL	STUDIES IN SCOTTISH LITERATURE
TLS	TIMES LITERARY SUPPLEMENT (London)
TN	THEATRE NOTEBOOK
TQ	TEXAS QUARTERLY
TSE	TEXAS STUDIES IN ENGLISH
UDR	UNIVERSITY OF DAYTON REVIEW
URLB	UNIVERSITY OF ROCHESTER LIBRARY BULLETIN
UTQ	UNIVERSITY OF TORONTO QUARTERLY
VN	VICTORIAN NEWSLETTER
VPN	VICTORIAN PERIODICALS NEWSLETTER
VS	VICTORIAN STUDIES
WHR	WESTERN HUMANITIES REVIEW
YES	YEARBOOK OF ENGLISH STUDIES

Chapter 1

BIBLIOGRAPHIES AND BIBLIOGRAPHICAL AIDS

1. Altick, Richard D. "Nineteenth-Century English Periodicals." NEWBERRY LIBRARY BULLETIN, 2d ser., 9 (1952), 255-64.

   Concerned generally with the Newberry Library's collection of nineteenth-century British periodicals.

2. Altick, Richard D., and William R. Matthews. GUIDE TO DOCTORAL DISSERTATIONS IN VICTORIAN LITERATURE, 1886-1958. Urbana: University of Illinois Press, 1960.

3. ANNUAL BIBLIOGRAPHY OF ENGLISH LANGUAGE AND LITERATURE [1920--]. Cambridge: Modern Humanities Research Association, 1921--.

4. "Appendix: Current Bibliographies." PQ, 50 (1971), 499-507.

5. Arber, Edward. "Contemporary Printed Lists of Books Produced in England." BIBLIOGRAPHICA, 3 (1897), 173-91.

   Includes data on such serial lists as the Term Catalogues, MERCURIUS LIBRARIUS (1680), and MONTHLY CATALOGUE (Lintot's and Wilford's).

6. Barwick, G.F. "Some Magazines of the Eighteenth Century." TRANSACTIONS OF THE BIBLIOGRAPHICAL SOCIETY, 10 (1901), 109-40.

   Lists sixty miscellaneous London magazines, eighteen provincial, fifteen Scottish, twenty-seven Irish, and one hundred on special subjects (agriculture and commerce, history and biography, literature, politics, religion, social, etc.) with remarks on the most important.

7. Bateson, F.W., ed. THE CAMBRIDGE BIBLIOGRAPHY OF ENGLISH LITERATURE. 4 vols. New York: Macmillan; Cambridge: At the University Press, 1941.

The following sections are relevant to this bibliography: "News-Sheets and News-Books" (vol. I, pages 736-63); "Essayists and Pamphleteers" (vol. II, pages 567-656); "Periodical Publications" (vol. II, pages 656-739); and "Newspapers and Magazines" (vol. III, pages 779-846). Reviews appear in MP, 39:303-12; PQ, 21:251-56; LIBRARY, 22:250-55. See also No. 117.

8. ______. THE CAMBRIDGE BIBLIOGRAPHY OF ENGLISH LITERATURE. Vol. V: SUPPLEMENT: A.D. 600-1900. Ed. George Watson. Cambridge: At the University Press, 1957.

Reviews appear in TLS, 4 October 1957, p. 600; LIBRARY, 13:208-10; PBSA, 52:68-70. See also No. 117.

9. Batho, Edith C., and Bonamy Dobrée. THE VICTORIANS AND AFTER: 1830-1914. Introductions to English Literature, no. 4. General ed. Bonamy Dobree. London: Cresset Press, 1940.

10. Berg, Virginia. "Holdings of 17th and 18th Century English Newspapers in the University of Illinois Library, Urbana." CORANTO, no. 2 (October 1950), pp. 4-7.

11. Bernbaum, Ernest. "Keats, Shelley, Byron, Hunt: A Critical Sketch of Important Books and Articles Concerning Them Published in 1940-1950." KSJ, 1 (1952), 73-85.

12. Besterman, Theodore. A WORLD BIBLIOGRAPHY OF BIBLIOGRAPHIES AND OF BIBLIOGRAPHICAL CATALOGUES, CALENDARS, ABSTRACTS, DIGESTS, INDEXES, AND THE LIKE. 3d and final ed. 4 vols. Geneva: Societas Bibliographical, 1955-56.

Reviewed in JOURNAL OF DOCUMENTATION, 12:44-46.

13. Bleackley, Horace. "A Bibliography of Forgotten Magazines." N&Q, 2 (1916), 143-45.

Describes briefly some of the ribald miscellanies of the late eighteenth and early nineteenth centuries.

14. Bolton, Henry Carrington. A CATALOGUE OF SCIENTIFIC AND TECHNICAL PERIODICALS, 1665-1895. 2d ed. Washington, D.C.: Smithsonian Institution, 1897.

15. Bond, Richmond P. "English Literary Periodicals to Form Microfilm Series." LIBRARY JOURNAL, 76 (1951), 125-28.

16. Bond, Richmond P., and Marjorie N. Bond, comps. 'THE TATLER' AND

'THE SPECTATOR' AND THE DEVELOPMENT OF THE EARLY PERIODIC PRESS IN ENGLAND: A CHECKLIST OF THE COLLECTION OF RICHMOND P. BOND AND MARJORIE N. BOND. Chapel Hill, N.C.: Privately printed, 1965.

A listing of 600 titles in a remarkable private collection which has now been purchased for the Kenneth Spencer Research Library of the University of Kansas at Lawrence.

17. Bristol Public Libraries. EARLY BRISTOL NEWSPAPERS: A DETAILED CATALOGUE OF BRISTOL NEWSPAPERS UP TO AND INCLUDING THE YEAR 1800 IN THE BRISTOL REFERENCE LIBRARY. Bristol: 1956.

A review appears in TLS, 28 September 1956, p. 574.

18. British Museum. Department of Printed Books. CATALOGUE OF PRINTED BOOKS: PERIODICAL PUBLICATIONS. London: William Clowes and Sons, 1885-86.

In six parts and an index. The items are entered under the place of publication; parts III-IV are devoted to London.

19. British Museum. Thomason Collection. "Newspapers, 1641-1663." CATALOGUE OF THE PAMPHLETS, BOOKS, NEWSPAPERS, AND MANUSCRIPTS RELATING TO THE CIVIL WAR, THE COMMONWEALTH, AND RESTORATION COLLECTED BY GEORGE THOMASON, 1640-1661. London: 1908. II, 371-440.

20. BRITISH PERIODICALS IN THE CREATIVE ARTS. Ann Arbor, Mich.: University Microfilms, 1972.

Includes British periodicals dealing with fine arts, architecture, archaeology, drama, and music published between 1770 and the early twentieth century and available through University Microfilms.

21. BRITISH PERIODICALS--LITERARY, 17TH-19TH CENTURIES. Ann Arbor, Mich.: University Microfilms, n.d.

22. BRITISH PERIODICALS, 17TH-19TH CENTURY, GENERAL. Ann Arbor, Mich.: University Microfilms, n.d.

Periodicals dealing with politics, economics, philosophy, and the social scene.

23. Buckley, Jerome H. VICTORIAN POETS AND PROSE WRITERS. Goldentree Bibliographies. New York: Appleton-Century-Crofts, 1966.

24. Burnett, Virginia S. "Seventeenth-Century English Newspapers and

Periodicals." JRUL, 7 (1943), 9-27.

An annotated bibliography of the Rutgers holdings. See also No. 46.

25. California. State Library. Sutro Branch. CATALOGUE OF ENGLISH PAMPHLETS IN THE SUTRO LIBRARY. Part II: SEVENTEENTH CENTURY PERIODICALS. Comp. Helen M. Brunner. San Francisco: Works Projects Administration, 1941. Mimeographed.

26. Cannon, Carl L. JOURNALISM: A BIBLIOGRAPHY. New York: New York Public Library, 1924.

Reprinted with additions from BNYPL, 27 (1923).

27. CATALOGUE OF A COLLECTION OF EARLY NEWSPAPERS AND ESSAYISTS, FORMED BY THE LATE JOHN THOMAS HOPE. Comp. Jacob Henry Burn. Oxford: Clarendon Press, 1865.

28. Chicago, University Library. Document Section. NEWSPAPERS IN LIBRARIES OF CHICAGO. A JOINT CHECK LIST. Chicago: 1936.

29. Cordasco, Francesco. A REGISTER OF 18TH CENTURY BIBLIOGRAPHIES AND REFERENCES: A CHRONOLOGICAL QUARTER-CENTURY SURVEY RELATING TO ENGLISH LITERATURE, BOOKSELLERS, NEWSPAPERS, PERIODICALS, PRINTING & PUBLISHING; AESTHETICS, ART & MUSIC; ECONOMICS, HISTORY & SCIENCE. Chicago: V. Giorgio; Milan: Sansoni; Rome: Vallecchi; Paris: Alberto Tallone, 1950.

More than 500 titles, grouped according to year of publication.

30. _____. EIGHTEENTH CENTURY BIBLIOGRAPHIES. HANDLISTS OF CRITICAL STUDIES RELATING TO SMOLLETT, RICHARDSON, STERNE, FIELDING, DIBDIN, 18TH CENTURY MEDICINE, THE 18TH CENTURY NOVEL, GODWIN, GIBBON, YOUNG, AND BLAKE. TO WHICH IS ADDED JOHN P. ANDERSON'S BIBLIOGRAPHY OF SMOLLETT. Metuchen, N.J.: Scarecrow, 1970.

31. Cotton, Henry. A TYPOGRAPHICAL GAZATTEER. Oxford: Clarendon Press, 1825. 2d ed., 1831.

32. Crane, R[onald]. S., and F.B. Kaye, with M.E. Prior. "A Census of British Newspapers and Periodicals, 1620-1800." SP, 24 (1927), 1-205.

Reviews appear in TLS, 20 October 1927, p. 739; TLS, 22 December 1927, p. 977; RES, 5:241-43. See also R.S. Crane and F.B. Kaye in TLS, 15 December 1927, p. 961.

33. Cranfield, G.A. A HAND-LIST OF ENGLISH PROVINCIAL NEWSPAPERS AND PERIODICALS, 1700-1760. Cambridge Bibliographical Society, Monographs no. 2. Cambridge: Bowes and Bowes, 1952.

A review appears in TLS, 13 March 1952, p. 176. See also next item and No. 119.

34. _____. "Handlist of English Provincial Newspapers and Periodicals, 1700-1760. Additions and Corrections." TRANSACTIONS OF THE CAMBRIDGE BIBLIOGRAPHICAL SOCIETY, 2, pt. III (1956), 269-74.

See also previous item and No. 119.

35. Crossley, J. "'Works of the Learned.'" N&Q, 6 (1852), 435-37.

A list of literary journals published in Great Britain from 1665-1749. In this same volume of N&Q, see the material by M. on page 271 and that by Arterus on page 327.

36. "Current Bibliography [of Keats, Shelley, Byron, Hunt, etc., 1950-]." KSJ, annually, 1952--.

Collected by David B. Green and Edwin C. Wilson in KEATS, SHELLEY, BYRON, HUNT, AND THEIR CIRCLES: A BIBLIOGRAPHY, JULY 1, 1950-JUNE 30, 1962 (Lincoln: University of Nebraska Press, 1964).

37. Dahl, Folke. "Short-Title Catalogue of English Corantos and Newsbooks, 1620-1642." LIBRARY, 19 (1938), 44-95.

38. Davies, Godfrey, ed. BIBLIOGRAPHY OF BRITISH HISTORY, STUART PERIOD, 1603-1714. 2d ed., rev. by Mary Frear Keeler. Oxford: Clarendon Press, 1970.

39. Dyson, J.V.D., and John Butt. "Journalism." AUGUSTANS AND ROMANTICS, 1689-1830. Introductions to English Literature, no. 3. General ed. Bonamy Dobrée. London: Cresset Press, 1940. Pp. 264-73.

40. Egoff, Shelia A. CHILDREN'S PERIODICALS OF THE NINETEENTH CENTURY: A SURVEY AND BIBLIOGRAPHY. Library Association Pamphlets, no. 8. London: Library Association, 1951.

41. Ehrsam, Theodore G., and Robert H. Deily, comps., under the direction of Robert M. Smith. BIBLIOGRAPHIES OF TWELVE VICTORIAN AUTHORS. New York: H.W. Wilson, 1936; rpt. New York: Octagon, 1968.

Includes M. Arnold, E.B. Browning, Clough, Fitzgerald,

Hardy, Kipling, Morris, C. Rossetti, D. Rossetti, Stevenson, Swinburne, and Tennyson. See also the "Supplement" to this work published as an addendum to the "Victorian Bibliography for 1937," MP, 37 (1938), 89-96.

42. "The Eighteenth Century: A Current Bibliography [1925-]." PQ, annually, 1926--.

Prior to 1971, this annual bibliography was titled "English Literature, 1660-1800: A Current Bibliography." Issues for 1925-70 were collected by Louis A. Landa and others for ENGLISH LITERATURE, 1660-1800: A BIBLIOGRAPHY OF MODERN STUDIES, published in six volumes (Princeton, N.J.: Princeton University Press, 1950-72).

43. ENGLISH LITERARY PERIODICALS. Ann Arbor, Mich.: University Microfilms, n.d.

A catalog of literary periodicals published in Britain from the seventeenth through the nineteenth centuries and now available on microfilm.

44. "Existing Newspapers and Periodicals of the Seventeenth & Eighteenth Centuries, Arranged Chronologically"; "Titular Changes and Amalgamations." WILLING'S PRESS GUIDE, 43 (1916), 419-20, 421-38.

45. Fielding K.J. "Edinburgh Check-List 1840-80." VPN, 2 (1968), 23.

A checklist concerning nineteenth-century newspapers and periodicals.

46. French, J. Milton. "Seventeenth-Century English Newsbooks." JRUL, 7 (1943), 1-8.

See also No. 24.

47. Gabler, Anthony J. "Check List of English Newspapers and Periodicals Before 1801 in the Huntington Library." HLB, no. 2 (November 1931), pp. 1-66.

48. Garrison, Fielding H. "The Medical and Scientific Periodicals of the 17th and 18th Centuries. With a Revised Catalogue and Check-List." BULLETIN OF THE INSTITUTE OF THE HISTORY OF MEDICINE, 2 (1934), 285-343.

Includes Europe and North America. See also No. 65.

49. Gerould, James Thayer. "Newspapers." SOURCES OF ENGLISH HISTORY OF THE SEVENTEENTH CENTURY, 1603-1689, IN THE UNIVER-

SITY OF MINNESOTA LIBRARY. Research Publications of the University of Minnesota, Bibliographical Series, no. 1. Minneapolis: University of Minnesota Press, 1921. Pp. 27-31.

50. Gibbons, G.S. "A Monthly Magazine of 1789." N&Q, 170 (1936), 458.

Describes a bound volume (with missing title page) of a magazine published by Alexander Hogg.

51. Graham, Robert X. A BIBLIOGRAPHY IN THE HISTORY AND BACKGROUND OF JOURNALISM. Pittsburgh: University of Pittsburgh, 1940.

52. Gregory, Winifred, ed. UNION LIST OF SERIALS IN LIBRARIES IN THE UNITED STATES AND CANADA. 2d ed. New York: H.W. Wilson, 1943.

See also the supplement for 1941-43, edited by Gabrielle E. Malikoff. (New York: H.W. Wilson, 1945), and No. 107.

53. Grose, Clyde Leclare. A SELECT BIBLIOGRAPHY OF BRITISH HISTORY, 1660-1760. Chicago: University of Chicago Press, 1939.

54. HANDLIST OF SEVENTEENTH CENTURY NEWSPAPERS IN THE GUILDHALL LIBRARY. London: Library Committee of the Corporation of London, 1954.

Reviewed in TLS, 12 November 1954, p. 726.

55. Haskell, Daniel C. CHECKLIST OF NEWSPAPERS AND OFFICIAL GAZETTES IN THE NEW YORK PUBLIC LIBRARY. New York: New York Public Library, 1915.

Reprinted from BNYPL, 18-19 (1914-15).

56. Houghton, Walter E. "British Periodicals of the Victorian Age: Bibliographies and Indexes." LIBRARY TRENDS, 7 (1969), 554-65.

57. _____, ed. THE WELLESLEY INDEX TO VICTORIAN PERIODICALS, 1824-1900. TABLES OF CONTENTS AND IDENTIFICATION OF CONTRIBUTORS WITH BIBLIOGRAPHIES OF THEIR ARTICLES AND STORIES. 2 vols. Toronto: University of Toronto Press; London: Routledge and Kegan Paul. Vol. I, 1966; vol. II, 1972.

Volume I includes BLACKWOOD'S MAGAZINE, CONTEMPORARY REVIEW, CORNHILL MAGAZINE, EDINBURGH REVIEW, HOME AND FOREIGN REVIEW, MACMILLAN'S MAGAZINE,

NORTH BRITISH REVIEW, and QUARTERLY REVIEW. Volume II includes BENTLEY'S QUARTERLY REVIEW, DUBLIN REVIEW, FOREIGN QUARTERLY REVIEW, FORTNIGHTLY REVIEW, FRASER'S MAGAZINE, LONDON REVIEW, NATIONAL REVIEW, NEW QUARTERLY MAGAZINE, NINETEENTH CENTURY, OXFORD AND CAMBRIDGE MAGAZINE, RAMBLER, and SCOTTISH REVIEW.

58. Jaryc, Marc. "Studies of 1935-1942 on the History of the Periodical Press," JMH, 15 (1943), 127-41.

59. Landon, Philip J. "A Proposal for Compiling a List of Victorian Periodical Holdings in the Baltimore-Washington Area." VPN, 3 (1968), 9-11.

60. ______. "Research in Victorian Periodicals: A Checklist of Doctoral Dissertations in the U.S., 1921-67." VPN, 5-6 (1969), 33-44.

61. Lang, W.J. "Unlocated British Newspapers and Periodicals (Ante 1801)." N&Q, 166 (1934), 83, 99-100, 116-17, 339-40, 423, 466; 167 (1934), 62-63, 83-84.

Other relevant material may be found in N&Q, volume 166, by H. Tapley-Soper (page 86), J. Ardagh (pages 124-25 and 141), G.E. Flack, R.S.B., and V.H. (pages 156-57), Corrigendum (page 180), J.W. Fawcett (page 124), H.I.A. (page 319), and F.C. Morgan and J.W. Fawcett (page 357). In volume 167 of N&Q, see also the material by Edward Bensly, R.T. Milford, and G.W. Wright (page 32), C.J. Hindle (page 100), and Alfred Welby (page 159). Lang was collecting data for a "Bibliographical Register of British and Irish Newspapers and Periodicals Printed in the United Kingdom Before 1801."

62. [Layton, W.E.] "Early Periodicals." BIBLIOGRAPHER, 3 (1883), 36-39.

Annotated list of eighty-two papers from TATLER to RAMBLER period, based in part on manuscript notes in Charles Miller's copy of the SPECTATOR.

63. Lee, W[illiam]. "Forgotten Periodical Publications." N&Q, 9 (1866), 53-54.

64. ______. "Periodical Publications During the Twenty Years 1712 to 1732." N&Q, 9 (1866), 72-75, 92-95.

See also N&Q, volume 9, for the material by Llewellynn

Jewitt (page 164) and C.N. (page 268). See volume 10 (1866), for other work by W. Lee (page 134) and J. McC. B. (page 134).

65. Lefanu, W.R. "British Periodicals of Medicine: A Chronological List. Part I: 1684-1899." BULLETIN OF THE INSTITUTE OF THE HISTORY OF MEDICINE, 5 (1937), 735-61, 827-55.

See also No. 48.

66. _____. BRITISH PERIODICALS OF MEDICINE: A CHRONOLOGICAL LIST. Baltimore, Md.: Johns Hopkins University Press, 1938.

67. Lloyd, George. "Newspapers of the Last Two Centuries." N&Q 5 (1870), 531.

Also in N&Q, volume 5, see the work by Charles Mason (page 591); in volume 6 (1870), see Llewellynn Jewitt (page 63) and Charles Vivian (page 123). Lloyd's work is a list of newspapers with the word "Post" in their titles.

68. Lowndes, William Thomas. THE BIBLIOGRAPHER'S MANUAL OF ENGLISH LITERATURE. New ed., rev., corrected, and enl. by Henry G. Bohn. 5 vols. London: Henry G. Bohn, 1857-63. VI, 1669-71.

List of "News."

69. Lysiak, Arthur W. "Victorian Periodicals and Newspapers in Microfilm." VPN, 16 (1972), 29-46.

70. MacMichael, J. Holden. "Periodicals for Women." N&Q, 1 (1904), 295.

See also N&Q, volume 1, for the material by John Pickford (page 397), and No. 379.

71. Madden, Lionel. "Proposed Bibliography of Writings About Victorian Periodicals." VPN, 2 (1968), 18-19.

72. "Microfilm of British Dramatic Periodicals at Loyola University, Chicago." RECTR, 2 (1963), 20-31; 3 (1964), 46-50.

73. Milford, R.T., and D.M. Sutherland. "A Catalogue of English Newspapers and Periodicals in the Bodleian Library, 1622-1800." [OXFORD] BIBLIOGRAPHICAL SOCIETY PROCEEDINGS & PAPERS, IV, pt. 2 (1935, 1936), 167-346.

Reviewed in TLS, 9 January 1937, p. 32.

74. MLA INTERNATIONAL BIBLIOGRAPHY OF BOOKS AND ARTICLES ON THE MODERN LANGUAGES AND LITERATURES. New York: Modern Language Association, 1922--.

Earlier titles of this continuing bibliography were AMERICAN BIBLIOGRAPHY and ANNUAL BIBLIOGRAPHY. Prior to the 1956 issue, the bibliography included only books and articles by American scholars.

75. Morgan, William Thomas. A BIBLIOGRAPHY OF BRITISH HISTORY (1700-1715), WITH SPECIAL REFERENCE TO THE REIGN OF QUEEN ANNE. 5 vols. (Vols. IV and V with Chloe Siner Morgan). Bloomington: University of Indiana Press, 1939.

76. Morison, Stanley. "The Bibliography of Newspapers and the Writing of History." LIBRARY, 9 (1954), 153-75.

77. Muddiman, J.G. "The History and Bibliography of English Newspapers." N&Q, 160 (1931), 3-6, 21-24, 40-43, 57-59, 207-9, 227-29, 298-300, 337-38, 375-76, 442-43.

See also N&Q, volume 160, for work by R.T. Milford (page 174), J.C. Burch (pages 174-75), E.E. Newton (pages 229-30 and 336-37), H. Kendra Baker (page 264), and Herbert Southam (page 391). Muddiman's series of articles was part of a debate initiated by criticism of the Crane and Kaye "Census" (see No. 32) written by the compiler of the TERCENTENARY HANDLIST (see No. 106). An acrimonious dispute developed over the comparative accuracy of the "Census" and the HANDLIST.

78. NATIONAL REGISTER OF MICROFILM MASTERS. Compiled by the Library of Congress with the Cooperation of the American Library Association and the Association of Research Libraries. Washington, D.C.: 1966-68.

79. NEWSPAPERS ON MICROFILM: A UNION CHECKLIST. Compiled under the direction of George A. Schwegmann, Jr. Philadelphia: Association of Research Libraries, 1949; 2d ed. Washington, D.C.: Library of Congress, 1953.

A review of the first edition appears in LIBRARY, 4:153-54.

80. NINETEENTH CENTURY READER'S GUIDE TO PERIODICAL LITERATURE, 1890-1899. WITH SUPPLEMENTARY INDEXING, 1900-1922. Ed. Helen G. Cushing and Adah V. Morris. 2 vols. New York: Wilson, 1944.

Reviewed in JEGP, 44:225-27. Includes only 51 periodicals,

compared to POOLE'S 187, but valuable nonetheless.

81. O'Neill, James. "Victorian Periodicals and Newspapers in Microform: A Preliminary List, and Proposals." VPN, 7 (1970), 14-28.

82. Oxford University, Bodleian Library. CATALOGUE OF PERIODICALS CONTAINED IN THE BODLEIAN LIBRARY. 2 vols. Oxford: Oxford University Press, 1878-80.

See also No. 73.

83. Pargellis, Stanley, and D.J. Medley, eds. BIBLIOGRAPHY OF BRITISH HISTORY: THE EIGHTEENTH CENTURY, 1714-1789. Oxford: Clarendon Press, 1951.

84. Parkes, Samuel. "An Account of the Periodical Literary Journals Which Were Published in Great Britain and Ireland, from the Year 1681 to the Commencement of the MONTHLY REVIEW, in the Year 1749." QUARTERLY JOURNAL OF SCIENCE, LITERATURE, AND THE ARTS, 13 (1822), 36-58, 289-312.

85. Peet, Hubert W. A BIBLIOGRAPHY OF JOURNALISM; A GUIDE TO THE BOOKS ABOUT THE PRESS AND PRESSMEN. London: Sells, 1915.

"Repr. from the 1915 edition of SELL'S WORLD'S PRESS," pages 34-44.

86. PERIODICAL POST-BOY (Chapel Hill, N.C., and Austin, Tex.), nos. 1-15 (March 1948-June 1955). Mimeographed.

A serial publication for the encouragement of the study of British periodicals.

87. Price, Warren C., and Calder M. Pickett. AN ANNOTATED JOURNALISM BIBLIOGRAPHY, 1958-1968. Minneapolis: University of Minnesota Press, 1970.

88. R[ansom], H.H. "Recent Studies in Eighteenth Century Periodicals." PERIODICAL POST-BOY, no. 3 (March 1949), pp. 2-4.

89. "Recent Publications: A Selected List. . . ." VN, semiannually (September through February in Spring issue; March through August in Fall issue), 1961--.

90. "Recent Studies in the Nineteenth Century." SEL, annually (autumn issues), 1961--.

91. "Recent Studies in the Restoration and Eighteenth Century." SEL, annually (summer issues), 1961--.

92. Riffe, Nancy Lee. "Contributions to a Finding List of Eighteenth-Century Periodicals." BNYPL, 67 (1963), 431-34.

93. "The Romantic Movement: A Selective and Critical Bibliography" [1936-]. ELH, annually, 1937-49; PQ, annually, 1950-64; ELN, annually, 1965--.

94. THE ROTHSCHILD LIBRARY: A CATALOGUE OF THE COLLECTION OF EIGHTEENTH-CENTURY PRINTED BOOKS AND MANUSCRIPTS FORMED BY LORD ROTHSCHILD. 2 vols. Cambridge: Privately printed at the University Press, 1954.

   Lord Rothschild's collection includes some periodicals in addition to important collections of Boswell, Cowper, Defoe, Fielding, Gay, Givvon, Goldsmith, Johnson, Swift, and others.

95. Scottish Central Library. SCOTTISH NEWSPAPERS HELD IN SCOTTISH LIBRARIES. Comp. Miss J.P.S. Ferguson. Edinburgh: Scottish Central Library, 1956.

   Reviewed in TLS, 21 September, 1956, p. 558.

96. Shepard, Douglas H. "Some Early Lists of Victorian Periodicals." VPN, 8 (1970), 9-11.

97. Sparke, Archibald. "Forgotten Periodicals of 1830-33." N&Q, 8 (1921), 465-66, 488.

98. Sper, Felix. THE PERIODICAL PRESS OF LONDON, THEATRICAL AND LITERARY (EXCLUDING THE DAILY NEWSPAPER), 1800-1830. Useful Reference Series, no. 60. Boston: F.W. Faxon, 1937.

   A bibliography and finding list of primary materials.

99. Stewart, James D., Muriel E. Hammond, and Erwin Saenger, eds. BRITISH UNION-CATALOGUE OF PERIODICALS. 4 vols. London: Butterworths Scientific Publications, 1955-58. SUPPLEMENT, 1962.

   A bibliographical listing of all of the periodical holdings of every major library in Great Britain; also gives information on availability for loan or photocopy.

100. Stewart, Powell, ed. BRITISH NEWSPAPERS AND PERIODICALS, 1632-1800: A DESCRIPTIVE CATALOGUE OF A COLLECTION AT THE UNI-

VERSITY OF TEXAS. Austin: University of Texas, 1950.

Reviewed in PQ, 30:229-30.

101. Stratman, Carl J. A BIBLIOGRAPHY OF BRITISH DRAMATIC PERIODICALS 1720-1960. New York: New York Public Library, 1962.

See also No. 363.

102. _____. BRITAIN'S THEATRICAL PERIODICALS, 1720-1967: A BIBLIOGRAPHY. 2d ed. New York: New York Public Library, 1972.

103. SUBJECT GUIDE TO MICROFILMS IN PRINT. Ed. Albert James Diaz. Washington, D.C.: Microcard Editions, 1962.

104. Taylor, Archer, and Frederic J. Mosher. THE BIBLIOGRAPHICAL HISTORY OF ANONYMA AND PSEUDONYMA. Chicago: Published for the Newberry Library by the University of Chicago Press, 1951.

105. Thwaite, M[ary]. F[lorence]., comp. HERTFORDSHIRE NEWSPAPERS, 1772-1955: A LIST COMPILED FOR THE COUNTY BIBLIOGRAPHY. Foreword by Sir Harold Williams. Bengo: Hertfordshire Local History Council, 1956.

106. THE TIMES, London. TERCENTENARY HANDLIST OF ENGLISH & WELSH NEWSPAPERS, MAGAZINES & REVIEWS. London: 1920.

A chronological list in two sections--London and suburban, and provincial--with separate indices of titles. Reviewed in TLS, 3 December 1920, pp. 785-86. See also Roland Austin, "Tercentenary Handlist of Newspapers," N&Q, 8 (1921), 118, and other material by Austin in N&Q, 10 (1922), 191-94 and 213-14. See also Nora Richardson in N&Q 8 (1921), 173-74, 246, and 252-53, and Archibald Sparke in N&Q, 8 (1921), 174-75.

107. Titus, Edna Brown, ed. UNION LIST OF SERIALS IN LIBRARIES OF THE UNITED STATES AND CANADA. 3d ed. 5 vols. New York: H.W. Wilson, 1965.

See also No. 52.

108. Tobin, James E. EIGHTEENTH CENTURY ENGLISH LITERATURE AND ITS CULTURAL BACKGROUND. A BIBLIOGRAPHY. New York: Fordham University Press, 1939.

Relevant material may be found in the section entitled "Journalism," pages 46-50.

109. UNION CATALOGUE OF THE PERIODICAL PUBLICATIONS IN THE UNIVERSITY LIBRARIES OF THE BRITISH ISLES. . . . Comp. Marion G. Roupell. London: National Central Library, 1937.

110. UNION LIST OF MICROFILM. Rev. ed. Ann Arbor, Mich.: J.W. Edwards, 1951.

See also the cumulation of supplements for 1949-59, edited by Eleanor E. Campion and published in two volumes by J.W. Edwards (Ann Arbor, 1961). The UNION LIST must be used in conjunction with Schwegmann, No. 79.

111. "Victorian Bibliography [1932-]." MP, annually, 1933-57; VICTORIAN STUDIES, annually, 1958--.

Issues for 1932-64 were collected by William D. Templeman for BIBLIOGRAPHIES OF STUDIES IN VICTORIAN LITERATURE FOR 1932-1944 (Urbana: University of Illinois Press, 1945), by Austin Wright for BIBLIOGRAPHIES OF STUDIES IN VICTORIAN LITERATURE FOR . . . 1945-1954 (Urbana: University of Illinois Press, 1956), and by Robert C. Stack for BIBLIOGRAPHIES OF STUDIES IN VICTORIAN LITERATURE FOR . . . 1955-1964 (Urbana: University of Illinois Press, 1967).

112. Ward, William S[mith], comp. INDEX AND FINDING LIST OF SERIALS PUBLISHED IN THE BRITISH ISLES, 1789-1832. Lexington: University of Kentucky Press, 1953.

113. ______. BRITISH PERIODICALS & NEWSPAPERS, 1789-1832: A BIBLIOGRAPHY OF SECONDARY SOURCES. Lexington: University of Kentucky Press, 1972.

Lists more than 3,000 items of secondary material.

114. ______. LITERARY REVIEWS IN BRITISH PERIODICALS, 1798-1820: A BIBLIOGRAPHY. 2 vols. New York: Garland, 1971.

115. ______. "Index and Finding List of Serials Published in the British Isles, 1789-1832: A Supplementary List." BNYPL, 77 (1974), 291-97.

116. Watson, George, ed. THE CONCISE CAMBRIDGE BIBLIOGRAPHY OF ENGLISH LITERATURE, 600-1950. Cambridge: At the University Press, 1958.

117. ______. THE NEW CAMBRIDGE BIBLIOGRAPHY OF ENGLISH LITERATURE. Vol. II: 1660-1800. Vol. III: 1800-1900. Cambridge: At the University Press, 1971, 1969.

A review of Volume II appears in PQ, 51:517-18. See also Nos. 7 and 8.

118. Weed, Katherine Kirtley, and Richmond P. Bond. STUDIES OF BRITISH NEWSPAPERS AND PERIODICALS FROM THEIR BEGINNING TO 1800: A BIBLIOGRAPHY. Studies in Philology, Extra Ser., no. 2. Chapel Hill: University of North Carolina Press, 1946.

119. Wiles, R[oy]. M[cKeen]. "Further Additions and Corrections to G.A. Cranfield's HANDLIST OF ENGLISH PROVINCIAL NEWSPAPERS AND PERIODICALS, 1700-1760." TRANSACTIONS OF THE CAMBRIDGE BIBLIOGRAPHICAL SOCIETY, II, pt. V (1958), 385-89.

See also Nos. 33 and 34.

120. Williams, Iolo A. SEVEN XVIIITH CENTURY BIBLIOGRAPHIES. London: Dulau, 1924; rpt. New York: Burt Franklin, 1968.

Includes Armstrong, Akenside, Churchill, Collins, Goldsmith, Shenstone, and Sheridan.

121. Wing, Donald G. SHORT-TITLE CATALOGUE OF BOOKS PRINTED IN ENGLAND, SCOTLAND, IRELAND, WALES, AND BRITISH AMERICA, AND OF ENGLISH BOOKS PRINTED IN OTHER COUNTRIES, 1641-1700. New York: Printed for the Index Society by Columbia University Press, 1945-51.

122. YEAR'S WORK IN ENGLISH STUDIES [1919-]. Comp. the English Association. London, 1921--.

An annual collection of essays surveying the previous year's scholarship in all areas of English and American language and literature.

Chapter 2

GENERAL STUDIES

123. Abbott, Wilbur C. "The First Newspaperman." PROCEEDINGS OF THE MASSACHUSETTS HISTORICAL SOCIETY, 61 (1941), 32-52.

124. Agate, James, ed. THE ENGLISH DRAMATIC CRITICS: AN ANTHOLOGY 1660-1932. New York: Hill and Wang, 1958.

 This paperbound reprint of an earlier work contains some criticism which appeared originally in periodicals.

125. Alden, Raymond MacDonald. CRITICAL ESSAYS OF THE EARLY NINETEENTH CENTURY. New York: Charles Scribner's Sons, 1921.

126. Altick, Richard D. "Nineteenth-Century English Periodicals." NEWBERRY LIBRARY BULLETIN, 2nd Ser., 9 (1952), 255-64.

 See No. 1.

127. _____. THE ENGLISH COMMON READER: A SOCIAL HISTORY OF THE MASS READING PUBLIC, 1800-1900. Chicago: University of Chicago Press, 1957.

128. Altman, Elizabeth C. "Some Observations on the French vs. the English Press, 1830-1848." VPN, 11 (1971), 30-31.

129. Ames, John Griffith, Jr. THE ENGLISH LITERARY PERIODICAL OF MORALS AND MANNERS. Mt. Vernon, Ohio: Republican Publishing Co., 1904.

130. Andrews, Alexander. THE HISTORY OF BRITISH JOURNALISM FROM THE FOUNDATION OF THE NEWSPAPER PRESS IN ENGLAND, TO THE REPEAL OF THE STAMP ACT IN 1855, WITH SKETCHES OF PRESS CELEBRITIES. 2 vols. London: Richard Bentley, 1859.

131. Andrews, John S. "The Reception of Gotthelf in British and American

Nineteenth-Century Periodicals." MLR, 51 (1956), 543-54.

132. App, A.J. "How Six Famous Poets Were Treated." CATHOLIC WORLD, 144 (1937), 582-89.

Discussed the reception of Wordsworth, Coleridge, Byron, Shelley, Keats, and Tennyson in the periodicals.

133. Aronson, A. "The Anatomy of Taste: A Note on Eighteenth-Century Periodical Literature." MLN, 61 (1946), 228-36.

134. Ashton, John. SOCIAL LIFE IN THE REIGN OF QUEEN ANNE TAKEN FROM ORIGINAL SOURCES. New York: Charles Scribner's Sons, 1920.

135. Aspinall, A. "The Social Status of Journalists at the Beginning of the Nineteenth Century." RES, 21 (1945), 216-32.

136. ______. "The Circulation of Newspapers in the Early Nineteenth Century." RES, 22 (1946), 29-43.

137. ______. "Statistical Accounts of the London Newspapers in the Eighteenth Century." EHR, 63 (1948), 201-32.

138. ______. POLITICS AND THE PRESS, c. 1780-1850. London: Home and Van Thal, 1949.

Reviewed in AHR, 55:133-34.

139. ______. "The Reporting and Publishing of the House of Commons' Debates, 1771-1834." ESSAYS PRESENTED TO SIR LEWIS NAMIER. Ed. R. Pares and A.J.P. Taylor. London: Macmillan, 1956. Pp. 227-57.

140. Atkins, J.W.H. ENGLISH LITERARY CRITICISM: 17TH AND 18TH CENTURIES. London: Methuen, 1951.

141. Babcock, R.W. "Benevolence, Sensiblity and Sentiment in Some Late Eighteenth Century Periodicals." MLN, 62 (1947), 394-97.

Documents references to the three terms.

142. ______. "A Note on Genius, Imagination and Enthusiasm in Some Late Eighteenth Century Periodicals." N&Q, 192 (1947), 93-95.

A list of references.

143. Bakeless, John. "Christopher Marlowe and the Newsbooks." JQ, 14 (1937), 18-22.

Newsbooks as a source for Marlowe's MASSACRE AT PARIS.

144. Baker, George M. "Some References to German Literature in English Magazines of the Early Eighteenth Century." MLN, 24 (1909), 111-14.

145. Baker, Harry T. "Early English Journalism." SR, 25 (1917), 396-411.

146. Barnes, Sherman B. "The Scientific Journal, 1665-1730." SCIENTIFIC MONTHLY, 38 (1934), 257-60.

147. _____. "The Editing of Early Learned Journals." OSIRIS, 1 (1936), 155-72.

148. Barwick, G.F. "The Magazines of the Nineteenth Century." TRANSACTIONS OF THE BIBLIOGRAPHICAL SOCIETY, 11 (1909-11), 237-49.

149. Bauer, William A. "The Letter Device in the Early English Essay Journal." DAI, 31 (1971), 6044A-45A.

150. Bayne-Powell, Rosamond. "Newspapers and Magazines." EIGHTEENTH-CENTURY LONDON LIFE. New York: Dutton, 1938. Pp. 357-68.

151. Behrman, Cynthia F. "The Creation of Social Myth: Journalism and the Empire." VPN, 11 (1971), 9-13.

See also No. 406.

152. Bennett, Scott. "The Bentley and Constable Records." VPN, 8 (1970), 12-15.

Concerning Victorian periodicals.

153. Bernbaum, Ernest. GUIDE THROUGH THE ROMANTIC MOVEMENT. Rev. ed. New York: Ronald Press, 1949.

154. Birrell, Augustine. "Life, 'Literature' and 'Literary' Journalism During the First Half of the Last Century (1800-1850)." LONDON MERCURY, 2 (May 1920), 42-54.

155. Blagden, Cyprian. "The Distribution of Almanacks in the Second Half of the Seventeenth Century." SB, 11 (1958), 107-16.

156. _____. THE STATIONERS' COMPANY: A HISTORY, 1403-1959. London: Allen and Unwin; Cambridge, Mass.: Harvard University Press, 1960.

157. Blake, Robert. "Criticism of Poetry in Selected Victorian Periodicals: 1850-1870." DA, 29 (1969), 1224A.

Includes the ATHENAEUM, the FORTNIGHTLY REVIEW, and the SATURDAY REVIEW.

158. Bleyer, Willard Grosvenor. "Answers to Correspondents in Early English Journalism." JQ, 7 (1930), 14-22.

On the question-and-answer periodicals.

159. _____. "The Beginnings of English Journalism." JQ, 8 (1931), 317-28.

160. Bloom, Edward A. "'Labors of the Learned': Neoclassic Book Reviewing--Aims and Techniques." SP, 54 (1957), 537-63.

161. Bond, Richmond P. "Some Early English Newspapers and Periodicals at Yale." YALE UNIVERSITY LIBRARY GAZETTE, 12 (1939), 69-75.

162. _____. "Notes on Advertising in Early Newspapers and Periodicals." ANTIQUARIAN BOOKSELLERS' ASSOCIATION ANNUAL: BOOKS AND THE MAN. London: Dawson, 1953. Pp. 52-62.

163. _____. GROWTH AND CHANGE IN THE EARLY ENGLISH PRESS. University of Kansas Publications, Library Series, no. 35. Lawrence: University of Kansas Libraries, 1969.

An eighteen-page pamphlet published by the library that purchased the Bond collection (see No. 16).

164. Bond, Richmond P., et al. STUDIES IN THE EARLY ENGLISH PERIODICAL. Chapel Hill: University of North Carolina Press, 1957.

Contains an important introductory essay by Bond and six essays by others on the TATLER and the GAZETTE, the BRITISH APOLLO, the FREE-THINKER, the PROMPTER, the FEMALE SPECTATOR, and the WORLD. Reviewed in PQ, 37:182-87, and JEGP, 57:813-15.

165. Bonner, Willard H. "Moll, Knapton, and Defoe: A Note on Early Serial Publication." RES, 10 (1934), 320-23.

On the interest in geographico-trade serials from 1708-27, examining Defoe's GENERAL HISTORY OF TRADE, Moll's ATLAS GEOGRAPHICUS (1708-17), and Knapton's NEW COLLECTION OF VOYAGES AND TRAVELS (1708-10). The last two are not listed in the Crane and Kaye "Census" (No. 32).

166. Bourne, H.R. Fox. ENGLISH NEWSPAPERS. CHAPTERS IN THE HISTORY OF JOURNALISM. 2 vols. London: Chatto and Windus, 1887.

See also W. Roberts, "Newspapers 'In Walpole's Days,'" ACADEMY, 33 (1888), 308-9. Roberts' paper notes some of Bourne's errors.

167. Boyce, Benjamin. "News from Hell: Satiric Communications with the Nether World in English Writing of the Seventeenth and Eighteenth Centuries." PMLA, 58 (1943), 402-37.

168. Brady, L.W. "'Penny a Liners' and Politics: The Growth of Journalistic Influence." VPN, 11 (1971), 17-22.

169. Bragg, Mary Jane. "American News in English Periodicals, 1783-1800." HLQ, 8 (1945), 393-403.

170. Bredvold, Louis I. "The Literature of the Restoration and Eighteenth Century." A HISTORY OF ENGLISH LITERATURE. Ed. Hardin Craig. New York: Oxford University Press, 1950. Pp. 343-459.

171. Brewster, William Tenney. "The Eighteenth Century Magazine." HARVARD MONTHLY, 14 (1892), 105-15.

172. Brinton, Crane. THE POLITICAL IDEAS OF THE ENGLISH ROMANTICISTS. London: Oxford University Press, 1926.

Chapter 5 concerns "Romanticism and the Press."

173. Brown, Stephen J. "Some Catholic Periodicals." STUDIES, AN IRISH QUARTERLY REVIEW, 25 (1936), 428-42.

174. Bush, George E., Jr. "The Fable in the English Periodical, 1660-1800." DA, 28 (1967), 189A-90A.

175. Butt, John. THE AUGUSTAN AGE. Hutchinson's University Library. London: Hutchinson, 1950.

Reviewed in QUEEN'S QUARTERLY, 57:573-74; DURHAM UNIVERSITY JOURNAL, 42:121-22.

176. Cairns, William B. BRITISH CRITICISMS OF AMERICAN WRITINGS, 1783-1815. A CONTRIBUTION TO THE STUDY OF ANGLO-AMERICAN LITERARY RELATIONSHIPS. University of Wisconsin Studies in Language and Literature, no. 1. Madison: University of Wisconsin Press, 1918.

177. CAMBRIDGE HISTORY OF ENGLISH LITERATURE. Ed. A.W. Ward

and A.R. Waller. Cambridge: At the University Press, 1907-17.

Relevant material is included in the following (numbers refer to volume and chapter): VII.xv: "The Beginnings of Journalism," by J.B. Williams; IX.i: "Defoe--The Newspaper and the Novel," by W.P. Trent; IX.ii: "Steele and Addison," by Harold Routh; X.viii: "Johnson and Boswell," by David Nichol Smith; X.ix: "Oliver Goldsmith," by Henry Austin Dobson; XII.vi: "Reviews and Magazines in the Early Years of the Nineteenth Century," by Arthur R.D. Elliot; XII.vii: "Hazlitt," by W.D. Howe; XIV.iv: "The Growth of Journalism," by J.S.R. Phillips; XIV.v: "University Journalism," by Vernon Horace Rendall; XIV.vi: "Caricature and the Literature of Sport: PUNCH," by Harold Child.

Although many of these essays are quite old, many of them still stand as classic treatments of their subjects.

178. Cannon, Garland H. "Freedom of the Press and Sir William Jones." JQ, 33 (1956), 179-88.

179. Carlson, C. Lennart. "Richard Lewis and the Reception of His Work in England." AL, 9 (1937), 301-16.

Discusses Lewis's WEEKLY REGISTER, BEE, LONDON MAGAZINE, and GENTLEMAN'S MAGAZINE.

180. Caskey, J. Homer. "Truth and Fiction in Eighteenth-Century Newspapers." MLN, 45 (1930), 438-40.

Uses Arthur Murphy's NEWS FROM PARNASSUS as illustration.

181. Chalmers, Alexander, ed. THE BRITISH ESSAYISTS; WITH PREFACES, HISTORICAL AND BIOGRAPHICAL. 45 vols. London: J. Johnson, 1803; rpt. London: Printed for Nichols, Son, and Bentley, 1823.

Contents: TATLER, SPECTATOR, GUARDIAN, RAMBLER, ADVENTURER, WORLD, CONNOISSEUR, IDLER, MIRROR, LOUNGER, OBSERVER, and LOOKER-ON.

182. Chew, Samuel C. "The Nineteenth Century and After." A LITERARY HISTORY OF ENGLAND. Ed. A.C. Baugh. New York: Appleton-Century-Crofts, 1948; rev. by Richard D. Altick, 1967.

183. Churchill, R.C. ENGLISH LITERATURE IN THE NINETEENTH CENTURY. London: University Tutorial Press, 1951.

See "The Great Reviews" and "Their Literary Attitude" (pages 56-62).

184. Clark, Dora Mae. BRITISH OPINION AND THE AMERICAN REVOLU-

TION. Yale Historical Publications, Miscellany no. XX. New Haven, Conn.: Yale University Press, 1930.

185. Clark, G.N. THE LATER STUARTS, 1660-1714. The Oxford History of England, vol. X. 2d ed. Oxford: At the University Press, 1956.

186. Clyde, William M. "Parliament and the Press, 1643-7." LIBRARY, 13 (1933), 399-424; 14 (1933), 39-58.

187. Coggeshall, W.T. THE NEWSPAPER RECORD, CONTAINING A COMPLETE LIST OF NEWSPAPERS AND PERIODICALS IN THE UNITED STATES, CANADA AND GREAT BRITAIN, TOGETHER WITH A SKETCH OF THE ORIGIN AND PROGRESS OF PRINTING, WITH SOME FACTS ABOUT NEWSPAPERS IN EUROPE AND AMERICA. Philadelphia: Lay & Brother, 1856.

188. Conant, Martha Pike. THE ORIENTAL TALE IN ENGLAND IN THE EIGHTEENTH CENTURY. Columbia University Studies in Comparative Literature. New York: Columbia University Press, 1908.

189. CONTEMPORARIES OF THE TATLER AND SPECTATOR. Intro. by Richmond P. Bond. Augustan Reprint Society, Publication no. 47. Los Angeles: Clark Memorial Library, University of California, 1954.

Contains facsimile reproductions of essays selected from rare periodicals, 1709-12.

190. Cooke, John D., and Lionel Stevenson. ENGLISH LITERATURE OF THE VICTORIAN PERIOD. Appleton-Century Handbooks of Literature. New York: Appleton-Century-Crofts, 1949.

191. Cox, R.G. "The Great Reviews." SCRUTINY, 6 (1937), 2-20, 155-75.

Their attitude towards the Romantic poets, the novel, the drama, and literary criticism.

192. _____. "The Reviews and Magazines." THE PELICAN GUIDE TO ENGLISH LITERATURE. Vol. VI: FROM DICKENS TO HARDY. Baltimore: Penguin Books, 1958. Pp. 188-204.

193. Cramer, Richard Sheldon. "The British Magazines and the United States, 1815-1848." DA, 21 (1961), 3075-76.

194. Cranfield, G.A. THE DEVELOPMENT OF THE PROVINCIAL NEWSPAPER, 1700-1760. Oxford: Clarendon Press, 1962.

Reviewed in JQ, 40:383, and HISTORY, 48:224-25.

195. CRITICAL ESSAYS AND LITERARY FRAGMENTS, WITH AN INTRODUCTION BY J. CHURTON COLLINS. (AN ENGLISH GARNER) New York: Dutton, [1903].

A volume of ARBER'S ENGLISH GARNER with contents rearranged and classified. Texts of especial interest are the Bickerstaff and Partridge Tracts, 1708; Gay's PRESENT STATE OF WIT, 1711; and the preface to Tickell's edition of Addison, 1721.

196. Cummings, Dorothea. "Prostitution as Shown in Eighteenth-Century Periodicals." BSUF, 12, pt. ii (1971), 44-49.

197. Davies, Bernice F. "The Social Status of the Middle-Class Victorian Woman as it is Interpreted in Representative Mid-Nineteenth Century Novels and Periodicals." ABSTRACTS OF DISSERTATIONS, STANFORD UNIVERSITY, 1942-43 (1944), 45-47.

Includes a discussion of PUNCH, FRASER'S MAGAZINE, and the WESTMINSTER REVIEW.

198. Davies, Godfrey. THE EARLY STUARTS, 1603-60. The Oxford History of England, vol. IX. 2d ed. Oxford: Oxford University Press, 1959.

199. Deering, Dorothy. "Computer Programming for the Victorian Periodicals Project." VPN, 7 (1970), 29-44.

200. Dix, E.R. McC. "Eighteenth Century Newspapers." IRISH BOOK LOVER, 1 (1909), 39-41.

A plea for libraries to consolidate their holdings and thus make available in one place complete files of eighteenth-century newspapers. Discusses briefly dates and files of various papers.

201. Dobrée, Bonamy. ENGLISH LITERATURE IN THE EARLY EIGHTEENTH CENTURY, 1700-1740. Oxford History of English Literature, vol. VII. Ed. F.P. Wilson and Bonamy Dobree. London and New York: Oxford University Press, 1959.

See particularly chapter IV: "Essayists and Controversialists" (pages 73-120). Reviewed in PQ, 39:293-95; ENGLISH, 13: 23-24; MLR, 56:105-6; RES, 12:84-85; MLN, 76:356-59; and MP, 60:138-41.

202. Drake, Nathan. ESSAYS, BIOGRAPHICAL, CRITICAL, AND HISTORICAL, ILLUSTRATIVE OF THE TATLER, SPECTATOR, AND GUARDIAN.

3 vols. London: John Sharpe, 1805.

Volumes I-II contain an essay on periodical writing and long studies of Steele and of Addison; Volume III gives sketches of forty-eight occasional contributors. Reviewed in BRITISH CRITIC, 28:147-58, and QR, 1:398-405.

203. ______. ESSAYS, BIOGRAPHICAL, CRITICAL, AND HISTORICAL, ILLUSTRATIVE OF THE RAMBLER, ADVENTURER, & IDLER, AND OF THE VARIOUS PERIODICAL PAPERS WHICH, IN IMITATION OF THE WRITINGS OF STEELE AND ADDISON, HAVE BEEN PUBLISHED BETWEEN THE CLOSE OF THE EIGHTH VOLUME OF THE SPECTATOR, AND THE COMMENCEMENT OF THE YEAR 1809. 2 vols. London: Seeley, 1809-10.

Reviewed in QR, 1:398-405.

204. Egoff, Shelia A. CHILDREN'S PERIODICALS OF THE NINETEENTH CENTURY: A SURVEY AND BIBLIOGRAPHY. Library Association Pamphlets, no. 8. London: Library Association, 1951.

205. Ehrenpreis, Irvin. "Personae." RESTORATION AND EIGHTEENTH-CENTURY LITERATURE. ESSAYS IN HONOR OF ALAN DUGALD McKILLOP. Ed. Carroll Camden. Chicago: University of Chicago Press, for William Marsh Rice University, 1963. Pp. 25-37.

Rejects the concept of "personae" in the periodical and elsewhere.

206. Ellegard, Alvar. "Public Opinion and the Press: Reactions to Darwinism." JHI, 19 (1958), 379-89.

207. ______. THE READERSHIP OF THE PERIODICAL PRESS IN MID-VICTORIAN BRITAIN. GUA, vol. LXIII, no. 3. Goteborg: 1957.

208. ______. "The Readership of the Periodical Press in Mid-Victorian Britain: II. Directory." VPN, 13 (1971), 3-22.

209. Ellis, James. "An Index to John Forbes Wilson's A FEW PERSONAL RECOLLECTIONS." VPN, 11 (1971), 22-27.

210. Ellis, Theodore R. III. "The Dramatist and the Comic Journal in England, 1830-1870." DA, 29 (1969), 2209A.

211. ______. "The Dramatist and the Comic Journal in England, 1830-1870." VPN, 14 (1972), 29-31.

212. Ensor, R.C.K. ENGLAND, 1870-1914. The Oxford History of England, vol. XIV. Oxford: Oxford University Press, 1936.

213. Escott, T.H.S. MASTERS OF ENGLISH JOURNALISM. A STUDY OF PERSONAL FORCES. London: T. Fisher Unwin, 1911.

214. Esdaile, Arundell. "Autolycus' Pack: The Ballad Journalism of the Sixteenth Century." QR, 208 (1913), 372-91.

215. ESSAYS ON THE THEATRE FROM EIGHTEENTH-CENTURY PERIODICALS. Sel., with intro., by John Loftis. Augustan Reprint Society, Publication nos. 85-86. Los Angeles: Clark Memorial Library, University of California, 1960.

216. Ewald, William Bragg, Jr. THE NEWSMEN OF QUEEN ANNE. Oxford: Blackwell, 1956; American ed. with title ROGUES, ROYALTY, AND REPORTERS: THE AGE OF QUEEN ANNE THROUGH ITS NEWSPAPERS. Boston: Houghton Mifflin, 1956.

An anthology of periodical articles.

217. Fetter, Frank. "Economic Controversy in the British Reviews, 1802-1850." ECONOMICS, 32 (1965), 424-37.

218. Ffrench, Yvonne, ed. NEWS FROM THE PAST: 1805-1877: THE AUTOBIOGRAPHY OF THE NINETEENTH CENTURY. Intro. by Sir John Squire. New York: Viking Press; London: Gollancz, 1934.

More than 2,000 extracts from English newspapers including social, artistic, political, and fashionable items.

219. Fleischmann, Wolfgang Bernard. LUCRETIUS AND ENGLISH LITERATURE 1680-1740. Paris: A.G. Nizet, 1964.

Reviewed in PQ, 44:320.

220. Fletcher, John R. "Early Catholic Periodicals in England." DUBLIN REVIEW, 198 (1936), 284-310.

221. Frank, Joseph. "Some Clippings from the Pre-Restoration Newspaper." HLQ, 22 (1959), 351-58.

222. _____. THE BEGINNINGS OF THE ENGLISH NEWSPAPER, 1620-1660. Cambridge, Mass.: Harvard University Press, 1961.

Reviewed in JMH, 34:437-38; AHR, 67:696-97; HISTORY, 47:312-14; and DALHOUSIE REVIEW, 42:378-84.

223. Fraser, Peter. THE INTELLIGENCE OF THE SECRETARIES OF STATE AND THEIR MONOPOLY OF LICENSED NEWS, 1660-1688. Cambridge: At the University Press, 1956.

Reviewed in HISTORY TODAY, 6:574-75; N&Q, 201:367-68; and TLS, 12 October 1956, p. 608.

224. Gillett, Charles Ripley. BURNED BOOKS. NEGLECTED CHAPTERS IN BRITISH HISTORY AND LITERATURE. 2 vols. New York: Columbia University Press, 1932.

225. THE GLEANER: A SERIES OF PERIODICAL ESSAYS; SELECTED AND ARRANGED FROM SCARCE OR NEGLECTED VOLUMES. Intro. and notes by Nathan Drake. 4 vols. London: Suttaby, Evance, 1811.

One hundred eighty-seven essays from forty-one journals of the eighteenth century; covers the period from 1713 to 1797.

226. Graham, Walter. "Some Infamous Tory Reviews." SP, 22 (1925), 500-517.

227. ______. ENGLISH LITERARY PERIODICALS. New York: Nelson, 1930.

Supersedes and incorporates the author's BEGINNINGS OF ENGLISH LITERARY PERIODICALS (1926). Covers from the beginnings of literary journalism in the seventeenth century down to about 1900.

228. Gray, Charles Harold. THEATRICAL CRITICISM IN LONDON TO 1795. Columbia University Studies in English and Comparative Literature. New York: Columbia University Press, 1931.

229. Gray, Donald J. "A List of Comic Periodicals Published in Great Britain, 1800-1900, with a Prefatory Essay." VPN, 15 (1972), 2-39.

230. Gross, John. THE RISE AND FALL OF THE MAN OF LETTERS: ASPECTS OF ENGLISH LITERARY LIFE SINCE 1800. London: Weidenfeld and Nicolson, 1969.

The opening chapter deals with "The Rise of the Reviewer."

231. Hampden, John, comp. AN EIGHTEENTH-CENTURY JOURNAL. BEING A RECORD OF THE YEARS 1774-1776. London: Macmillan, 1940.

Many of the entries in this "journal," such as "might have been kept in London," are taken from newspapers and periodicals.

232. Haney, J.L. EARLY REVIEWS OF ENGLISH POETS: 1757-1885. Philadelphia: Egerton Press, 1904.

233. Hart, Jeffrey, ed. POLITICAL WRITERS OF EIGHTEENTH-CENTURY ENGLAND. Borzoi Series in Eighteenth-Century Literature. New York: Knopf, 1964.

234. Hathaway, Lillie V. GERMAN LITERATURE OF THE MID-NINETEENTH CENTURY IN ENGLAND AND AMERICA AS REFLECTED IN THE JOURNALS, 1840-1914. Boston: Chapman & Grimes, 1935.

235. Hayden, John O. THE ROMANTIC REVIEWERS, 1802-1824: A STUDY OF LITERARY REVIEWING IN THE EARLY NINETEENTH CENTURY. Chicago: University of Chicago Press; London: Routledge & Kegan Paul, 1969.

236. Hazlitt, William. "On the Periodical Essayists." LECTURES ON THE ENGLISH COMIC WRITERS. COLLECTED WORKS OF WILLIAM HAZLITT. Ed. A.R. Waller and Arnold Glover. 12 vols. London: Dent, 1902-4. VIII, 91-105.

237. ______. "The Periodical Press." THE COLLECTED WORKS OF WILLIAM HAZLITT. Ed. A.R. Waller and Arnold Glover. 12 vols. London: Dent, 1902-4. X, 202-30.

Reprinted from the EDINBURGH REVIEW, 38 (1823).

238. Henderson, Alfred James. LONDON AND THE NATIONAL GOVERNMENT, 1721-1742: A STUDY OF CITY POLITICS AND THE WALPOLE ADMINISTRATION. Durham, N.C.: Duke University Press, 1945.

Includes a discussion of Defoe's defence of the government in the DAILY POST and APPLEBEE'S WEEKLY JOURNAL as well as of the activities of the CRAFTSMAN group.

239. Herd, Harold. THE MARCH OF JOURNALISM: THE STORY OF THE BRITISH PRESS FROM 1622 TO THE PRESENT DAY. London: Allen and Unwin, 1952.

240. Hill, Peter Murray. TWO AUGUSTAN BOOKSELLERS: JOHN DUNTON AND EDMUND CURLL. University of Kansas Publications, Library Series, no. 3. Lawrence: University of Kansas Libraries, 1958.

241. Hodgart, Patricia, and Theodore Redpath, eds. ROMANTIC PERSPECTIVES: THE WORK OF CRABBE, BLAKE, WORDSWORTH, AND COLERIDGE AS SEEN BY THEIR CONTEMPORARIES AND BY THEMSELVES. London: Barnes and Noble, 1964.

The lengthy introduction (pages 16-83) discusses periodical criticism.

242. Hodgins, James Raymond. "A Study of the Periodical Reception of the Novels of Thomas Hardy, George Gissing, and George Moore." DA, 21 (1960), 196-97.

243. Hollis, Patricia. THE PAUPER PRESS: A STUDY IN WORKING-CLASS RADICALISM OF THE 1830'S. London: Oxford University Press, 1970.

244. Hooker, Edward Niles. "The Reviewers and the New Criticism, 1754-1770." PQ, 13 (1934), 189-202.

245. Houghton, Walter E. "British Periodicals of the Victorian Age: Bibliographies and Indexes." LIBRARY TRENDS, 7 (1959), 554-65.

246. _____. "Report from THE WELLESLEY INDEX." VN, 15 (Spring 1959), 30-31.

See also "Victorian Periodicals," TLS, 6 March 1959, p. 133.

247. _____. "Reflections on Indexing Victorian Periodicals." VS, 7 (1963), 192-96.

248. _____. "THE WELLESLEY INDEX, Volumes II and III: Plans and Problems." VPN, 4 (1969), 3-6.

249. _____. "Victorian Periodicals." TLS, 3 September 1971, p. 1057.

250. Houtchens, Carolyn Washburn, and Lawrence Huston Houtchens, eds. THE ENGLISH ROMANTIC POETS AND ESSAYISTS: A REVIEW OF RESEARCH AND CRITICISM. New York: Modern Language Association, 1957.

251. Howe, Ellic. NEWSPAPER PRINTING IN THE NINETEENTH CENTURY. London: Privately printed, 1943.

252. Howse, W.H. "Literary Tastes in 1797." N&Q, 195 (1950), 537-38.

A newspaper advertisement of books.

253. Hudson, Derek. BRITISH JOURNALISTS AND NEWSPAPERS. Britain in Pictures. London: Collins, 1945.

254. Hughes, Helen Sard. "English Epistolary Fiction before PAMELA." THE

MANLY ANNIVERSARY STUDIES IN LANGUAGE AND LITERATURE. Chicago: University of Chicago Press, 1923. Pp. 156-69.

255. Inglis, Brian. THE FREEDOM OF THE PRESS IN IRELAND, 1784-1841. Studies in Irish History, vol. VI. London: Faber & Faber, 1954.

Reviewed in STUDIES, 45:254-55, and CATHOLIC HISTORICAL REVIEW, 41:492-93.

256. Innis, Harold A. "The English Press in the Nineteenth Century: An Economic Approach." UTQ, 15 (1945), 37-53.

257. Jack, Ian. ENGLISH LITERATURE, 1815-1832. Oxford History of English Literature, vol. X. London and New York: Oxford University Press, 1963.

258. Jack, Jane H. "The Periodical Essayists." THE PELICAN GUIDE TO ENGLISH LITERATURE. Ed. Boris Ford. Vol. IV: FROM DRYDEN TO JOHNSON. Baltimore: Penguin Books, 1957. Pp. 217-29.

259. Jackson, Alfred. "Play Notices from the Burney Newspapers 1700-1703." PMLA, 48 (1933), 815-49.

260. ______. "The Stage and the Authorities, 1700-1714 (As Revealed in the Newspapers)." RES, 14 (1938), 53-62.

261. Jackson, Ian. "Towards a Study of the Victorian Provincial Press." VPN, 5-6 (1969), 14-16.

262. James, Louis. "'Economic' Literature: The Emergence of Popular Journalism." VPN, 14 (1972), 13-20.

263. Jones, Calvin P. "Spanish-America in Selected British Periodicals, 1800-1830." DAI, 30 (1969), 1941A.

264. Jones, Linda B. "The Kenealy Collection at the Huntington Library." VPN, 14 (1972), 20-22.

265. Jones, W.P. "The Vogue of Natural History in England, 1750-1770." ANNALS OF SCIENCE, 2 (1937), 345-52.

266. Joshi, K.L. "Some Conditions of the Production of Periodical Literature about the Year 1720." JOURNAL OF THE UNIVERSITY OF BOMBAY, 8, pt. ii (1939), 11-28.

267. Jump, J.D. "Weekly Reviewing in the Eighteen-Fifties." RES, 24 (1948), 42-57.

See annotation for next item.

268. ______. "Weekly Reviewing in the Eighteen-Sixties." RES, 3 (1952), 244-62.

Surveys the contemporary reputations of numerous Victorian authors.

269. Kronick, David A. "Scientific Journal Publication in the Eighteenth Century." PBSA, 59 (1965), 28-44.

270. Lamar, Lillie B. "The Eighteenth-Century 'Filler': A Key to Popular Taste." JPC, 6 (1972), 178-203.

271. L'Ami, C.E. "The Philosophy of Journalism." DALHOUSIE REVIEW, 29 (1949), 314-26.

Largely concerned with Defoe and Wilkes.

272. Laprade, William T. "The Power of the English Press in the Eighteenth Century." SAQ, 27 (1928), 426-34.

273. ______. PUBLIC OPINION AND POLITICS IN EIGHTEENTH CENTURY ENGLAND TO THE FALL OF WALPOLE. New York: Macmillan, 1936.

274. Lemay, J.A. Leo. A CALENDAR OF AMERICAN POETRY IN THE COLONIAL NEWSPAPERS AND MAGAZINES AND IN THE MAJOR ENGLISH MAGAZINES THROUGH 1765. Worcester, Mass.: American Antiquarian Society, 1972.

275. Lewis, W.S., and Ralph M. Williams, with the assistance of John M. Webb and A. Stuart Daley. PRIVATE CHARITY IN ENGLAND, 1747-1757. New Haven, Conn.: Yale University Press, 1938.

Includes hundreds of illustrative passages from the GENTLEMAN'S MAGAZINE, LONDON CHRONICLE, LONDON EVENING POST, DAILY ADVERTISER, and OLD ENGLAND.

276. Long, Ralph Bernard. "Dryden's Importance as a Spokesman of the Tories." UNIVERSITY OF TEXAS STUDIES IN ENGLISH, 1941. Pp. 79-99.

Includes a discussion of Whig and Tory journals during the years of the Popish and Whig Plots, 1677-84.

277. Lutnick, Solomon. THE AMERICAN REVOLUTION AND THE BRITISH PRESS. Columbia: University of Missouri Press, 1967.

278. Macaulay, Thomas Babington. THE HISTORY OF ENGLAND FROM THE ACCESSION OF JAMES THE SECOND. Boston: Houghton, 1901. I, 382-86; V, 64-69.

Newsletters and newspapers of the Restoration.

279. McCutcheon, Roger P. "The Beginnings of Book-Reviewing in English Periodicals." PMLA, 37 (1922), 691-706.

280. McKillop, Alan Dugald. ENGLISH LITERATURE FROM DRYDEN TO BURNS. New York: Appleton-Century-Crofts, 1948.

Reviewed in PQ, 28:371.

281. MacLeod, Roy M. "Printing Under the Golden Lamp: Taylor and Francis Ltd., and Work in Progress on Scientific Periodical Publishing." VPN, 5-6 (1969), 11-12.

282. Madden, Lionel. "Technical Processes in Victorian Office Practice." VPN, 14 (1972), 22-23.

283. "Magazines of the Last Century." CHAMBERS'S EDINBURGH JOURNAL, 18 (1852), 334-36.

284. Marillier, Harry Currie. UNIVERSITY MAGAZINES AND THEIR MAKERS. BEING A PAPER READ BEFORE THE SETTE OF ODD VOLUMES. London: Howard Wilford Bell, 1902.

285. Marr, George S. THE PERIODICAL ESSAYISTS OF THE EIGHTEENTH CENTURY. WITH ILLUSTRATIVE EXTRACTS FROM THE RARER PERIODICALS. New York: D. Appleton, 1924.

286. Matthews, William Roberts. "Late Victorian Journalistic Criticism: A Study of Gosse, Lang, Saintsbury, and Churton Collins." DA, 22 (1961), 574-75.

287. Maurer, Oscar, Jr. "Anonymity vs. Signature in Victorian Reviewing." TEXAS STUDIES IN ENGLISH, 27 (1948), 1-27.

288. ______. "Victorian Periodicals at Texas University." LIBRARY CHRONICLE OF THE UNIVERSITY OF TEXAS, 5, no. 3 (1955), 18-23.

289. Mayo, Robert D. "The Gothic Short Story in the Magazines." MLR, 37 (1942), 448-54.

290. _____. "Gothic Romance in the Magazines." PMLA, 65 (1950), 762-89.

A study of serials from 1770-1820, an area neglected by Gothic bibliographers, which printed or reprinted, and often pirated, Gothic romance and poetry. Includes discussion of LADY'S MAGAZINE, THEATRICAL INQUISITOR, LADIES POCKET MAGAZINE, and POCKET MAGAZINE.

291. _____. THE ENGLISH NOVEL IN THE MAGAZINES 1740-1815, WITH A CATALOGUE OF 1375 MAGAZINE NOVELS AND NOVELETTES. Evanston, Ill.: Northwestern University Press, 1962.

Reviewed in PQ, 42:322-24; PBSA, 57:261-62; MLR, 59:278; COLLEGE ENGLISH, 25:634; and RES, 15:208-10.

292. Miller, Mary R. "The Crimean War in British Periodical Literature, 1854-1859." DA, 27 (1967), 3055A-56A.

293. Mineka, Francis E. "The Critical Reception of Milton's DE DOCTRINA CHRISTIANA." UNIVERSITY OF TEXAS STUDIES IN ENGLISH, no. 23 (1943), 115-47.

A survey of periodical criticism following the publication in 1825 of Milton's "heretical" work.

294. _____. THE DISSIDENCE OF DISSENT. THE MONTLY REPOSITORY, 1806-1838. Chapel Hill: University of North Carolina Press, 1944.

Chapter II (pages 27-97) attempts to "furnish a brief survey of the development of religious journalism in the eighteenth century and to describe in somewhat more detail the various denominational periodicals from the time of the French Revolution to 1825."

295. Moore, John Robert. "On the Use of Advertisements as Bibliographic Evidence." LIBRARY, 9 (1954), 134-35.

Since advertisements were at times erroneous, misleading, or deliberately false, and were often repeated unchanged, they should be used with caution.

296. Mordell, Albert. NOTORIOUS LITERARY ATTACKS. New York: Boni & Liveright, 1926.

297. Morgan, Bayard Quincy, and A.R. Hohlfeld, eds. GERMAN LITERA-

TURE IN BRITISH MAGAZINES, 1750-1860. Madison: University of Wisconsin Press, 1949.

298. Morgan, F.G. "Eighteenth-Century Journals." TLS, 22 May 1953, p. 333.

Notes a copy of the HEREFORD JOURNAL extant.

299. Morgan, Peter F. "Problems in Examining Periodical Criticism." VPN, 7 (1970), 9-11.

300. Mullet, Charles F. "Englishmen Discover Herculaneum and Pompeii." ARCHAEOLOGY, 10 (1957), 31-38.

The discoveries reported in English periodicals.

301. Murray, Donald M. "Henry James and the English Reviewers, 1882-1890." AL, 24 (1952), 3-20.

302. Newlin, Claude M. "The English Periodicals and the Novel, 1709-40." PAPERS OF THE MICHIGAN ACADEMY OF SCIENCE, ARTS AND LETTERS, 16 (1931), 467-76.

Discusses work in TATLER, SPECTATOR, GUARDIAN, and later periodicals which contributed to the development of a moralized English novel.

303. Nichols, John. LITERARY ANECDOTES OF THE EIGHTEENTH CENTURY; COMPRIZING BIOGRAPHICAL MEMOIRS OF WILLIAM BOWYER, PRINTER, F. S. A. AND MANY OF HIS LEARNED FRIENDS: AN INCIDENTAL VIEW OF THE PROGRESS AND ADVANCEMENT OF LITERATURE IN THIS KINGDOM DURING THE LAST CENTURY; AND BIOGRAPHICAL ANECDOTES OF A CONSIDERABLE NUMBER OF EMINENT WRITERS AND INGENIOUS ARTISTS; WITH A VERY COPIOUS INDEX. 9 vols. London: Printed for the Author, 1812-15.

See especially "Of publick news and weekly papers; when they first began; their progress, increase, and uses and abuses to the people. (From the Harl. MSS. 5910)," IV, 33-97; "Additions to the list of periodical publications," VIII, 495-99 and IX, 710; "Edward Cave," V, 1-58; and "John Dunton," V, 59-83.

304. ______. ILLUSTRATIONS OF THE LITERARY HISTORY OF THE EIGHTEENTH CENTURY. CONSISTING OF AUTHENTIC MEMOIRS AND ORIGINAL LETTERS OF EMINENT PERSONS; AND INTENDED AS A SEQUEL TO THE 'LITERARY ANECDOTES.' 8 vols. London: Printed for the Author, 1817-58.

305. Palmegiano, Eugenia. "Feminist Propaganda in the 1850s and 1860s." VPN, 11 (1971), 5-8.

See also No. 406.

306. Pebody, Charles. ENGLISH JOURNALISM, AND THE MEN WHO HAVE MADE IT. Cassell's Popular Library. London: Cassell, Petter, Galpin & Co., 1882.

307. Pinkus, Philip. GRUB ST. STRIPPED BARE: THE SCANDALOUS LIVES & PORNOGRAPHIC WORKS OF THE ORIGINAL GRUB ST. WRITERS. London: Constable, 1968.

308. Plomer, Henry R. A DICTIONARY OF THE BOOKSELLERS AND PRINTERS WHO WERE AT WORK IN ENGLAND, SCOTLAND AND IRELAND FROM 1641 TO 1667. London: for the Bibliographical Society, by Blades, East & Blades, 1907.

309. Plomer, Henry R., with H.G. Aldis, E.R. McC. Dix, G.J. Gray, and R.B. McKerrow. A DICTIONARY OF THE PRINTERS AND BOOKSELLERS WHO WERE AT WORK IN ENGLAND, SCOTLAND AND IRELAND FROM 1668 TO 1725. Ed. Arundell Esdaile. Oxford: for the Bibliographical Society, at the Oxford University Press, 1922.

310. Plomer, Henry R., G.H. Bushnell, and E.R. McC. Dix. A DICTIONARY OF THE PRINTERS AND BOOKSELLERS WHO WERE AT WORK IN ENGLAND, SCOTLAND AND IRELAND FROM 1726 TO 1775. Oxford: for the Bibliographical Society, Oxford University Press, 1932 [for 1930].

311. POLITICAL BALLADS ILLUSTRATING THE ADMINISTRATION OF SIR ROBERT WALPOLE. Ed. Milton Percival. Oxford Historical and Literary Studies, vol. 8. Oxford: Clarendon Press, 1916.

Introduction includes sketch of the political journalism of the Walpole period.

312. Pollard, Graham. "Serial Fiction." NEW PATHS IN BOOK COLLECTING. BY VARIOUS HANDS. Ed. John Carter. London: Constable, 1934. Pp. 247-77.

313. ______. "Notes on the Size of the Sheet." LIBRARY, 22 (1941), 105-37.

Concerns the legal loophole in the Stamp Act of 1712 which permitted publishers of newspapers to halve their stamp duty by using double sheets and cutting them in half after printing.

314. Price, J.M. "A Note on the Circulation of the London Press, 1704-1714." BIHR, 31 (1958), 215-24.

Concerns figures based on stamp purchases recorded in the Harley papers.

315. PROGRESS OF BRITISH NEWSPAPERS IN THE NINETEENTH CENTURY. London: Simpkin, Marshall, Hamilton, Kent & Co., [1901].

Illustrated.

316. Quinlan, Maurice J. "Anti-Jacobin Propaganda in England, 1792-1794." JQ, 16 (1939), 9-15.

317. Rea, Robert R. "'The Liberty of the Press' as an Issue in English Politics, 1792-1793." HISTORIAN, 24 (1961), 26-43.

318. ______. THE ENGLISH PRESS IN POLITICS, 1760-1774. Lincoln: University of Nebraska Press, 1963.

Reviews appear in COLLEGE ENGLISH 25:232; PBSA 57:388; PQ 43:307-10.

319. Read, Donald. "Reform Newspapers and Northern Opinion." PLPLS-LHS, 8 (1959), 301-14.

320. ______. PRESS AND PEOPLE, 1790-1850: OPINION IN THREE ENGLISH CITIES. London: E. Arnold, 1961.

Concerns Leeds, Manchester, and Sheffield.

321. Reidy, James E. "The Higher Criticism in England and the Periodical Debate of the 1860's." DAI, 32 (1972), 6390A.

322. Renwick, W[illiam]. L[indsay]. ENGLISH LITERATURE, 1789-1815. Oxford History of English Literature, vol. IX. Ed. F.P. Wilson and Bonamy Dobrée. Oxford: Oxford University Press, 1963.

Reviews appear in TLS, 1 March 1964, p. 154; MLR 59:643-45; EHR 79:866-67.

323. Richards, James O. PARTY PROPAGANDA UNDER QUEEN ANNE: THE GENERAL ELECTIONS OF 1702-1713. Athens: University of Georgia Press, 1972.

324. Riffe, Nancy Lee. "Milton in the Eighteenth-Century Periodicals: 'Hail, Wedded Love!'" N&Q, 210 (1965), 18-19.

325. ______. "Milton's Minor Poetry in British Periodicals before 1740." N&Q, 210 (1965), 453-54.

326. Ritcheson, Charles R. "The London Press and the First Decade of American Independence, 1783-1793." JOURNAL OF BRITISH STUDIES, 2 (1963), 88-109.

327. Roberts, David F. "Early Victorian Newspaper Editors." VPN, 14 (1972), 1-12.

328. ______. "More Early Victorian Newspaper Editors." VPN, 16 (1972), 15-28.

329. Roberts, Helene E. "British Art Periodicals of the Eighteenth and Nineteenth Centuries." VPN, 9 (1970), 2-56.

330. Roe, F. Gordon. "The Lighter Side of Collecting: Some 'Comics' of Yesteryear." CONNOISSEUR, 108 (1941), 22-26, 35, 184-86.

Discusses artists whose work appeared in FUN and HOOD'S COMIC ANNUAL.

331. Rogal, Samuel J. "Religious Periodicals in England During the Restoration and Eighteenth Century." JRUL, 35 (1971), 27-33.

Includes a checklist of fifty-one entries.

332. Rogers, Pat. GRUB STREET: STUDIES IN A SUBCULTURE. New York: Barnes & Noble; London: Methuen, 1972.

333. Roscoe, Christopher. "Haydn and London in the 1780's." MUSIC AND LETTERS, 49 (1968), 203-12.

An account derived primarily from contemporary periodicals and newspapers.

334. Rosenberg, Henry, and Sheila Rosenberg. "Bibliography of Writings on Nineteenth-Century Periodicals." VPN, 7 (1970), 11-13.

Not a bibliography at all, but a brief and very general statement of the difficulties of such a project.

335. Rosenfield, Sybil. "Dramatic Advertisements in the Burney Newspapers 1660-1700." PMLA, 51 (1936), 123-52.

336. ______. "The Restoration Stage in Newspapers and Journals, 1660-1700." MLR, 30 (1935), 445-59.

337. Ross, John F. "The Character of Poor Richard: Its Source and Alteration." PMLA, 55 (1940), 785-94.

Concerns Richard's debt to Bickerstaff and Partridge.

338. Rygh, Andrew Robert. "English Periodicals and the Democratic Movement." DA, 21 (1960), 1547.

339. Schalack, Harry G. "Fleet Street in the 1880's: The Old Journalism and the New." JQ, 41 (1964), 421-26.

340. Segar, M.G., ed. ESSAYS FROM EIGHTEENTH CENTURY PERIODICALS. London: Methuen, 1947.

341. Shaaber, Matthias A. SOME FORERUNNERS OF THE NEWSPAPER IN ENGLAND, 1476-1622. Philadelphia: University of Pennsylvania Press, 1929.

342. Sherburn, George. "The Restoration and Eighteenth Century (1660-1789)." A LITERARY HISTORY OF ENGLAND. Ed. Albert C. Baugh. New York and London: Appleton-Century-Crofts, 1948; 2d ed. with bibliographical supplement by Donald F. Bond. New York: Appleton-Century-Crofts, 1967. 1st ed., [697]-1108.

The first edition was reviewed in PQ, 28:373-75, the second in PQ, 47:344-45.

343. Shine, Hill. "Recent Studies of Nineteenth Century English Periodicals." PERIODICAL POST-BOY, no. 1 (March 1948), 2-6.

344. Shugrue, Michael. "The Rise of the Weekly Journal." N&Q, 207 (1962), 246-47.

Comment on journals established following the Stamp Act (1712).

345. Siebert, Fred S. "The Regulation of Newsbooks, 1620-1640." JQ, 16 (1939), 151-60.

Origin and growth of corantos; Nicholas Bourne and Nathaniel Butter; patents for news (1632-40).

346. ______. FREEDOM OF THE PRESS IN ENGLAND, 1476-1776: THE RISE AND DECLINE OF GOVERNMENT CONTROLS. Urbana: University of Illinois Press, 1952.

347. Smith, D. Nichol. "The Newspaper." JOHNSON'S ENGLAND. AN

ACCOUNT OF THE LIFE & MANNERS OF HIS AGE. Ed. A.S. Turberville. 2 vols. Oxford: Clarendon Press, 1933. II, 331-67.

348. Smith, Preserved. A HISTORY OF MODERN CULTURE. 2 vols. New York: Henry Holt, 1930.

For comment on censorship, see I, 511-12; for scientific academies, journals, and museums, see II, 126-40; and for material on newspapers and magazines, see II, 279-94.

349. Snyder, Henry L. "The Circulation of Newspapers in the Reign of Queen Anne." LIBRARY, 23 (1968), 206-35.

Includes extensive statistical material.

350. ______. "The Collection of Richmond P. Bond and Marjorie N. Bond." BOOKS AND LIBRARIES AT THE UNIVERSITY OF KANSAS, 7, no. 1 (1970), 1-8.

A general description of a rich private collection of early periodicals and related material recently acquired by the University of Kansas. See also No. 16.

351. Somers, Wayne. "Aids to the Use of Poole's Index." VPN, 8 (1970), 15-22.

For research in Victorian periodicals.

352. Speck, W.A. "Political Propaganda in Augustan England." ROYAL HISTORICAL SOCIETY TRANSACTIONS, 22 (1972), 17-32.

353. Spector, Robert D. "English Literary Periodicals and the Climate of Opinion, 1756-1763." DA, 28 (1967), 1450A.

354. ______. ENGLISH LITERARY PERIODICALS AND THE CLIMATE OF OPINION DURING THE SEVEN YEARS WAR. Studies in English Literature, no. XXXIV. The Hague: Mouton, 1966.

Reviewed in PQ, 47:345-46.

355. Sper, Felix. THE PERIODICAL PRESS OF LONDON, THEATRICAL AND LITERARY (EXCLUDING THE DAILY NEWSPAPER), 1800-1830. Useful Reference Series, no. 60. Boston: F.W. Faxon, 1937.

A list of literary and theatrical periodicals.

356. Stearnes, Bertha Monica. "Early English Periodicals for Ladies (1700-1760)." PMLA, 48 (1933), 38-60.

357. Stewart, Powell. "The Loyal London Mercuries." University of Texas Studies in English, no. 28. Austin: University of Texas Press, 1949. Pp. 105-23.

An account of two newspapers of 1682.

358. ______. "Typographical Characteristics of 'The Loyal London Mercuries.'" N&Q, 194 (1949), 118-19.

359. Stewart, Powell, and W.O.S. Sutherland, Jr. "Techniques for a Subject Index to 18th-Century Journals." LIBRARY CHRONICLE OF THE UNIVERSITY OF TEXAS, 5 (Spring 1956), 6-15.

360. Stokoe, Frank W. GERMAN INFLUENCE IN THE ENGLISH ROMANTIC PERIOD, 1788-1818, WITH SPECIAL REFERENCE TO SCOTT, COLERIDGE, SHELLEY, AND BYRON. Cambridge: At the University Press, 1926.

Chapter 3 concerns periodical literature.

361. Stone, George Winchester, Jr. "Shakespeare in the Periodicals, 1700-1740." 2 pts. SHAKESPEARE QUARTERLY, 2 (1951), 221-31; 3 (1952), 313-28.

362. Stone, J[ames]. A., ed. PERIODICAL ESSAYS OF THE EIGHTEENTH CENTURY. Sheldonian English Series. London: Oxford University Press, 1954.

363. Stratman, Carl J. "Preparing a Bibliography of English Dramatic Periodicals, 1720-1960." BNYPL, 23 (1962), 405-8.

See also No. 101.

364. Strickland, Geoffrey, ed. SELECTED JOURNALISM FROM THE ENGLISH REVIEWS BY STENDHAL WITH TRANSLATIONS OF OTHER CRITICAL WRITINGS. London: Calder, 1959.

Several essays concern Byron.

365. Sugden, E.H. "Some References to Methodism in the Periodical Literature of the Eighteenth Century." PROCEEDINGS OF THE WESLEY HISTORICAL SOCIETY, 12 (1920), 152-58.

366. Sutherland, James R. "Lost Journals." PERIODICAL POST-BOY, no. 6 (March 1950), 1-4.

Titles "advertised in contemporary newspapers, but of which nothing appears to be known."

367. _____. ENGLISH LITERATURE OF THE LATE SEVENTEENTH CENTURY. Oxford History of English Literature, vol. VI. Ed. Bonamy Dobrée and Norman Davis. Oxford: Oxford University Press, 1969.

See especially "The Periodical" (pages 233-44). Reviews appear in ECS 2:454-63; PQ 49:319-21; RES 21:501-4; ELN 7:222-25.

368. _____. "Some Aspects of Eighteenth-Century Prose." ESSAYS ON THE EIGHTEENTH CENTURY PRESENTED TO DAVID NICHOL SMITH ON HIS SEVENTIETH BIRTHDAY. Oxford: Clarendon Press, 1945. Pp. 94-110.

Includes illustrative quotations from Defoe's REVIEW.

369. Sydney, William Connor. "The Literary World." ENGLAND AND THE ENGLISH IN THE EIGHTEENTH CENTURY. 2d ed. 2 vols. Edinburgh: John Grant, [1891]. II, 113-56.

370. Symonds, Emily Morse. "The Illustrated Magazine of the Georgian Period." SIDE-LIGHTS ON THE GEORGIAN PERIOD. New York: Dutton, 1903. Pp. 57-75.

371. Symonds, R.V. THE RISE OF ENGLISH JOURNALISM. English Inheritance Series. Exeter: A. Wheaton, 1953.

Contains selections from seventeenth- and eighteenth-century newspapers.

372. Tave, Stuart M. THE AMIABLE HUMORIST: A STUDY IN THE COMIC THEORY AND CRITICISM OF THE EIGHTEENTH AND EARLY NINETEENTH CENTURIES. Chicago: University of Chicago Press, 1960.

373. Thomas, Peter D.G. "The Beginning of Parliamentary Reporting in Newspapers, 1768-1774." EHR, 74 (1959), 623-36.

374. Thompson, Denys. "A Hundred Years of the Higher Journalism." SCRUTINY, 4 (1935), 25-34.

375. Thompson, Leslie M., and John R. Ahreus. "Satire in Eighteenth Century Reviews of Fiction: Or, Guffaws of the Grave Reviewer." SATIRE NEWSLETTER, 9 (1972), 113-21.

Concerns reviews from the 1780s and 90s.

376. Thornton, Richard Hurt. "The Periodical Press and Literary Currents in England, 1785-1802." [UNIVERSITY OF CHICAGO] ABSTRACTS OF THESES, Humanistic Series, IV (1925-26), 347-52.

377. Todd, William B. "On the Use of Advertisements in Bibliographical Studies." LIBRARY, 8 (1953), 174-87.

378. _____. "The Printing of Eighteenth-Century Periodicals: With Notes on the EXAMINER and the WORLD." LIBRARY, 10 (1955), 49-54.

379. Torfrida. "Periodicals for Women." N&Q, 1 (1904), 228.

See also No. 70.

380. Turberville, A.S. ENGLISH MEN AND MANNERS IN THE EIGHTEENTH CENTURY. AN ILLUSTRATED NARRATIVE. Oxford: Clarendon Press, 1926.

381. VICTORIAN PERIODICALS NEWSLETTER. Bloomington: University of Indiana Press, 1968--.

Considers any periodical whose run falls in part or entirely within the years 1824-1900.

382. Wain, John, ed. CONTEMPORARY REVIEWS OF ROMANTIC POETRY. New York: Barnes and Noble; London: Harrap, 1953.

383. Wallins, Roger P. "The Emerging Victorian Social Conscience." DAI, 33 (1972), 1699A.

384. Ward, William Smith. THE CRITICISM OF POETRY IN BRITISH PERIODICALS, 1793-1820. WITH A HANDLIST OF PERIODICALS AND A CHECKLIST OF REVIEWS. Microcard Series A; MLA Series, no. 3. SAMLA. Lexington, Ky.: 1935.

385. _____. "Some Aspects of the Conservative Attitude toward Poetry in English Criticism, 1798-1820." PMLA, 60 (1945), 386-98.

386. _____. "Wordsworth, the Lake Poets, and Their Contemporary Reviewers." SP, 42 (1945), 87-113.

387. _____. "Unrecorded Journals." PERIODICAL POST-BOY, 7 (June 1950), 6-7; 8 (December 1950), 1-2.

388. _____. "Periodical Literature." SOME BRITISH ROMANTICS. Ed. James V. Logan, John E. Jordan, and Northrop Frye. Columbus: Ohio State University Press, 1966. Pp. 292-331.

A survey article examining the development of new forms of the review, the magazine, and the weekly journal of scholarly and critical interest in them.

389. Watson, J. Steven. THE REIGN OF GEORGE III, 1760-1815. The Oxford History of England, vol. XII. Oxford: Oxford University Press, 1960.

390. Watson, Melvin R. MAGAZINE SERIALS AND THE ESSAY TRADITION, 1745-1820. Louisiana State University Studies, Humanities Series, no. 6. Baton Rouge: Louisiana State University Press, 1956.

"The purpose of the study is to relate the serials to the tradition established by Addison and Steele. . . . The final chapter of the book develops the thesis that the early work of Lamb and Hazlitt (and to a lesser extent that of Hunt) exhibited a change from the Addison and Steele tradition to that of the familiar essay." (PQ, 36:337). Other reviews appeared in JEGP 51:496-99; MLR 53:141; RES 9:345.

391. Welker, John J. "The Position of the Quarterlies on Some Classical Dogmas." SP, 37 (1940), 542-62.

392. Werkmeister, Lucyle. THE LONDON DAILY PRESS, 1772-1792. Lincoln: University of Nebraska Press, 1963.

Reviews appear in PQ 43:307-10; COLLEGE ENGLISH 25: 232-33; PBSA 57-388.

393. _____. A NEWSPAPER HISTORY OF ENGLAND, 1792-1793. Lincoln: University of Nebraska Press, 1968.

394. Wiener, Joel H. "The Press and the Working Class, 1815-1840." VPN, 11 (1971), 1-4.

See also No. 406.

395. Wiles, Roy McKeen. "Prose Fiction in English Periodical Publications before 1750." HARVARD UNIVERSITY SUMMARIES OF THESES, 1935. Cambridge, Mass.: Harvard University Press, 1937. Pp. 289-92.

396. _____. "Freshest Advices, Foreign and Domestick." DALHOUSIE REVIEW, 38 (1958), 8-17.

Popular account of an eighteenth-century provincial paper.

397. _____. FRESHEST ADVICES: EARLY PROVINCIAL NEWSPAPERS IN ENGLAND. Columbus: Ohio State University Press, 1965.

Reviews appear in PQ 45:506-7; UTQ 35:259-61; AHR 71:

1332-33; MP 64:367-68; MLR 62:704-5.

398. ______. "Crowd-Pleasing Spectacles in Eighteenth-Century England." JPC, 1 (1967), 90-105.

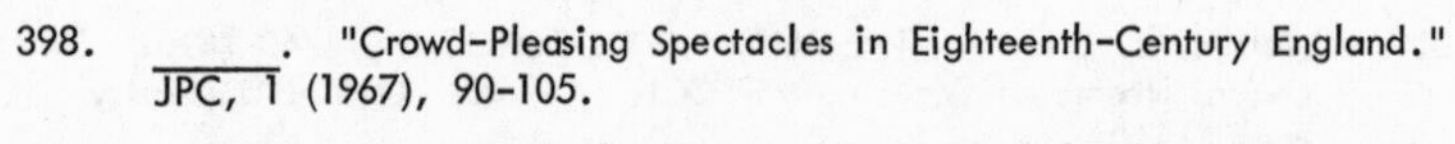

Based on news and advertisements in provincial newspapers.

399. ______. "Weekly Entertainments for the Mind." JPC, 2 (1968), 119-35.

"Non-news" items in provincial papers.

400. ______. "Middle-Class Literacy in Eighteenth-Century England: Fresh Evidence." STUDIES IN THE EIGHTEENTH CENTURY: PAPERS PRESENTED AT THE DAVID NICHOL SMITH MEMORIAL SEMINAR, CANBERRA, 1966. Ed. R.F. Brissenden. Canberra: Australian National University Press, 1968. Pp. 49-65.

401. ______. "The Periodical Essay: Lures to Readership." ENGLISH SYMPOSIUM PAPERS II. Ed. Douglas Shepard. Fredonia: State University of New York, Department of English, 1972. Pp. 3-40.

402. Wilkerson, Marjorie. NEWS AND THE NEWSPAPERS. London: Batesford, 1970.

403. Williams, Basil. THE WHIG SUPREMACY, 1714-60. The Oxford History of England, vol XI. 2d ed., rev. by C.H. Stuart. Oxford: Oxford University Press, 1962.

404. Williams, J.B. A HISTORY OF ENGLISH JOURNALISM TO THE FOUNDATION OF THE GAZETTE. London: Longmans, Green, 1908.

Appendix D is an excellent chronological list of periodicals flourishing in 1641-66. A review appeared in ATHENAEUM, 20 February, 1909, pp. 219-20, and a reply followed in the 27 February issue (pp. 255-56).

405. Wolff, Michael. "Victorian Reviewers and Cultural Responsibility." 1859: ENTERING AN AGE OF CRISIS. Ed. Philip Appleman, William A. Madden, and Michael Wolff. Bloomington: Indiana University Press, 1959. Pp. 269-89.

406. ______. "Comments." VPN, 11 (1971), 13-16.

Related to the subject of Nos. 151, 305, and 394.

407. ______. "Charting the Golden Stream: Thoughts on a Directory of

Victorian Periodicals." VPN, 13 (1971), 23-38.

408. Woodward, Sir Llewellyn. THE AGE OF REFORM, 1815-70. The Oxford History of England, vol. XIII. 2d ed. Oxford: Oxford University Press, 1962.

409. Wright, C. Hagberg. "The Evolution of the Periodical." NINETEENTH CENTURY AND AFTER, 101 (1927), 320-29.

410. Young, G.M., ed. EARLY VICTORIAN ENGLAND, 1830-1865. 2 vols. Oxford: Oxford University Press, 1934.

Contains a chapter on "The Press."

Chapter 3
PERIODICALS

ABERDEEN JOURNAL (1747-1900+; ABERDEEN'S JOURNAL, 1747-48)

411. THE ABERDEEN JOURNAL, 1747-1897: OUR 150TH YEAR. Aberdeen: Aberdeen Journal Office, 1897.

Contains a table of British newspapers after 1718 in addition to a history of the ABERDEEN JOURNAL.

412. Bulloch, J.M. "Aberdeen Newspaper Index." N&Q, 157 (1929), 422.

Refers to an index to the JOURNAL for the years 1747-1847, compiled by John A. Henderson.

413. ______. "Aberdeen Journal, 1747-1847, Indexed." N&Q, 11 (1933), 136.

Concerns a typewritten index at King's College.

414. McDonald, William R. "Circulating Libraries in the Northeast of Scotland in the Eighteenth Century." BIBLIOTHECK, 5 (1968), 119-37.

New information derived in part from advertisements in this periodical.

ABERDEEN MAGAZINE (1788-1791)

415. Roy, G. Ross. "Robert Burns and the ABERDEEN MAGAZINE." BIBLIOTHECK, 5 (1968), 102-5.

Concerns early printings of Burns's poems in periodicals, 1789-91.

ACADEMY (1869-1900+)

416. Roll-Hansen, Diderik. "Matthew Arnold and the ACADEMY: A Note

on English Criticism in the Eighteen-Seventies." PMLA, 68 (1953), 384-96.

417. _____. THE ACADEMY, 1869-1879; VICTORIAN INTELLECTUALS IN REVOLT. ANGLISTICA, vol. VIII. Copenhagen: Rosenkilde & Bagger; New York: G. Lounze, 1957.

ADVENTURER (1752-54)

See also JOHNSON, SAMUEL (chapter 4) and Nos. 185, 199, 2066, and 2074.

418. Griffith, Philip Malone. "A Study of the ADVENTURER." DA, 22 (1962), 3662-63.

419. _____. "The Authorship of the Papers Signed 'A' in Hawkesworth's ADVENTURER: A Strong Case for Dr. Richard Bathurst." TULANE STUDIES IN ENGLISH, 12 (1962), 63-70.

See also No. 420.

420. Lams, Victor J., Jr. "The 'A' Papers in the ADVENTURER: Bonnell Thornton, Not Dr. Bathurst, Their Author." SP, 64 (1967), 83-96.

See also No. 419.

421. Powell, L.F. "Johnson's Part in THE ADVENTURER." RES, 3 (1927), 420-29.

422. Sherbo, Arthur. "The Translation of the Motto for 'The Adventurer.' No. 126." N&Q, 196 (1951), 497-98.

The translation is by Rowe rather than Johnson.

423. _____. "Two Notes on Johnson's Revisions." MLR, 50 (1955), 311-15.

One note is concerned with revisions of essays in the ADVENTURER.

424. _____. SAMUEL JOHNSON, EDITOR OF SHAKESPEARE. WITH AN ESSAY ON 'THE ADVENTURER.' Illinois Studies in Language and Literature, vol. 42. Urbana: University of Illinois Press, 1956.

The "Essay" concerns translation of the mottoes and quotations in the ADVENTURER.

ADVERTISER (Edinburgh, 1764?)

425. Quaintance, Richard E., Jr. "Charles Churchill as Man of Feeling: A Forgotten Poem by Mackenzie." MLR, 56 (1961), 73-77.

ALBION MAGAZINE (1830)

426. Thoms, William J. "THE ALBION MAGAZINE." N&Q, 2 (1880), 9.

ALL THE YEAR ROUND (1859-95)

See also No. 1002.

427. Casey, Ellen M. "Novels in Teaspoonfuls: Serial Novels in ALL THE YEAR ROUND, 1859-1895." DAI, 30 (1969), 1521A.

428. Grubb, Gerald G. "The American Edition of ALL THE YEAR ROUND." PBSA, 47 (1953), 301-4.

429. Morley, M. "ALL THE YEAR ROUND Plays." DICKENSIAN, 52 (1956), 128-31, 177-80.

ANALYTICAL REVIEW (1788-99)

430. Roper, Derek. "Mary Wollstonecraft's Reviews." N&Q, 203 (1958), 37-38.

Criticism of Wardle's attributions (see No. 432).

431. Russell, Norma. A BIBLIOGRAPHY OF WILLIAM COWPER TO 1837. Oxford Bibliographical Society Publications, XII (1963).

See pages 158-61 for reviews by Cowper published in the ANALYTICAL REVIEW.

432. Wardle, Ralph M. "Mary Wollstonecraft, ANALYTICAL REVIEWER." PMLA, 62 (1947), 1000-1009.

Attempts attribution of reviews for 1788-91, 1796-97. See No. 430.

433. _____. MARY WOLLSTONECRAFT: A CRITICAL BIOGRAPHY. Lawrence: University of Kansas Press, 1951.

See especially pages 98-99, 101, 102-3, and 366 concerning periodical contributions.

ANNALS OF THE FINE ARTS (1816-20)

See also No. 2089.

434. Bellinger, Rossiter. "The First Publication of 'Ode on a Grecian Urn.'" N&Q, 194 (1949), 478-79.

The poem appeared in the issue for 19 January 1820.

435. Olney, Clarke. "ANNALS OF THE FINE ARTS, 1816-1820: An Annotated Set of." N&Q, 165 (1933), 416-18.

ANNUAL REGISTER (1758-1900+)

See also BURKE, EDMUND (chapter 4).

436. "The Annual Register." TLS, 29 May 1959, p. 321.

On the bicentenary.

437. Bryant, Donald C. "Letter to the Editor." QJS, 39 (1953), 351-52.

Describes newly discovered papers bearing on Burke's part in editing the ANNUAL REGISTER.

438. Copeland, Thomas W. "Burke and Dodsley's ANNUAL REGISTER." PMLA, 54 (1939), 223-45.

439. _____. "Edmund Burke and the Book Reviews in Dodsley's ANNUAL REGISTER." PMLA, 58 (1942), 446-68.

440. _____. OUR EMINENT FRIEND EDMUND BURKE. New Haven, Conn.: Yale University Press, 1949.

See especially chapter 3.

441. _____. "Edmund Burke's Friends and THE ANNUAL REGISTER." LIBRARY, 18 (1963), 29-39.

Burke continued to influence editorial policy through friends after he ceased to serve as editor.

442. Crossley, James. "Edmund Burke, and the 'Annual Register.'" N&Q, 3 (1851), 441-42.

443. GENERAL INDEX TO DODSLEY'S ANNUAL REGISTER, VOLS. 1-61, 1758-1819. London: 1826.

444. H.,A.M. "THE ANNUAL REGISTER: A Bibliographical Note." N&Q, 84 (1943), 99-100.

445. Havens, Raymond D. "A Theft in the Annual Register." PQ, 29 (1950), 416-17.

A passage reprinted from John Brown's ESSAYS ON THE CHARACTERISTICS (1751).

446. L. "The 'Annual Register.'" N&Q, 12 (1855), 62-63.

Also in this issue of N&Q, see the material by Philip Bliss (page 92) and that by Henry Cotton (page 171).

447. ______. "Annual Register." N&Q, 7 (1859), 156.

448. Meyerstein, E.H.W. "The Forged Letter from Peele to Marlowe." TLS, 29 June 1940, p. 315.

Meyerstein suggests that a letter appearing in the ANNUAL REGISTER for 1770 was forged by Chatterton. See also, in the issue of TLS for 20 July 1940, the material by E. St. John Brooks (page 351).

449. Mullen, Jay C. "Lecky as Plagiarist: THE ANNUAL REGISTER and the American Revolution." SBHT, 13 (1972), 2193-202.

450. Ryan, A.P. "Rambling Readings in the ANNUAL REGISTER." LISTENER (BBC), 29 July 1954, pp. 176-77.

451. Sarason, Bertram D. "Edmund Burke and the Two ANNUAL REGISTERS." PMLA, 68 (1953), 496-508.

452. ______. "Editorial Mannerisms in the Early 'Annual Register.'" PBSA, 52 (1958), 131-37.

Suggests that Burke ended his editorship in 1764.

453. Seitz, R.W. "Goldsmith and the ANNUAL REGISTER." MP, 31 (1933), 183-94.

On Goldsmith's borrowings from the ANNUAL REGISTER for his HISTORY OF ENGLAND, IN A SERIES OF LETTERS FROM A NOBLEMAN TO HIS SON.

454. Todd, William B. "A Bibliographical Account of THE ANNUAL REGISTER, 1758-1825." LIBRARY, 16 (1961), 104-20.

455. Weston, John C., Jr. "Predecessors to Burke's and Dodsley's ANNUAL REGISTER." SB, 17 (1964), 215-220.

456. ______. "Burke's Authorship of the 'Historical Articles' in Dodsley's 'Annual Register.'" PBSA, 51 (1957), 244-49.

Includes 1764 in the period during which Burke wrote for Dodsley.

ANTI-JACOBIN (1797-98)

See also CANNING, GEORGE and GIFFORD, WILLIAM (chapter 4).

457. THE ANTI-JACOBIN; OR WEEKLY EXAMINER. 2 vols. Hildeshiem, W. Germany: Georg Olms, 1967.

A reprint of the 1797 edition.

458. Bagot, Josceline, ed. "The 'Anti-Jacobin.'" GEORGE CANNING AND HIS FRIENDS. 2 vols. London: John Murray, 1909. I, 135-52.

459. Bourne, H.R. Fox. "Anti-Jacobins and Reformers." GENTLEMAN'S MAGAZINE, 263 (1887), 559-84.

460. C., J.D. "Coleridge and the Anti-Jacobins." ATHENAEUM, 31 May 1890, pp. 703-4.

Attack on Coleridge and Lamb in the BEAUTIES OF THE ANTI-JACOBIN, 1799.

461. ______. "The 'Anti-Jacobin.'" ATHENAEUM, 14 June 1890, p. 769.

462. "Canning and the Anti-Jacobin." CORNHILL MAGAZINE, 15 (1867), 63-74.

463. Duffield, W.B. "The Anti-Jacobin. An Anniversary Article." CORNHILL MAGAZINE, 5 (1898), 17-32.

464. Fraser, W. "THE OLD ENGLISHMAN AND ANTI-JACOBIN EXAMINER." N&Q, 12 (1885), 229.

465. Greenwood, Frederick. "Canning's 'Anti-Jacobin.'" ACADEMY, 68 (1905), 275-76.

See also No. 477.

466. Hanson, L.W. "Canning's Copy of 'The Anti-Jacobin.'" BRITISH MUSEUM QUARTERLY, 11 (1936), 19.

467. Hawkins, Edward. "Authors of the Poetry of the Anti-Jacobin." N&Q, 3 (1851), 348-49.

Also in this issue of N&Q, see the material by Bolton Corney (page 349), the material signed C.B. (page 396), and that signed C. (page 431). See also the material by J.H. Markland (page 334) for writers of some of the numbers of ANTI-JACOBIN.

468. Head, Emory L. "A Study of the ANTI-JACOBIN; OR, WEEKLY EXAMINER." DAI, 32 (1972), 4565A.

469. Holloway, Owen E. "George Ellis, the ANTI-JACOBIN and the QUARTERLY REVIEW." RES, 10 (1934), 55-66.

470. Makrocheir. "Rogero's Song in THE ANTI-JACOBIN." N&Q 2 (1868), 374, 521-22.

See also No. 476.

471. "'The Needy Knife-Grinder.'" ATHENAEUM, 24 May 1890, p. 674.

Authorship of the poem, which appeared in ANTI-JACOBIN, 27 November 1797.

472. Perkinson, Richard H. "THE ANTI-JACOBIN." N&Q, 172 (1937), 164.

473. "The Poetry of THE ANTI-JACOBIN." WESTMINSTER REVIEW, 58 (1852), 247-57.

474. POETRY OF THE ANTI-JACOBIN. Ed., intro., and notes by L. Rice-Oxley. Percy Reprints, no. 8. Oxford: Blackwell, 1924.

See also review of 1890 edition in ATHENAEUM, 3 May 1890, pp. 561-63. For discussion of the sources used by Rice-Oxley, see No. 472.

475. Pollin, Burton Ralph. "Verse Satire on William Godwin in the Anti-Jacobin Period." SNL, 2 (1964), 31-40.

476. R., A.B. "Rogero's Song in 'The Anti-Jacobin.'" N&Q, 6 (1858), 324, 521-22.

477. Temperley, H.W.V. "The ANTI-JACOBIN, Gillray, and Canning." ACADEMY, 68 (25 March 1905), 345.

APPLEBEE'S ORIGINAL WEEKLY JOURNAL (1713?-37)

See also Nos. 238 and 1926.

478. Shugrue, Michael Francis. "A Study of APPLEBEE'S ORIGINAL WEEKLY JOURNAL, 1714-1731." DA, 21 (1961), 2278-79.

479. ______. "APPLEBEE'S ORIGINAL WEEKLY JOURNAL: An Index to Eighteenth-Century Taste." NEWBERRY LIBRARY BULLETIN, 6 (1964), 108-21.

ARBROATH MAGAZINE (1799-1800)

480. McBain, J.M. "The Arbroath Magazine." N&Q, 2 (1888), 66-67.

Reprinted in McBain's BIBLIOGRAPHY OF ARBROATH PERIODICAL LITERATURE AND POLITICAL BROADSIDES (Arbroath: 1889).

ARMINIAN MAGAZINE (1788-1900+)

Title changes. See also No. 2243.

481. Brooks, Elmer L. "Cowper's Periodical Contributions." TLS, 17 August 1956, p. 487.

Letter to editor suggesting Cowper contributed to this periodical.

482. Harrison, A.W. "The Arminian Magazine." PROCEEDINGS OF THE WESLEY HISTORICAL SOCIETY, 12 (1920), 150-52.

483. Herbert, Thomas Walter. JOHN WESLEY AS EDITOR AND AUTHOR. Princeton Studies in English, no. 17. Princeton, N.J.: Princeton University Press, 1940.

The ARMINIAN MAGAZINE is discussed in chapter 5.

484. Wallington, A. "THE ARMINIAN AND METHODIST MAGAZINE. British and Irish Editions." PROCEEDINGS OF THE WESLEY HISTORICAL SOCIETY, 13 (1921), 11-13.

ARTIST (1855)

485. Oswald, O.S.B., et al. "THE ARTIST." N&Q, 6 (1894), 476.

ASIATICK MISCELLANY (1785-86)

486. Cannon, Garland H. "A New Probable Source for 'Kubla Kahn.'" COLLEGE ENGLISH, 17 (1955), 136-42.

ATHENAEUM (1828-1900+)

See also Nos. 157 and 986.

487. Booth, Bradford A. "Trollope and LITTLE DORRIT." TROLLOPIAN, 2 (1948), 237-40.

Trollope submitted an article, which ATHENAEUM did not accept (1856), concerning Dickens' novel.

488. Fahnestock, Jeanne. "Authors of Book Reviews in the ATHENAEUM, 1830-1900: A Preview and Sample." VPN, 15 (1972), 47-52.

489. Marchand, Leslie. 'THE ATHENAEUM': A MIRROR OF VICTORIAN CULTURE. Chapel Hill: University of North Carolina Press, 1940.

490. R.,V. "THE ATHENAEUM and Bulwer Lytton." N&Q, 168 (1935), 128-29.

491. Ward, Humphry. HISTORY OF 'THE ATHENAEUM,' 1828-1925. London: Printed for the Club, 1926.

ATHENIAN GAZETTE; after first issue, ATHENIAN MERCURY (1691-96, 1697)

See also Nos. 1033 and 1938.

492. Bensly, Edward. 'ATHENIAN GAZETTE.' N&Q, 147 (1924), 158.

Discussion of beginning date and description of first issue.

493. Cooper, Charles Henry. "Some Account of Richard Sault, Mathematician, and One of the Editors of the ATHENIAN MERCURY." CAMBRIDGE ANTIQUARIAN COMMUNICATIONS: BEING PAPERS PRESENTED AT THE MEETINGS OF THE CAMBRIDGE ANTIQUARIAN SOCIETY, 3 for 1864 (1879), 37-45.

494. G.,P.A. "'The Athenian Mercury.'" N&Q, 5 (1864), 77.

495. McEwen, Gilbert D. ORACLE OF THE COFFEE HOUSES: JOHN DUNTON'S ATHENIAN MERCURY. San Marino, Calif.: Huntington Library, 1972.

496. Merritt, H.C. "The Smithfield Muses: The Literary Influence of the ATHENIAN MERCURY." ENGLISH, 20 (1971), 7-10.

497. N. "The 'Athenian Oracle.'" N&Q, 5 (1852), 230.

See also the material by Uneda in N&Q, 6 (1853), 521.

498. Smith, C.J. "How History Repeats itself. London in 1661 [sic] a Counterpart of New York in 1902." JOURNALIST, 30 (1902), 317-18.

Uses excerpt from ATHENIAN MERCURY.

499. Starr, G.A. "From Casuistry to Fiction: The Importance of the ATHENIAN MERCURY." JHI, 28 (1967), 17-32.

Examines John Dunton's ATHENIAN MERCURY "as a medium through which traditional casuistry found its way into Defoe's fiction."

ATHENIAN MERCURY (1691-96, 1697)

See ATHENIAN GAZETTE.

ATLAS GEOGRAPHICUS (1708-17)

See No. 165.

AUDITOR (1762-63)

See No. 1269.

AUNT JUDY'S MAGAZINE (1866-85)

500. "Twenty Years with Aunt Judy." TLS, 7 December 1946, p. i [of children's book section].

BABLER [or BABBLER]

See No. 641.

BAPTIST ANNUAL REGISTER (1790-1802)

501. Whitley, W.T. "The Baptist Annual Register, 1790." BAPTIST QUARTERLY, 10 (1940), 122-26.

BATH CHRONICLE (1755-1900+)

Title changes.

502. Price, Cecil. "Hymen and Hirco: A Vision." TLS, 11 July 1958, p. 396.

Suggests an article in the BATH CHRONICLE (9 May 1771) may be by Sheridan.

503. Wienholt, E.C. "Old Newspapers." N&Q, 11 (1922), 108.

See also page 157 in the same issue of N&Q.

BEACON (1821)

504. Marshall, William H. "Comments on Shelley in THE BEACON and THE KALEIDOSCOPE (1821)." N&Q, 6 (1959), 224-26.

BEE (1733-35)

See also No. 179.

505. Riffe, Nancy Lee. "Budgell's BEE, 1733-1734." N&Q, 11 (1964), 57.

See also page 296.

BEE (1759)

See also GOLDSMITH, OLIVER (chapter 4).

506. Friedman, Arthur. "The First Edition of Goldsmith's BEE, No. 1." SB, 11 (1958), 255-59.

507. Knight, Douglas. "Two Issues of Goldsmith's 'Bee.'" N&Q, 187 (1944), 276.

508. Starkey, James. "Goldsmith and 'The Bee.'" ESSAYS AND RECOLLECTIONS, BY SEUMAS O'SULLIVAN. Dublin and Cork: Talbot Press, 1944. Pp. 24-28.

BEE; OR, LITERARY WEEKLY INTELLIGENCER (1790-94)

509. Cook, Davidson. "The Editor of 'The Bee.'" TLS, 27 August 1920, pp. 552-53.

510. Currie, A.W. "Literary Views of Adam Smith." N&Q, 207 (1962), 269.

In the BEE, 1791.

511. Mullett, Charles F. "THE BEE (1790-1794): A Tour of Crochet Castle." SAQ, 66 (1967), 70-86.

BELFAST NEWS-LETTER (1796-1900+)

See No. 2282.

BELL'S NEW WEEKLY MESSENGER (1832-55)

See No. 1857.

BELL'S WEEKLY MESSENGER (1796-1896)

See No. 1857.

BENTLEY'S MISCELLANY (1837-68)

512. Littlewood, L.M. "A Victorian Magazine." CR, 151 (1937), 331-39.

BENTLEY'S, founded in 1837, was absorbed by TEMPLE BAR, 1868.

BENTLEY'S QUARTERLY REVIEW (1859-60)

See No. 57.

BIBLIOTHECA UNIVERSALIS (1688)

513. Menzies, Walter. "'Bibliotheca Universalis' and the Rev. John Cockburn." SN&Q, 8 (1930), 50-51.

See also the material by J.W. Fawcett (pages 56-57). Excellent description of a rare review journal of which only one number was published.

BINGLEY'S JOURNAL (1770-90)

See No. 1860

BIRCH (1865-66)

See No. 2293.

BLACKWOOD'S MAGAZINE (1817-1900+)

See also Nos. 57, 1499, and 2154.

514. Batt, Max. "Contributions to the History of English Opinion of German Literature: Gillies and BLACKWOOD'S MAGAZINE." MLN, 18 (1903), 65-69.

515. Besterman, Theodore. "Hazlitt and MAGA." TLS, 22 August 1935, p. 525.

516. ______. "The Cost of Libel and Maga." TLS, 25 April 1936, p. 356.

517. Brooks, E.L. "Coleridge's Second Packet for BLACKWOOD'S MAGAZINE." PQ, 30 (1951), 426-30.

    Concerning articles on witchcraft.

518. Byrns, Richard H. "De Quincey's First Article in BLACKWOOD'S MAGAZINE." BNYPL, 60 (1955), 333-37.

519. C.,J.P. "The Story of 'Maga' and the Blackwoods." LIVING AGE, 253 (1907), 778-85.

520. Carson, James C. "Contributions to 'Blackwood's Magazine.'" N&Q, 195 (1950), 63.

521. "A Causerie--Sir Walter Scott and 'Maga.'" BLACKWOOD'S MAGAZINE, 232 (1932), 1-15.

522. Daghlian, Philip B. "Byron's 'Observations on an Article in BLACKWOOD'S MAGAZINE.'" RES, 23 (1947), 123-30.

523. Davis, Kenneth W. "George Henry Lewes's Introduction to the Blackwood Circle." ELN, 1 (1963), 113-14.

524. _____. "A Note on the Ruskin-BLACKWOOD'S Controversy." VN, 30 (1966), 26-27.

525. Fetter, Frank Whitson. "The Economic Articles in BLACKWOOD'S EDINBURGH MAGAZINE, and Their Authors, 1817-1853." SCOTTISH JOURNAL OF POLITICAL ECONOMY, 7, no. 2 (1960), 85-107; 7, no. 3 (1960), 213-31.

526. Francis, John C. "BLACKWOOD'S MAGAZINE." N&Q, 3 (1899), 81-82.

527. G.,S. "A Ghost Story in BLACKWOOD'S." N&Q, 185 (1943), 109.

528. Gecker, Gerald E. "The Coleridgean Context of Poe's BLACKWOOD Satires." ESQ, no. 60, Supp. (Fall 1970), 87-91.

529. Griffith, Clark. "Poe's 'Ligeia' and the English Romantics." UTQ, 24 (1954), 8-25.

Argues that "Ligeia" is an allegorized jest at the Germanization of writers in BLACKWOOD'S.

530. Grundy, J. Owen. "R.L.S. in Greenwich Village." BNYPL, 67 (1963), 152-54.

531. Howe, P.P. "Hazlitt and BLACKWOOD'S." FR, 112 (1919), 165-66.

532. Kilbourne, William G., Jr. "The Role of Fiction in BLACKWOOD'S MAGAZINE from 1817-1845." DA, 27 (1967), 3428A-29A.

533. Massey, Irving. "Mary Shelley, Walter Scott, and 'Maga.'" N&Q, 9 (1962), 420-21.

534. Murray, Brian M. "The Authorship of Some Unidentified of Disputed Articles in BLACKWOOD'S MAGAZINE." SSL, 4 (1967), 144-54.

535. Needler, G.H. THE LONE SHIELING. Toronto: University of Toronto Press, 1942.

The origin and authorship of a poem entitled "Canadian Boat Song" which appeared in BLACKWOOD'S in 1829.

536. Nolte, Eugene. "David Macbeth Moir as Morgan Odoherty." PMLA, 72 (1957), 803-6.

537. Parker, William. "Charles Ollier to William Blackwood." TLS, 7 June 1947, p. 288.

Confidential letters concerning, among other things, the dispute between BLACKWOOD'S and the LONDON MAGAZINE.

538. Ricks, Christopher. "'Peace and War' and MAUD." N&Q, 9 (1962), 230.

"Peace and War, A Dialogue" appeared in BLACKWOOD'S, November 1854.

539. Stevenson, Thomas G. "BLACKWOOD'S MAGAZINE." N&Q, 10 (1966), 158.

540. Strout, Alan Lang. "'Maga,' Champion of Shelley." SP, 29 (1932), 95-119.

541. _____. "Samuel Taylor Coleridge and John Wilson of BLACKWOOD'S MAGAZINE." PMLA, 48 (1933), 100-128.

542. _____. "John Wilson, Champion of Wordsworth." MP, 31 (1934), 383-94.

543. _____. "James Hogg and 'Maga.'" TLS, 14 December 1935, p. 859.

544. _____. "A Note on BLACKWOOD'S MAGAZINE of October 1817." N&Q, 169 (1935), 452-54.

545. _____. "Purple Patches in the 'Noctes Ambrosianae.'" ELH, 2 (1935), 327-31.

546. _____. "Concerning the 'Noctes Ambrosianae.'" MLN, 51 (1936), 493-505.

547. _____. "The Cost of Libel and Maga." TLS, 28 March 1936, p. 278.

548. _____. "Unidentified Quotations in 'Noctes Ambrosianae.'" N&Q, 170 (1936), 66.

549. _____. "Hunt, Hazlitt, and MAGA." ELH, 4 (1937), 151-59.

Concerns attacks by BLACKWOOD'S and the QUARTERLY REVIEW on the "Cockneys."

550. _____. "'The Noctes Ambrosianae' and James Hogg." RES 13 (1937), 46-63, 177-89.

551. ______. "BLACKWOOD'S MAGAZINE, Lockhart, and John Scott." N&Q, 175 (1938), 290-94.

552. ______. "Walter Scott and 'Maga.'" TLS, 5 February 1938, p. 92.

553. ______. "Authorship of the Review ON HOGG'S MEMOIRS IN BLACKWOOD'S." N&Q, 181 (1941), 302-3.

554. ______. "BLACKWOOD'S MAGAZINE, Lockhart, and John Scott: A Whig Satirical Broadside." N&Q, 180 (1941), 22-24.

555. ______. "'Timothy Tickler' of BLACKWOOD'S MAGAZINE." N&Q, 180 (1941), 61.

556. ______. "BLACKWOOD'S MAGAZINE, Lockhart and John Scott." N&Q, 181 (1941), 22-24, 61.

557. ______. "THE RECREATIONS OF CHRISTOPHER NORTH, 1842." N&Q, 182 (1942), 314-15; 183 (1942), 69-71.

558. ______. "A Study in Periodical Patchwork: John Wilson's RECREATIONS OF CHRISTOPHER NORTH, 1842." MLR, 38 (1943), 88-105.

559. ______. "Contributors to BLACKWOOD'S MAGAZINE." N&Q, 194 (1949), 541-43; 195 (1950), 71-72.

560. ______. "George Croly and BLACKWOOD'S MAGAZINE." TLS, 6 October 1950, p. 636.

561. ______. "BLACKWOOD'S MAGAZINE, 1817-25." N&Q, 198 (1953), 130.

A query concerning authorship of certain articles.

562. ______. "Knights of the Burning Epistle (the Blackwood Papers in the National Library of Scotland)." STUDIA NEOPHILOLOGICA, 26 (1953/54), 77-98.

563. ______. "Some Miscellaneous Letters Concerning 'Blackwood's Magazine.'" N&Q, n.s. (1954), 216-17, 309-12.

564. ______. "Writers on German Literature in BLACKWOOD'S MAGAZINE: With a Footnote on Thomas Carlyle." LIBRARY, 9 (1954), 35-44.

565. ______. "BLACKWOOD'S MAGAZINE." N&Q, 200 (1955), 545-46.

566. ______. "The Authorship of Articles in BLACKWOOD'S MAGAZINE, Numbers XVII-XXIV (August 1818-March 1819)." LIBRARY, 11 (1956), 187-201.

567. ______. "Blunders about Blackwood." N&Q, 4 (1957), 263-65, 307-8.

Strout claims that Maginn wrote neither the review of Shelley's ADONAIS nor the "Critique on Lord Byron".

568. ______. "The First Twenty-Three Numbers of the 'Noctes Ambrosianae.'" LIBRARY, 12 (1957), 108-18.

569. ______. A BIBLIOGRAPHY OF ARTICLES IN 'BLACKWOOD'S MAGAZINE, 1817-1825.' Lubbock: Texas Technological College, 1959.

570. ______. "Maga and the Ettrick Shepherd: Two Unpublished Letters to William Blackwood." SSL, 4 (1967), 48-52.

571. Tredrey, F.D. THE HOUSE OF BLACKWOOD 1804-1954: THE HISTORY OF A PUBLISHING FIRM. Edinburgh and London: Blackwood, 1954.

572. Usrey, Malcolm Orthell. "The Letters of Sir Edward Bulwer-Lytton to the Editors of BLACKWOOD'S MAGAZINE, 1840-1873, in the National Library of Scotland [with] Volume II." DA, 24 (1964), 5392.

573. Wardle, Ralph M. "Noctes Ambrosianae." TLS, 9 October 1937, p. 735.

574. ______. "William Maginn and BLACKWOOD'S MAGAZINE." Ph.D. dissertation, Harvard University, 1940.

575. ______. "The Authorship of 'Noctes Ambrosianae.'" MP, 42 (1944), 9-17.

576. Whibley, Charles. "A Retrospect." BLACKWOOD'S MAGAZINE, 201 (1917), 433-46; rpt. LIVING AGE, 293 (1917), 793-803.

577. ______. "Hazlitt vs. BLACKWOOD'S MAGAZINE." BLACKWOOD'S MAGAZINE, 204 (1918), 388-98.

578. Williams, McDonald. "Blackwood's Magazine: A Selective and Critical Bibliography of Reviews (with an Introductory Essay), 1850-1880."

DA, 20 (1960), 2815-17.

579. Woolen, Wilfrid H. "BLACKWOOD'S on ADONAIS." TLS, 14 May 1925, p. 335.

BORDERLAND (1893-97)

580. Baylen, Joseph O. "W.T. Stead's BORDERLAND: A Quarterly Review and Index of Psychic Phenomena, 1893-97." VPN, 4 (1969), 30-35.

BREWSTER'S JOURNAL (1819-85)

581. Forsythe, Robert S., and A.M. Colman. "BREWSTER'S JOURNAL." N&Q, 171 (1936), 68.

BRISTOL JOURNAL (1752-1853)

582. Perry, Norma. "A Forged Letter from Frederick to Voltaire." STUDIES ON VOLTAIRE AND THE EIGHTEENTH CENTURY, vol. 60. Ed. Theodore Besterman. Geneva: Droz, 1968. Pp. 225-27.

583. ______. "John Vansommer of Spitalfields: Huguenot, Silk-Designer, and Correspondent of Voltaire." STUDIES ON VOLTAIRE AND THE EIGHTEENTH CENTURY, vol. 60. Ed. Theodore Besterman. Geneva: Droz, 1968. Pp. 289-310.

584. ______. "Voltaire and Felix Farley's BRISTOL JOURNAL." STUDIES ON VOLTAIRE AND THE EIGHTEENTH CENTURY, vol. 62. Ed. Theodore Besterman. Geneva: Droz, 1968. Pp. 137-50.

BRITISH AND FOREIGN REVIEW (1835-44)

585. DeGroot, H.B. "Lord Brougham and the Founding of the BRITISH AND FOREIGN REVIEW." VPN, 8 (1970), 22-32.

586. Winegarner, Lela. "Thackeray's Contributions to the BRITISH AND FOREIGN REVIEW." JEGP, 47 (1948), 237-45.

BRITISH APOLLO (1708-11)

See also Nos. 164 and 1991.

587. Niven, G.W. "The Authorship of 'The British Apollo.'" N&Q, 8

(1901), 97-99, 158-59, 432-33.

Discusses the probabilities that Arbuthnot wrote the APOLLO articles on the Hungarian Twins. See also the material by John Hebb, in the same issue of N&Q, page 291.

588. SELECTIONS FROM THE BRITISH APOLLO. CONTAINING ANSWERS TO CURIOUS QUESTIONS IN LITERATURE, SCIENCE, FOLKLORE, AND LOVE, PERFORMED BY A SOCIETY OF GENTLEMEN IN THE REIGN OF QUEEN ANNE. A STUDY IN THE EVOLUTION OF PERIODICAL LITERATURE. Ed. G.W. Niven. Paisley, Scotland: Alexander Gardner, 1903.

Based on the 1740 edition of selections.

589. Y.,E.H. "'The British Apollo.'" N&Q, 6 (1852), 148.

See also W.J. Bernhard Smith (page 230) and J. Crossley (page 416).

BRITISH CONTROVERSIALIST AND LITERARY MAGAZINE (1850-72)

590. Wolff, Michael. "THE BRITISH CONTROVERSIALIST AND LITERARY MAGAZINE: DEVOTED TO THE IMPARTIAL AND DELIBERATE DISCUSSION OF IMPORTANT QUESTIONS IN RELIGION, PHILOSOPHY, HISTORY, POLITICS, SOCIAL ECONOMY, ETC., AND TO THE PROMOTION OF SELF-CULTURE AND GENERAL EDUCATION." VPN, 2 (1968), 27-45.

A description of an index to this periodical.

BRITISH CRITIC (1793-1843)

591. Houghton, Esther Rhoades. "THE BRITISH CRITIC and the Oxford Movement." SB, 16 (1963), 119-37.

592. Matthews, Albert. "Richard Rolle's 'Prick of Conscience': 'The British Critic.'" N&Q, 4 (1911), 11-12.

Changes in title and numbering 1793-1843. See also Charles Higham (pages 73-74).

BRITISH JOURNAL (1722-31)

593. Anderson, Paul Bunyan. "Cato's Obscure Counterpart in THE BRITISH JOURNAL 1722-25." SP, 34 (1937), 412-28.

BRITISH LIBRARY (dates unknown)

See No. 1857.

BRITISH MAGAZINE; OR, THE LONDON AND EDINBURGH INTELLIGENCER (1747-48)

594. J.,G. "'The British Magazine,' 1747." N&Q, 7 (1859), 217.

BRITISH MAGAZINE; OR, MONTHLY REPOSITORY FOR GENTLEMEN AND LADIES (1760-67)

See also Nos. 674, 2007, 2020, and 2167.

595. Golden, Morris. "Two Essays Erroneously Attributed to Goldsmith." MLN, 74 (1959), 13-16.

The two essays were published in August 1760.

BRITISH QUARTERLY REVIEW (1845-86)

596. Osbourn, R.V. "THE BRITISH QUARTERLY REVIEW." RES, 1 (1950), 147-52.

BRITISH REVIEW AND LONDON CRITICAL JOURNAL (1811-25)

597. Ward, W.S. "Lord Byron and 'My Grandmother's Review.'" MLN, 64 (1949), 25-29.

BRITON (1762-63)

See Nos. 1269 and 2167.

CALEDONIAN MERCURY (1720-1867)

598. Murray, John. "Notes on Johnson's Movements in Scotland. Suggested Attributions to Boswell in the CALEDONIAN MERCURY." N&Q, 178 (1940), 3-5.

599. ______. "Boswell and the CALEDONIAN MERCURY. Further Suggested Attributions to Him in this Journal, January 1772-March 1774." N&Q, 178 (1940), 182-85.

CAMBRIDGE CHRONICLE (1744-1900+)

See No. 1298.

CENSOR (1715-17)

600. Golding, C. "Lewis Theobald." N&Q, 2 (1886), 215-16.

See also additional notes by C.A. Ward, and G.F.R.B. (page 216).

601. Jones, Richard Foster. LEWIS THEOBALD: HIS CONTRIBUTION TO ENGLISH SCHOLARSHIP WITH SOME UNPUBLISHED LETTERS. Columbia University Studies in English and Comparative Literature. New York: Columbia University Press, 1919.

CENTURY GUILD HOBBY HORSE (1884-92)

602. Hunt, Lorraine Rose Lively. "THE CENTURY GUILD HOBBY HORSE: A Study of a Magazine." DA, 26 (1966), 3954.

CHAMBERS'S EDINBURGH JOURNAL (1832-1900+)

See also No. 1314.

603. "End of CHAMBERS'S JOURNAL." THE TIMES, 7 December 1956, p. 7.

604. Gray, W. Forbes. "A Hundred Years Old: CHAMBERS'S JOURNAL, 1832-1932." CHAMBERS'S JOURNAL, 1 (1932), 81-96.

CHAMPION (1813-21?)

605. Bauer, Josephine. "The Champion." TLS, 26 September 1952, p. 269.

A request for information.

606. Gifford, Gordon. "Thomas Barnes and THE CHAMPION." TLS, 1 January 1944, p. 7.

607. Hudson, Derek. "Thomas Barnes and 'The Champion.'" TLS, 15 January 1944, p. 31.

See also No. 609.

608. Jones, Leonidas M. "Keats's Theatrical Reviews in the CHAMPION." KSJ, 3 (1954), 55-65.

609. Parker, W.M. "Thomas Barnes and 'The Champion.'" TLS, 1 January 1944, p. 7.

See also No. 607.

610. Turnbull, John M. "Keats, Reynolds, and THE CHAMPION." LONDON MERCURY, 19 (1929), 384-94.

CHAMPION; OR, BRITISH MERCURY (1739-43)

See also FIELDING, HENRY (chapter 4).

611. Battestin, Martin C. THE MORAL BASIS OF FIELDING'S ART: A STUDY OF 'JOSEPH ANDREWS.' Middletown, Conn.: Wesleyan University Press, 1959.

Occasional references to the CHAMPION.

612. Coley, William B. "The 'Remarkable Queries' in the CHAMPION." PQ, 41 (1962), 426-36.

613. Fielding, Henry. 'THE VOYAGES OF MR. JOB VINEGAR' FROM 'THE CHAMPION' (1740). Ed., with intro., by S.J. Sackett. Augustan Reprint Society, Publication no. 67. Los Angeles: Clark Memorial Library, 1958.

614. Graham, Walter. "The Date of the 'Champion.'" TLS, 4 February 1932, pp. 9, 76.

Appeared also in N&Q, 156 (1932), 150.

615. Kishler, Thomas C. "Fielding's Experiments with Fiction in the CHAMPION." JNT, 1 (1971), 95-107.

616. Shipley, J.B. "On the Date of the 'Champion.'" N&Q, 198 (1953), 441.

617. ______. "Essays from Fielding's 'Champion.'" N&Q, 198 (1953), 468-69.

618. ______. "Fielding's CHAMPION and a Publishers' Quarrel." N&Q, 200 (1955), 25-28.

619. ______. "The 'M' in Fielding's 'Champion.'" N&Q, 200 (1955), 240-45, 345-51.

620. ______. "A New Fielding Essay from the CHAMPION." PQ 42 (1963), 417-22.

621. Wells, John Edwin. "Fielding's Choice of Signature for 'The Champion.'" MLR, 7 (1912), 374-75.

622. ______. "Fielding's Signatures in 'The Champion' and the Date of His 'Of Good-Nature.'" MLR, 7 (1912), 97-98.

623. ______. "The 'Champion' and Some Unclaimed Essays by Henry Fielding." ENGLISCHE STUDIEN, 46 (1913), 355-66.

624. ______. "Fielding's 'Champion' and Captain Hercules Vinegar." MLR, 8 (1913), 165-72.

625. ______. "News for Bibliophiles." NATION (New York), 96 (1913), 53-54.

On Hercules Vinegar: libels and defenses.

626. ______. "Fielding's CHAMPION--More Notes." MLN, 35 (1920), 18-23.

CHIT-CHAT (1839?)

See No. 2188.

CHIT-CHAT IN A LETTER TO A LADY IN THE COUNTRY (1716)

See No. 2178.

CHRISTIAN GUARDIAN (1802-52)

627. Ellis, James, and Michael Wolff. "The CHRISTIAN GUARDIAN in 1853: An Unrecorded Volume." VPN, 16 (1972), 51-52.

CHRISTIAN MONTHLY HISTORY (1743-46)

628. Austin, Roland. "The Christian Monthly History." PROCEEDINGS OF THE WESLEY HISTORICAL SOCIETY, 12 (1919), 15-20.

629. S.,W. "Robe's Monthly History." SN&Q, 7 (1905), 95.

CHRISTIAN'S AMUSEMENT (1740)

See also No. 2107.

630. Jones, M.H. "'The Christian's Amusement.'" PROCEEDINGS OF THE WESLEY HISTORICAL SOCIETY, 11 (1917-18), 68-70, 181-86.

631. ______. "References to the Wesleys in the First Calvinistic Methodist Newspaper." PROCEEDINGS OF THE WESLEY HISTORICAL SOCIETY, 12 (1920), 158-63.

CHRISTIAN'S MAGAZINE (1760-67)

See also No. 2016.

632. Sherbo, Arthur. "Two Pieces Newly Ascribed to Christopher Smart." MLR, 62 (1967), 214-20.

A letter in the CHRISTIAN MAGAZINE (September 1762) and a poem in the LITERARY MAGAZINE (May 1758).

CITIZEN (1739)

See No. 2144.

"Citizen of the World" (1760-61)

See GOLDSMITH, OLIVER (chapter 4), and PUBLIC LEDGER (below).

COBBETT'S GRIDIRON (1822)

633. Perkins, W. Frank. "COBBETT'S GRIDIRON, London, 1822." N&Q, 171 (1936), 332.

COMIC TIMES (1850)

634. Ellis, James. "The COMIC TIMES." VPN, 12 (1971), 14-15.

COMPLETE MAGAZINE (1764)

635. Golden, Morris. "A Goldsmith Essay in the COMPLETE MAGAZINE."

N&Q, 5 (1958), 465-66.

CONJUROR'S MAGAZINE (1791-93)

636. "The Conjuror's Magazine." BIBLIOGRAPHER, 4 (1883), 132-34.

637. Salt, S. "Rosycrucians." BIBLIOGRAPHER, 1 (1882), 158.

An extract from volume I (1791).

CONNOISSEUR (1754-56)

See also Nos. 181 and 1906.

638. Lams, Victor J., Jr. "A Study of the CONNOISSEUR (1754-56)." DA, 26 (1965), 3304-5.

639. Sherbo, Arthur. "Cowper's CONNOISSEUR Essays." MLN, 70 (1955), 340-42.

640. Spector, Robert D. "The CONNOISSEUR: A Study of the Functions of a Persona." ENGLISH WRITERS OF THE EIGHTEENTH CENTURY. Ed. John H. Middendorf. New York and London: Columbia University Press, 1971. Pp. 109-21.

641. Tucker, Susie I. "Pre-Datings and Additions." N&Q, 206 (1961), 262-64.

Presents quotations from CONNOISSEUR and BABLER to show usages earlier than those given in THE OXFORD ENGLISH DICTIONARY. (The BRITISH UNION-CATALOGUE OF PERIODICALS, no. 99, lists two BABBLERS--one for 1763 and one for 1767. Tucker apparently confuses the two here.)

CONTEMPORARY REVIEW (1866-1900+)

See also No. 57.

642. Brown, A.W. THE METAPHYSICAL SOCIETY: VICTORIAN MINDS IN CRISIS. New York: Columbia University Press, 1947.

See chapter IX (pages 167-83) concerning the years 1866-77.

643. Lowe, Robert L. "Matthew Arnold and Percy William Bunting: Some New Letters, 1884-1887." SB, 7 (1955), 199-207.

CORK GAZETTE (1772-97)

See No. 2282.

CORNHILL MAGAZINE (1860-1900+)

See also No. 57.

644. Bicanic, Sonia. "Writing for the Magazines: A Study Based on the Novels of the CORNHILL MAGAZINE (1860-1880)." SRAZ, nos. 13-14 (1962), 13-30.

645. Eddy, Spencer L., Jr. THE FOUNDING OF THE 'CORNHILL MAGAZINE.' Ball State Monograph 19; Publications in English 13. Muncie, Ind.: Ball State University Press, 1970.

646. ______. "A History of the Editorship of the CORNHILL MAGAZINE: 1860-1896." DAI, 31 (1971), 6051A.

647. "Editorial Note." CORNHILL MAGAZINE, 167 (1954), 237-43.
    In its 1,000th number, the CORNHILL looks back at its history since 1860.

648. Hamilton, Richard. "The 'Cornhill.'" NEW STATESMAN AND NATION, 7 August 1954, p. 158.

649. Hyde, Ralph W. "The Short Story in CORNHILL MAGAZINE, 1860-1900: A Study in Form and Content." DA, 27 (1966), 1337A-38A.

650. Maurer, Oscar. "Leslie Stephen and the CORNHILL MAGAZINE, 1871-82." UNIVERSITY OF TEXAS STUDIES IN ENGLISH, 33 (1954), 67-95.

651. Smith, Peter. "The Cornhill Magazine--Number I." REL, 4, ii (1963), 23-34.

652. Tiemersma, Richard Robert. "Fiction in the CORNHILL MAGAZINE, January 1860-March 1871." DA, 23 (1963), 3358.

653. Tindall, Samuel J., Jr. "Leslie Stephen as Editor of the CORNHILL MAGAZINE." DAI, 30 (1970), 5422A.

COTES'S WEEKLY JOURNAL (1734)

654. Milford, R.T. "Cotes's Weekly Journal." TLS, 19 March 1931, p. 234.

Not entered in the Crane & Kaye CENSUS (No. 32).

655. Stratman, Carl J. "Cotes's Weekly Journal; or, The English Stage-Player." PBSA, 56 (1962), 104-6.

A newspaper of 1734 which promised to print "all the plays in the English language," but printed only two in its nine issues.

COURIER (1792-1842)

See also Nos. 1698 and 1855.

656. Cline, C.L. "Byron and Southey: A Suppressed Rejoinder." KSJ, 3 (1954), 27-38.

A letter from Byron to the editor.

657. Erdman, David V. "A New Discovery: The First Review of CHRISTABEL." TSE, 37 (1958), 53-60.

A long and laudatory review reprinted from the TIMES.

658. ______. "Coleridge on Coleridge: The Context (and Text) of His Review of 'Mr. Coleridge's Lay Sermon.'" SIR, 1 (1961), 47-64.

659. Southam, B.C. "Jane Austen." TLS, 30 November 1962, p. 944; 14 December 1962, p. 980.

Her obituary (22 July 1817), possibly by Cassandra; evidence for her authorship of "Venta."

COURT MAGAZINE (1806-32)

See No. 700.

COVENT-GARDEN JOURNAL (1752)

See also FIELDING, HENRY (chapter 4), No. 1729 and COVENT GARDEN JOURNAL EXTRAORDINARY (below).

660. Coley, William B. "Fielding and the Two 'Covent-Garden Journals.'"

MLR, 58 (1962), 386-87.

Hostile relations between Fielding and the two COVENT-GARDEN JOURNALS and OLD ENGLAND.

661. THE COVENT-GARDEN JOURNAL. BY SIR ALEXANDER DRAWCANSIR, KNT. CENSOR OF GREAT BRITAIN (HENRY FIELDING). Ed. Gerard Edward Jensen. 2 vols. New Haven, Conn.: Yale University Press, 1915.

662. Dobson, [Henry] Austin. "The Covent-Garden Journal. Being a Hitherto-Unwritten Chapter in the Life of Henry Fielding." NATIONAL REVIEW, 37 (1901), 383-96; rpt. SIDE-WALK STUDIES. By Austin Dobson. London: Chatto & Windus, 1902. Pp. 63-92.

Also reprinted in Dobson's EIGHTEENTH CENTURY STUDIES (1914).

663. Rogers, Pat. "Fielding's Parody of Oldmixon." PQ, 49 (1970), 262-66.

In the issue for 29 January 1752.

COVENT-GARDEN JOURNAL EXTRAORDINARY (1752)

664. Jensen, Gerard E[dward]. "The Covent-garden Journal Extraordinary." MLN, 34 (1919), 57-59.

CRACKLING GOOSE (dates unknown)

665. Brushfield, T.N. "Extinct Devonshire Periodicals: THE CRACKLING GOOSE." WESTERN ANTIQUARY; OR, DEVON AND CORNWALL NOTE-BOOK, 11 (1891), 71-73.

CRAFTSMAN (1726-47)

See also No. 238.

666. Avery, Emmett L. "THE CRAFTSMAN of July 2, 1737, and Colley Cibber." RESEARCH STUDIES OF THE STATE COLLEGE OF WASHINGTON, 7 (1939), 91-103.

667. "The 'Craftsman' and Its Contributors." BOOKWORM, 2 (1889), 13-17.

668. F.,W. "The 'Craftsman' on Chess: L. Rou." N&Q, 10 (1902), 41-43.

No. 376 of the CRAFTSMAN and the replies that it provoked, especially concerning the manuscript of Lewis Rou.

669. Powell, G.H. "'Craftsman.'" N&Q, 3 (1887), 8.

A manuscript duplicate of No. 63.

CRITICAL REVIEW (1756-1817)

See also Nos. 2010 and 2016.

670. Bouce, Paul-Gabriel. "Smollett's Libel." TLS, 30 December 1965, p. 1218.

Smollett's attack on Admiral Knowles is not printed in full in some copies for May 1758.

671. Erdman, David V. "Immoral Acts of a Library Cormorant: The Extent of Coleridge's Contributions to the CRITICAL REVIEW." BNYPL, 63 (1959), 433-54, 515-30, 575-87.

672. Foster, James R. "Smollett's Pamphleteering Foe Shebbeare." PMLA, 57 (1942), 1053-1100.

Attributes to Smollett a series of articles related to Shebbeare which appeared in the CRITICAL REVIEW.

673. Friedman, Arthur. "Goldsmith's Contributions to the CRITICAL REVIEW." MP, 44 (1946), 23-52.

674. Golden, Morris. "Notes on Three Goldsmith Attributions." N&Q, 203 (1958), 24-26.

Accepts one essay in the BRITISH MAGAZINE (February 1760); rejects one in BRITISH MAGAZINE (June 1760) and one in CRITICAL REVIEW (June 1759).

675. Jones, Claude E. "Smollett and the 'Critical Review.'" SMOLLETT STUDIES. University of California Publications in English, IX, ii. Berkeley: University of California Press, 1942. Pp. 77-102.

See also "Appendix B1, Attacks on the 'Critical,' 1756-1771" (pages 107-10).

676. ______. "Contributors to 'The Critical Review,' 1756-1785." MLN, 61 (1946), 433-41.

"Lists and discusses known and supposed contributions. The

discussion of Goldsmith is inaccurate in some of its details" (PQ, 26:107).

677. ______. "Poetry and the CRITICAL REVIEW, 1756-1785." MLQ, 9 (1948), 17-36.

678. ______. "'The Critical Review's' First Thirty Years (1756-1785)." N&Q, 201 (1956), 78-80.

679. ______. "'The Critical Review,' and Some Major Poets." N&Q, 201 (1956), 114-15.

The poets include Spenser, Milton, and Pope.

680. ______. "Dramatic Criticism in the CRITICAL REVIEW, 1756-1785." MLQ, 20 (1959), 18-26, 133-44.

681. Klukoff, Philip J. "A Smollett Attribution in the 'Critical Review.'" N&Q, 210 (1965), 221.

The editorial preface to volume XI (January 1761).

682. ______. "Smollett and the CRITICAL REVIEW: Criticism of the Novel." DA, 27 (1966), 748A.

683. ______. "Smollett as the Reviewer of 'Jeremiah Grant.'" N&Q, 211 (1966), 466.

684. ______. "Two Smollett Attributions in the 'Critical Review': 'The Reverie' and 'Tristram Shandy.'" N&Q, 211 (1966), 465-66.

685. ______. "New Smollett Attributions in the 'Critical Review.'" N&Q, 212 (1967), 418-19.

686. ______. "Smollett's Defense of Dr. Smellie in the Critical Review." MEDICAL HISTORY, 14 (1970), 31-41.

687. ______, comp. "Novels Reviewed in the CRITICAL REVIEW, 1756-1763." BULLETIN OF BIBLIOGRAPHY, 28, no. 1 (1971), 35-36; 28, no. 2 (1971), 40-41.

Smollett was editor during these years.

688. Noyes, Edward S. "THE CRITICAL REVIEW." TLS, 4 December 1930, p. 1042.

689. Patterson, Charles I. "The Authenticity of Coleridge's Reviews of Gothic Romances." JEGP, 50 (1951), 517-21.

Opposed by Roper (see No. 693).

690. _____. "An Unidentified Criticism by Coleridge Related to CHRISTABEL." PMLA, 67 (1952), 973-88.

691. Roper, Derek. "Tobias Smollett and the Founders of His 'Review.'" CALL NUMBER (Library of the University of Oregon), 19 (1957), 4-9.

Concerns a marked copy of the CRITICAL REVIEW at the University of Oregon.

692. _____. "Smollett's 'Four Gentlemen': The First Contributors to the CRITICAL REVIEW." RES, 10 (1959), 38-44.

Identifies Smollett's four assistants on the basis of early pencilled annotations in the University of Oregon copy of the first two volumes of the CRITICAL REVIEW, and includes a list of works reviewed by Smollett in 1756.

693. _____. "Coleridge and the CRITICAL REVIEW." MLR, 55 (1960), 11-16.

694. _____. "The Politics of the CRITICAL REVIEW, 1756-1817." DURHAM UNIVERSITY JOURNAL, 53 (1961), 117-22.

695. Sparke, Archibald. "Southey's Contributions to THE CRITICAL REVIEW." N&Q, 5 (1919), 187-88.

A response to Zeitlin (see No. 701).

696. Spector, Robert D. "Language Control in the Eighteenth Century." WORD STUDY, 27 (1951), 1-2.

Standards of language in the CRITICAL REVIEW.

697. _____. "Further Attacks on the 'Critical Review.'" N&Q, 200 (1955), 535.

698. _____. "Additional Attacks on the 'Critical Review.'" N&Q, 201 (1956), 425.

699. _____. "Attacks on the 'Critical Review' (1964-1765)." N&Q, 202 (1957), 121.

700. _____. "Attacks on the 'Critical Review' in the 'Court Magazine.'"

N&Q, 203 (1958), 308.

701. Zeitlin, Jacob. "Southey's Contributions to 'The Critical Review.'" N&Q, 4 (1918), 35-36, 66-67, 94-96, 122-25.

The reviews discussed appeared between 1798 and 1803.

CRITICK (1718; rpt. 1719 as THE CRITICKS)

702. Gorham, James J. "The Critics." N&Q, 154 (1928), 317; 155 (1928), 339.

Information given is largely taken from the TIMES HANDLIST and the BURN CATALOGUE. Also in this issue of N&Q, see the material by Archibald Sparke (page 357) and E.E. Newton (pp. 409-10).

703. Naugle, Helen H. "THE CRITICKS: An Annotated Edition." DA, 29 (1969), 3183A.

DAILY ADVERTISER (1730-1803)

See Nos. 275, 1982, and 2083.

DAILY GAZETTEER (1735-48)

See also No. 2144.

704. McKenzie, D.F. "Samuel Richardson, Mr. W., and Lady T. . ." N&Q, 209 (1964), 299-300.

Why Richardson severed his connection with the DAILY GAZETTEER in 1746.

DAILY JOURNAL (1720-42)

See also No. 2144.

705. Eaves, T.C. Duncan, and Ben D. Kimpel. "Two Notes on Samuel Richardson: Richardson's Chapel Rules; the Printer of the DAILY JOURNAL." LIBRARY, 23 (1968), 242-47.

DAILY NEWS (1846-1900+)

706. "THE DAILY NEWS and Charles Dickens." JRLB, 19 (1946), 247-49.

707. Grubb, Gerald Giles. "Dickens and the DAILY NEWS: The Origin of the Idea." BOOKER MEMORIAL STUDIES. Ed. Hill Shine. Chapel Hill: University of North Carolina Press, 1950. Pp. 61-77.

". . . [D]isposes of the legend that Dickens originated the DAILY NEWS" (MP, 48:243-44).

708. _____. "Dickens and the DAILY NEWS: Preliminaries to Publication." NCF, 6 (1951), 174-94.

709. _____. "Dickens and the DAILY NEWS: Resignation." NCF, 7 (1952), 234-46.

710. S.,L.C. "THE DAILY NEWS Centenary." DICKENSIAN, 42 (1946), 78-79.

DAILY POST (1719-46)

See Nos. 238 and 1926.

DAILY TELEGRAPH (1826)

711. Coulling, Sidney M.B. "Matthew Arnold and the DAILY TELEGRAPH." RES, 12 (1961), 173-79.

DEFOE'S REVIEW (1704-13)

See REVIEW (Defoe's).

DODSLEY'S ANNUAL REGISTER (1758-1900+)

See ANNUAL REGISTER.

DOME (1897-1900)

712. West, Paul. "THE DOME: An Aesthetic Periodical of the 1890's." BC, 6 (1957), 160-69.

713. Ziegler, Arthur P., Jr. "THE DOME and Its Editor Publisher: An Exploration." ABC, 15, vii (1965), 19-21.

DUBLIN LIBRARY MAGAZINE (dates unknown)

714. Abhba. "'The Dublin Library.'" N&Q, 6 (1870), 174.
Not entered in the Crane & Kaye CENSUS, (No. 32).

DUBLIN REVIEW (1836-1900+)

See also No. 57.

715. Fletcher, John R. "Early Catholic Periodicals in England." DUBLIN REVIEW, 198 (April-June 1936), 284-310.

716. McLaughlin, P.J. "Dr. Russell and the DUBLIN REVIEW." STUDIES, AN IRISH QUARTERLY REVIEW, 41 (1952), 175-88.

717. Walsh, Leo Joseph. "William G. Ward and the DUBLIN REVIEW." DA, 26 (1966), 6028.

DUBLIN UNIVERSITY MAGAZINE (1833-80)

718. Chuto, Jacques. "Mangan and the 'Irys Herfner': Articles in the DUBLIN MAGAZINE." HERMATHENA, 111 (Spring 1971), 55-58.

DUBLIN WEEKLY ORACLE (1735-36)

719. M[ortimer]., R[ussell]. S. "The Quaker's Dublin Weekly Oracle, 1721." JOURNAL OF THE FRIENDS' HISTORICAL SOCIETY, 49 (1961), 244-47.
This periodical, no longer extant, was edited by John Crabb.

DUNDEE MAGAZINE (1775)

See No. 2267.

DUNDEE WEEKLY INTELLEGENCER (dates unknown)

See No. 2267.

ECLECTIC REVIEW (1805-68)

720. Taylor, Henry. "THE ECLECTIC REVIEW." N&Q, 3 (1899), 27.

Also in this issue, see page 118.

EDINBURGH COURANT (1705-20; SCOTS COURANT after 1709)

721. Burch, Charles Eaton. "Defoe's Connections with the EDINBURGH COURANT." RES, 5 (1929), 437-40.

722. S.,J. "Scotch Newspaper of the Age of Queen Anne." N&Q, 7 (1883), 386.

EDINBURGH EVENING POST (1827-32?)

See Nos. 776 and 1948.

EDINBURGH GAZETTEER (1792-94)

723. Clarke, John S. "Burns and the EDINBURGH GAZETTEER." THE ROBERT BURNS ANNUAL AND CHRONICLE, 2d ser., 21 (1946), 25-28.

724. M. "'The Edinburgh Gazetteer.'" N&Q, 4 (1863), 161-62.

Quotes poem from the issue for March 1793.

EDINBURGH LITERARY JOURNAL (1828-32)

725. Cochrane, Robert. "EDINBURGH LITERARY JOURNAL, 1829-31." N&Q, 2 (1910), 267.

Also in this issue, see pages 317 and 338.

726. Glasheen, Adaline E., and Francis J. Glasheen. "The Publication of THE WANDERING JEW." MLR, 28 (1943), 11-17.

Concludes that the version in FRASER'S MAGAZINE is a garbled corruption of the LITERARY JOURNAL'S MS.

EDINBURGH MAGAZINE; OR, LITERARY MISCELLANY (1785-1803); continued as SCOTS MAGAZINE AND EDINBURGH LITERARY MISCELLANY (1804-17)

727. Hayden, John O. "Hazlitt Reviews Hazlitt?" MLR, 64 (1969), 20-26.

Argues that Hazlitt reviewed his own work in November 1817.

728. Walford, Cornelius. "'Edinburgh Magazine and Literary Miscellany.'" N&Q, 6 (1882), 188-89.

Replies appear on pages 333-34.

EDINBURGH MAGAZINE AND REVIEW (1757-62)

729. Kerr, Robert. MEMOIRS OF THE LIFE, WRITINGS & CORRESPONDENCE OF WILLIAM SMELLIE. 2 vols. Edinburgh: Printed for John Anderson, 1811.

EDINBURGH REVIEW (1755-56)

See No. 2301.

EDINBURGH REVIEW (1802-1900+)

See also Nos. 57 and 2154.

730. Bell, A.S. "An Unpublished Letter on the EDINBURGH REVIEW." TLS, 9 April 1970, p. 388.

From S. Smith to J. Mackintosh.

731. Blagden, Cyprian. "EDINBURGH REVIEW Authors, 1830-49." LIBRARY, 7 (1952), 212-14.

A supplement to No. 759 below.

732. Brogan. D.W. "The Intellectual Review." ENCOUNTER, November 1963, pp. 7-15.

733. Buckingham, Leroy H. "THE EDINBURGH REVIEW." N&Q, 173 (1937), 441.

734. _____. THE AUTHORSHIP OF THE FIRST TWENTY-FIVE NUMBERS OF THE 'EDINBURGH REVIEW,' 1802-1808. Ann Arbor, Mich.: University Microfilms, 1938.

735. Carver, P.L. "Hazlitt's Contributions to the EDINBURGH REVIEW." RES, 4 (1928), 385-93.

736. Clive, John. "The Earl of Buchan's Kick: A Footnote to the History of the EDINBURGH REVIEW." HARVARD LIBRARY BULLETIN 5 (1951), 326-70.

737. _____. "The EDINBURGH REVIEW: 150 Years After." HISTORY TODAY, 2 (1952), 844-50.

738. _____. SCOTCH REVIEWERS: THE EDINBURGH REVIEW, 1802-1815. London: Faber and Faber; Cambridge, Mass.: Harvard University Press, 1957.

739. Collins, Philip. "Dickens and the EDINBURGH REVIEW." RES, 14 (1963), 167-72.

740. Crawford, Thomas. THE EDINBURGH REVIEW AND ROMANTIC POETRY (1802-29). Auckland University College Bulletin no. 47; English Series no. 8. Auckland, New Zealand: Auckland University College, 1955.

741. de Beer, E.S. "Macaulay and Croker: The Review of Croker's Boswell." RES, 10 (1959), 388-97.

The review appeared in EDINBURGH REVIEW (August-December 1831).

742. Dowden, Wilfred S. "Thomas Moore and the Review of CHRISTABEL." MP, 60 (1962), 47-50.

In EDINBURGH REVIEW (September 1816). Denies Moore's authorship. See also Nos. 761, 771, and 772.

743. "The EDINBURGH REVIEW (1802-1902)." EDINBURGH REVIEW, 196 (1902), 275-318.

744. "1802-1929." EDINBURGH REVIEW, 250 (1929), 193-94.

745. "End of the EDINBURGH." LIVING AGE, 337 (1929), 420.

746. Fetter, Frank W. "The Authorship of Economic Articles in the EDINBURGH REVIEW, 1802-47." JPE, 61 (1953), 232-59.

747. _____. "A Probable Source of Copinger's 'On the Authorship of the First Hundred Numbers of the Edinburgh Review.'" LIBRARY, 9 (1954), 49-53.

748. _____. "Biographical Aids to Research, XIII: The Authorship of Articles in the EDINBURGH REVIEW." BIHR, 30 (1957), 76-79.

749. _____. THE ECONOMIC WRITINGS OF FRANCIS HORNER IN THE

EDINBURGH REVIEW. Reprints of Scarce Works on Political Economy, no. 13. London: 1957.

750. Goldberg, Maxwell H. "Jeffrey: Mutilator of Carlyle's 'Burns.'" PMLA, 56 (1941), 466-71.

751. ______. "Thomas Carlyle's Relationships with the EDINBURGH REVIEW." DAI, 32 (1971), 429A.

752. Greig, James A. FRANCIS JEFFREY OF THE EDINBURGH REVIEW. London: Oliver and Boyd, 1948.

753. Griggs, Earl Leslie. "Robert Southey and the EDINBURGH REVIEW." MP, 30 (1932), 100-103.

754. Griggs, Irwin, John D. Kern, and Elisabeth Schneider. "Early EDINBURGH REVIEWERS: A New List." MP, 42 (1945), 152-73; 43 (1946), 192-210.

755. Halpern, Sheldon. "Sydney Smith in the EDINBURGH REVIEW: A New List." BNYPL, 66 (1962), 589-602.

756. Hatch, Ronald B. "'This Will Never Do.'" RES, 21 (1970), 57-62.

Concerns alterations by Francis Jeffrey to the text of his CONTRIBUTIONS TO THE EDINBURGH REVIEW, 1844 (No. 758).

757. Ireland, Alexander. "William Hazlitt's Contributions to the EDINBURGH REVIEW." N&Q, 11 (1879), 165.

758. Jeffrey, Francis. CONTRIBUTIONS TO THE EDINBURGH REVIEW. 4 vols. London: 1844.

See also No. 756.

759. Johnson, L.G. "On Some Authors of EDINBURGH REVIEW, 1830-1849." LIBRARY, 7 (1952), 38-50.

See also No. 731.

760. Jones, Stanley. "Hazlitt, Cobbett, and the EDINBURGH REVIEW." NEOPHILOLOGUS, 53 (1969), 69-76.

761. Jordan, Hoover H. "Thomas Moore and the Review of CHRISTABEL." MP, 54 (1956), 95-105.

Rejects attribution to Moore in favor of Hazlitt and Jeffrey. See also Nos. 742, 771, and 772.

762. Karminski, Anne. "The EDINBURGH REVIEW after 150 Years." LISTENER (BBC), 30 October 1952, pp. 728-29.

763. Millgate, Jane. "Father and Son: Macaulay's EDINBURGH Debut." RES, 21 (1970), 159-67.

764. Morgan, P[eter]. F. "Carlyle, Jeffrey, and the EDINBURGH REVIEW." NEOPHILOLOGUS, 54 (1970), 297-310.

765. _____. "Carlyle and Macaulay as Critics of Literature and Life in the EDINBURGH REVIEW." SGG, 12 (1971), 131-44.

766. Murphy, James. "Sydney Smith's Contributions to the EDINBURGH REVIEW." LIBRARY, 8 (1953), 275-78.

767. New, Chester William. THE LIFE OF HENRY BROUGHAM TO 1830. Oxford: Oxford University Press, 1961.

See expecially chapters 2 and 5.

768. Qureshi, Ahmad Hasan. "The Attitude of Some English Liberals toward Napoleon as Reflected in the EDINBURGH REVIEW and Leigh Hunt's EXAMINER." DA, 19 (1959), 2604.

769. Rossi, Sergiol. THE EDINBURGH REVIEW (1802-1830). Milan: Marzorati, 1955.

770. Schneider, Elisabeth. "Thomas Moore and the EDINBURGH REVIEW." MLN, 61 (1946), 177-79.

771. _____. "The Unknown Reviewer of CHRISTABEL: Jeffrey, Hazlitt, Tom Moore." PMLA, 70 (1955), 417-32.

A reopening of the case against Moore. See also Nos. 742, 761, and 772.

772. _____. "Tom Moore and the EDINBURGH Review of 'Christabel.'" PMLA, 77 (1962), 71-76.

In EDINBURGH REVIEW (September 1816). Moore is the author rather than Hazlitt or Jeffrey, but see also Nos. 742, 761, and 771.

773. Schneider, Elisabeth, Irwin Griggs, and John D. Kern. "Brougham's Early Contributions to the EDINBURGH REVIEW: A New List." MP, 42 (1945), 152-73.

774. Watkins, Lloyd I. "Lord Brougham's Authorship of Rhetorical Articles in the EDINBURGH REVIEW." QJS, 42 (1956), 55-63.

775. Wheeler, Paul Mowbray. AMERICA THROUGH BRITISH EYES; A STUDY OF THE ATTITUDE OF THE 'EDINBURGH REVIEW' TOWARD THE UNITED STATES OF AMERICA FROM 1802 UNTIL 1861. Rock Hill, S.C.: 1935.

A lithoprint of a 1930 Johns Hopkins University doctoral dissertation.

EDINBURGH SATURDAY POST (1827-28)

See also No. 1948.

776. Tave, Stuart M. NEW ESSAYS BY DEQUINCEY: HIS CONTRIBUTIONS TO THE 'EDINBURGH SATURDAY POST' AND THE 'EDINBURGH EVENING POST,' 1827-28. Princeton, N.J.: Princeton University Press, 1966.

Thirty-nine articles added to the DeQuincey canon including reviews of the EDINBURGH REVIEW and BLACKWOOD'S MAGAZINE.

EDINBURGH THEATRICAL CENSOR (1803)

777. Stratman, Carl J. "Scotland's First Dramatic Periodical: THE EDINBURGH THEATRICAL CENSOR." TN, 17 (1963), 83-86.

EDINBURGH WEEKLY JOURNAL (1757-1847)

778. C.,W.J. "Provost Brown of Aberdeen and the EDINBURGH WEEKLY JOURNAL." SN&Q, 7 (1906), 190.

See also SN&Q, 8 (1906), 16, 30.

ENGLISH FREEHOLDER (1791)

779. Roberts, W. "THE ENGLISH FREEHOLDER, 1791." N&Q, 2 (1910), 108, 216.

ENGLISHMAN (1713-14, 1715)

See also STEELE, RICHARD (chapter 4).

780. THE ENGLISHMAN: A POLITICAL JOURNAL BY RICHARD STEELE. Ed. Rae Blanchard. Oxford: Clarendon Press, 1955.

An excellent and important modern edition. Reviewed in PQ 35:326-27; MLR 51:423-24; MP 54:64-66; RES 8:315-16.

781. Friedman, Arthur. "Goldsmith and Steele's ENGLISHMAN." MLN, 55 (1940), 294-96.

ENTERTAINING GAZETTE (dates unknown)

782. Levy, M. "ENTERTAINING GAZETTE." N&Q, 10 (1890), 228.

See also N&Q, (1898), 505.

ENTHUSIAST (dates unknown)

783. McKillop, Alan D. "Shaftesbury in Joseph Warton's ENTHUSIAST." MLN, 70 (1955), 337-39.

EUROPEAN MAGAZINE (1782-1825)

784. Durant, W. Clark. "Mary Wollstonecraft." N&Q, 9 (1921), 490.

A scurrilous review in the EUROPEAN MAGAZINE.

785. Maxwell, J.C. "Hazlitt and 'The European Magazine for the Year 1761.'" N&Q, 15 (1968), 25.

Hazlitt's memory slipped; there was no EUROPEAN MAGAZINE in 1761.

786. Race, Sydney. "The Authenticity of Keeling's Journal Entries on HAMLET and RICHARD II." N&Q, 196 (1951), 513-15.

The entries first appeared in the EUROPEAN MAGAZINE for 1825.

787. Whiting, George W. "A Sonnet Addressed to the Physicians of Exeter on the Ill Health of a Beautiful Lady." N&Q, 202 (1957), 322.

EVANGELICAL MAGAZINE (1793-1812)

788. Lindsay, Jack. "The Evangelical Magazine." TLS, 12 November 1938, p. 725.

Publication of Cowper's "Stanzas for the Northampton Bill of Mortality for 1792" in the issue for February 1794.

EXAMINER (1808-81)

See also HUNT, LEIGH (chapter 4) and Nos. 768 and 2089.

789. Blunden, Edmund. LEIGH HUNT'S 'EXAMINER' EXAMINED. New York and London: Harper, 1928.

790. Cameron, Kenneth Neill. "A Reference to Shelley in the EXAMINER." N&Q, 184 (1943), 42.

791. Erdman, David V. "Blake's 'Nest of Villains.'" KSJ, 2 (1953), 61-71.

Concerns Blake's quarrel with the editors.

792. Fenner, Theodore L. "Leigh Hunt on Opera: The EXAMINER Years." DA, 28 (1968), 5013A.

793. Fielding, K.J. "Re-Reading THE EXAMINER, 1832-55." VPN, 1 (January 1968), 24-25.

794. Graham, Walter. "Shelley's Debt to Leigh Hunt and the EXAMINER." PMLA, 40 (1925), 185-92.

795. Grittings, Robert. "Leigh Hunt's EXAMINER." TLS, 23 November 1967, p. 1111.

An account of four years spent reading this periodical.

796. Hainds, J.R. "J.S. Mill's EXAMINER Articles on Art." JHI, 11 (1950), 215-34.

797. King, Helen G., ed. "Trollope's Letters to the EXAMINER." PULC, 26 (1965), 71-101.

798. Legge, J.G. "THE EXAMINER and William Blake." LONDON MERCURY, 20 (May 1929), 70-71.

799. "Leigh Hunt's 'Examiner.'" COLBY LIBRARY QUARTERLY, 4th ser., February 1958, pp. 244-45.

Concerns the acquisition of "a small run."

800. Peck, Walter Edwin. "Shelley's Reviews Written for THE EXAMINER." MLN, 39 (1924), 118-19.

801. Stout, George D. THE POLITICAL HISTORY OF LEIGH HUNT'S 'EXAMINER.' Washington University Studies, New Series, Language and Literature, no. 19. St. Louis: Washington University Press, 1949.

802. Strout, Alan Lang. "A Libellous Inscription." N&Q, 196 (1951), 215.

In the EXAMINER and the WESTMINSTER REVIEW.

803. Thomas, Donald. "Leigh Hunt's EXAMINER." CENSORSHIP, 2 (Spring 1966), 38-42.

804. Tillotson, Kathleen, and Nina Burgis. "Forster's Reviews in the EXAMINER, 1840-1841." DICKENSIAN, 68 (1972), 105-8.

805. Turnbull, John M. "Lamb (?) and London Fogs." N&Q, 192 (1947), 360-61.

Strengthens a doubtful attribution printed over Lamb's name in the issue for 18 December 1831.

EXAMINER; OR, REMARKS ON PAPERS AND OCCURRENCES (1710-14)

See also SWIFT, JONATHAN (chapter 4) and Nos. 378, 821, and 1471.

806. Allen, Robert J. "William Oldisworth: 'The Author of THE EXAMINER.'" PQ, 26 (1947), 159-80.

Reviewed in PQ, 29:288-89.

807. Cook, Richard I. "'Mr. Examiner' and 'Mr. Review': The Tory Apologetics of Swift and Defoe." HLQ, 29 (1966), 127-46.

Swift and Defoe, both defending the Harley administration but to different audiences, used differing rhetoric.

808. Davis, Herbert. THE SATIRE OF JONATHAN SWIFT. New York: Macmillan, 1947.

Includes a discussion of Swift's EXAMINER. Reviewed in ES,

29:22-24; MLN, 63:578; PQ, 28:404-5.

809. Lindstrom, David H. "THE EXAMINER, Vol. I (1710-1711): Introduction and Notes." DAI, 31 (1970), 1805A.

810. Swift, Jonathan. THE EXAMINER AND OTHER PIECES WRITTEN IN 1710-11. [Ed. Herbert Davis.] Oxford: Blackwell, 1940.

Contains Nos. 13-45 of EXAMINER.

EXTRAORDINARY NORTH BRITON (1768-70)

811. Crossley, James. "Extraordinary North Briton." N&Q 3 (1851), 432.

See also the material signed F.S.A. (page 409).

812. Rhodon. "THE EXTRAORDINARY OF NORTH BRITON: A Lost Journal." N&Q, 66 (1934), 187-89, 225, 264.

See also R.T. Milford, Andrew Stewart, and F.W. Read (pages 230-31).

FELIX FARLEY'S BRISTOL JOURNAL (1752-1853)

See BRISTOL JOURNAL.

FEMALE SPECTATOR (1744-46)

See also HAYWOOD, ELIZA (chapter 4) and No. 164.

813. THE FEMALE SPECTATOR. BEING SELECTIONS FROM MRS. ELIZA HEYWOOD'S [sic] PERIODICAL (1744-1746). Sel. and ed. by Mary Priestley. Intro. by J.B. Priestley. Decorations by Constance Rowlands. London: John Lane, 1929.

FEMALE TATLER (1709-10)

See also MANLEY, MRS. MARY DE LA RIVIÈRE (chapter 4) and No. 1670.

814. Anderson, Paul Bunyan. "The History and Authorship of Mrs. Crackenthorpe's FEMALE TATLER." MP, 28 (1931), 354-60.

See also No. 821.

815. ______. "Splendor out of Scandal: the Lucinda-Artesia Papers in

THE FEMALE TATLER." PQ, 15 (1936), PQ, 15 (1936), 286-300.

See also No. 824.

816. _____. "Innocence and Artifice: or, Mrs. Centlivre and THE FEMALE TATLER." PQ, 16 (1937), 358-75.

817. _____. "La Bruyère and Mrs. Crackenthorpe's FEMALE TATLER." PMLA, 52 (1937), 100-103.

818. Bowyer, John Wilson. THE CELEBRATED MRS. CENTLIVRE. Durham, N.C.: Duke University Press, 1952.

Proposes her as author for a portion of this periodical.

819. Graham, Walter. "Thomas Baker, Mrs. Manley, and the FEMALE TATLER." MP, 34 (1937), 267-72.

820. Milford, R.T. "The Female Tatler." MP, 29 (1932), 350-51.

A correction to No. 814.

821. Needham, Gwendolyn B. "Mary de la Rivière Manley: Tory Defender." HLQ, 12 (1949), 253-88.

Concerns the career of the woman who may have written the FEMALE TATLER and who did edit the EXAMINER for a time. Reviewed in PQ, 29:286.

822. Smith, John Harrington. "Thomas Baker and the FEMALE TATLER." MP, 49 (1952), 182-88.

Evidence for ascribing Nos. 1-51 to Baker.

823. Vichert, Gordon S. "Some Recent Mandeville Attributions." PQ, 45 (1966), 459-63.

Confirms Anderson's attribution of a portion of the FEMALE TATLER to Mandeville (see No. 815).

824. White, Robert B., Jr. "A Study of the FEMALE TATLER (1709-1710)." DA, 27 (1967), 3021A-22A.

825. _____. "An Eighteenth Century Allusion to Chaucer's COOK'S TALE." ELN, 7 (1970), 190-92.

826. _____. "The Rivalry of the FEMALE TATLERS: Periodical Piracy in the Early Eighteenth Century." QUICK SPRINGS OF SENSE: STUDIES IN THE EIGHTEENTH CENTURY [IN HONOR OF LODWICK HARTLEY].

Ed. Larry S. Champion. Athens: University of Georgia Press, 1974. Pp. 51-59.

FLAPPER (1796-97)

827. Graham, Walter. "The Authorship of the FLAPPER, 1796." N&Q, 162 (1932), 25, 246.

See also the material by R.T. Milford, (page 122) and T.O. Mabbott (page 340).

828. Stockwell, La Tourette. "The Flapper." IRISH BOOK LOVER, 17 (1929), 94-95.

FOG'S WEEKLY JOURNAL (1716-37)

See WEEKLY JOURNAL; OR, SATURDAY'S POST.

FOREIGN QUARTERLY REVIEW (1827-47)

See also No. 57.

829. Batt, Max. "Contributions to the History of English Opinion of German Literature: Gillies and the FOREIGN QUARTERLY REVIEW." MLN, 17 (1902), 166-70.

830. Curran, Eileen Mary. "The FOREIGN QUARTERLY REVIEW (1827-1846): A British Interpretation of Modern European Literature." DA, 19 (1958), 137-38.

831. ______. "The FOREIGN QUARTERLY REVIEW on Russian and Polish Literature." SLAVONIC AND EAST EUROPEAN REVIEW, 40 (December 1961), 206-19.

832. ______. "Carlyle's First Contribution to the FOREIGN QUARTERLY REVIEW: A Small Identification." VPN, 2 (1968), 25-26.

833. McCray, John. "List of Writers in the FOREIGN QUARTERLY REVIEW, Vols. I-XIV, a Contribution to Literary History." N&Q, 8 (1859), 124-27.

FOREIGN REVIEW (1828-30)

834. Havens, Raymond D. "Southey's Contributions to the FOREIGN RE-

VIEW." RES, 8 (1932), 210-11.

FORTNIGHTLY REVIEW (1865-1900+)

See also Nos. 57 and 157.

835. Everett, Edwin Mallard. THE PARTY OF HUMANITY: THE 'FORTNIGHTLY REVIEW' AND ITS CONTRIBUTORS, 1865-1874. Chapel Hill: University of North Carolina Press, 1939.

836. Houghton, Esther R. "John Verschoyle and the FORNIGHTLY REVIEW." VPN, 3 (1968), 17-21.

837. Lyons, Edward. "THE FORTNIGHTLY REVIEW and France: Politics and Literature, 1865-1882." DA, 20 (1959), 1017-18.

838. Waugh, Arthur. "The Fortnightly's Seventieth Birthday." FR, 137 (1935), 627-29.

FRASER'S MAGAZINE (1830-82)

See also THACKERAY, WILLIAM MAKEPEACE (chapter 4) and Nos. 57, 197, and 726.

839. Green, David Bonnell. "George Meredith's 'Austrian Poets': A Newly Identified Review Essay with Translations." MLR, 54 (1959), 321-26.

On Grinnparzer, Lenau, and others in FRASER'S for August 1852.

840. Maurer, Oscar, Jr. "Froude and FRASER'S MAGAZINE, 1860-1874." UNIVERSITY OF TEXAS STUDIES IN ENGLISH, 28 (1949), 213-43.

841. Nitchie, Elizabeth. "Shelley in FRASER'S and the Annuals." TLS, 26 August 1939, p. 503.

842. Senex and others. "Frazier's [sic] Magazine, 'Regina.'" N&Q, 178 (1940) 425; 179 (1940), 159.

843. Shine, Hill. "Articles in FRASER'S MAGAZINE Attributed to Carlyle." MLN, 51 (1936), 142-45.

844. Stokes, Geoffrey C. "Thackeray as Historian: Two Newly Identified Contributions to FRASER'S MAGAZINE." NCF, 22 (1967), 281-88.

845. Thrall, Miriam. REBELLIOUS FRASER'S: NOL YORKE'S MAGAZINE IN THE DAYS OF MAGINN, THACKERAY, AND CARLYLE. New York: Columbia University Press, 1934.

846. White, Edward M. "Thackeray's Contributions to FRASER'S MAGAZINE." SB, 19 (1966), 67-84.

FREE BRITON (1729-35)

See No. 847.

FREE BRITON; OR, THE OPINION OF THE PEOPLE (1727-?)

847. Carlson, C. Lennart. "THE FREE BRITON; OR, THE OPINION OF THE PEOPLE, and F. Walsingham's FREE BRITON." N&Q, 169 (1935), 166-68.

FREEHOLDER (1715-16)

See also ADDISON, JOSEPH (chapter 4).

848. Lehney, James P. "Joseph Addison's FREEHOLDER: A Critical Edition." DA, 29 (1968), 1871A.

849. Lynn, Robert Hill. "THE FREEHOLDER by Joseph Addison: A Critical Edition." DA, 20 (1959), 1353.

850. McDonald, Daniel. "The 'Logic' of Addison's FREEHOLDER." PLL, 4 (1968), 20-34.

851. SIR RICHARD BLACKMORE'S 'ESSAY UPON WIT' (1716) AND JOSEPH ADDISON'S 'FREEHOLDER,' NO. 45 (1716). Intro. Richard C. Boys. Augustan Reprint Society, 1st Ser.: Essays on Wit, no. 1. Los Angeles: Clark Memorial Library, 1946.

FREELANCE [Manchester] (1866-78)

852. Fielding, K.J. "Skimpole and Leigh Hunt Again." N&Q, 200 (1955), 174-75.

An account of Hunt in the issue for April 1868.

FREE-THINKER (1718-21)

See also Nos. 164 and 2188.

853. Joost, Nicholas. "Henry Stephens: A Bibliographical and Biographical Note." N&Q, 194 (1949), 379-80.

Stephens contributed to Ambrose Philips' FREE-THINKER.

854. ______. "Gulliver and the FREE-THINKER." MLN, 45 (1950), 197-99.

Argues that Swift took the rope dancing idea from Philips' FREE-THINKER, no. 144. See also No. 856.

855. ______. "The FABLES of Fenelon and Philips' FREE-THINKER." SP, 47 (1950), 51-61.

856. Rosenheim, Edward, Jr. "A 'Source' for the Rope Dancing in GULLIVER'S TRAVELS." PQ, 31 (1952), 208-11.

Argues that the FREE-THINKER is probably not the source for the passage in GULLIVER'S TRAVELS because Swift had used the same figure in a similar way in a work written between 1707-9. See also No. 854.

FRIEND (1809-19)

857. Bailey, Dudley. "Coleridge's Revisions of THE FRIEND: A Study of His Thought and Method." DA, 15 (1955), 120-21.

858. ______. "Coleridge's Revision of THE FRIEND." MP, 59 (1961), 89-99.

859. Griggs, Earl Leslie. "THE FRIEND: 1809 and 1818 Editions." MP, 35 (1938), 369-73.

860. Hunter, Parks C., Jr. "Coleridge's THE FRIEND as the Probable Source of the Wordsworth Quotation in the Preface to Shelley's ALASTOR." N&Q, 5 (1958), 474.

861. Rooke, Barbara E. "THE FRIEND." TLS, 24 January 1948, p. 51.

See also TLS, 7 February 1948, p. 79.

862. ______, ed. SAMUEL TAYLOR COLERIDGE: 'THE FRIEND.' 2 vols. Princeton, N.J.: Princeton University Press, 1969.

863. Wells, John Edwin. "Printer's Bills for Coleridge's FRIEND and Wordsworth's CINTRA." SP, 36 (1939), 521-23.

864. Werkmeister, Lucyle. "The First Two Editions of Coleridge's FRIEND." DA, 17 (1957), 1560.

FRIEND OF THE PEOPLE (1850-51)

See RED REPUBLICAN.

FUN (1861-1900+)

See also No. 330.

865. Jones, John B. "W.S. Gilbert's Contributions to FUN, 1865-1874." BNYPL, 73 (1969), 253-66.

866. Lauterback, Edward Stewart. "FUN and Its Contributors: The Literary History of a Victorian Humor Magazine." DA, 22 (1961), 565.

GAZETTE [Oxford and London] (1665-1900+)

See also Nos. 164, 1986, and 2199.

867. H.,H. "The 'London Gazette,' 1665-1965." ManR, 10 (1965), 226-27.

Describes nearly complete run in the Manchester Central Library.

868. Handover, P.M. A HISTORY OF THE LONDON GAZETTE, 1665-1965. London: The London Gazette, 1965.

Reviewed in TLS, 10 February 1966, p. 108.

869. Hatton, Ragnhild. "The 'London Gazette' in 1718: Supply of News from Abroad." BIHR, 18 (1941), 108-11.

Sheds new light on efforts during the reign of George I to improve the foreign news service for the LONDON GAZETTE."

870. Hill, Arthur. "The Government's Newspaper." STRAND MAGAZINE, 26 (1903), 88-94.

871. Hulme, E. Wyndham. "'London Gazette': Early Advertisements." N&Q, 2 (1910), 203-4.

872. Leach, Douglas E. "Benjamin Batten and the LONDON GAZETTE Report on King Philip's War." NEW ENGLAND QUARTERLY, 34 (1963), 502-17.

The report in the GAZETTE (16-19 August 1675) based on a letter from Benjamin Batten in New England to Sir Thomas Allen.

873. _____. "The 'Gazette de Londres.'" N&Q, 5 (1894), 309.

On the French edition of the LONDON GAZETTE. See also the material by E[vard]. H[ome]. Coleman (page 418).

874. P.,R.B. "Advertisements in the 'London Gazette.'" N&Q 7 (1896), 365.

875. Stevens, David Harrison. "Beginnings of Modern Journalism. Early Records of the 'London Gazette.'" NATION, 101 (1915), 69-70.

876. Theta. "La Gazette de Londres." N&Q, 6 (1852), 223.

877. Wall, C.H. "The London Gazette." BIBLIOGRAPHER, 3 (1883), 153-56.

GAZETTEER (1735-96?)

878. Haig, Robert L. "The Last Years of the GAZETTEER." LIBRARY, 7 (1952), 242-61.

879. _____. 'THE GAZETTEER,' 1735-1797: A STUDY IN THE EIGHTEENTH-CENTURY NEWSPAPER. Carbondale: Southern Illinois University Press, 1960.

An important and informative study of one of the half dozen important early London dailies; it "was established in 1735 as a subsidized party journal but from 1742 was continued as an independent paper, becoming for a time London's most popular daily" (PQ, 40:352-53). Other reviews appear in JEGP, 60: 594; RES, 12:426-28; TLS, 3 March 1962, p. 136.

GENTLEMAN'S DIARY; OR, THE MATHEMATICAL REPOSITORY (1741-1840)

See also No. 1032.

880. Pedersen, Olaf. "The 'Philomaths' of 18th Century England: A Study in Amateur Science." CENTAURUS, 8 (1963), 238-62.

GENTLEMAN'S JOURNAL; OR, THE MONTHLY MISCELLANY (1692-94)

See also MOTTEUX, PETER (chapter 4).

881. C.,S. "'The Gentleman's Journal.'" N&Q, 11 (1861), 489.

882. Foster, Dorothy. "The Earliest Precursor of Our Present-Day Monthly Miscellanies." PMLA, 32 (1917), 22-58.

883. Workard, Job J. Bardwell. "'Gentleman's Journal,' 1693." N&Q, 3 (1863), 251.

GENTLEMAN'S MAGAZINE (1731-1900+)

See also SMART, CHRISTOPHER (chapter 4) and Nos. 179, 275, 1982, 2083, 2085, and 2164.

884. Abbott, John L. "John Hawkesworth: Friend of Samuel Johnson and Editor of Captain Cook's VOYAGES and of the GENTLEMAN'S MAGAZINE." ECS, 3 (1970), 339-50.

885. Anderson, P.J. "'Gentleman's Magazine': Numbering of Volumes." N&Q, 2 (1910), 338; 3 (1911), 16.

See also Alfred Sydney Lewis in N&Q, 2 (1910), 477.

886. Atkinson, Edward R. "Samuel Johnson's 'Life of Boerhaave.'" JOURNAL OF CHEMICAL EDUCATION, 19 (1942), 103-8.

Text of the "Life" from the GENTLEMAN'S MAGAZINE for 1739.

887. Aylward, J.D. "The Gentleman's Magazine." N&Q, 192 (1947), 437.

Concerns "births, marriages, and deaths."

888. Bernard, F.V. "Johnson's Address 'To the Reader.'" N&Q, 210 (1965), 455.

Supports attribution to Johnson of May 1739 issue.

889. ______. "The Hermit of Paris and the Astronomer in RASSELAS." JEGP, 67 (1968), 272-78.

Johnson drew on his translation of the life of Lewis Morin, French botanist and physician, which had appeared in the GENTLEMAN'S MAGAZINE (1741).

890. _____. "A Possible Source for Johnson's LIFE OF THE KING OF PRUSSIA." PQ, 47 (1968), 206-15.

The foreign history section of the GENTLEMAN'S MAGAZINE.

891. Buckler, William E. "Henry Kingsley and THE GENTLEMAN'S MAGAZINE." JEGP, 50 (1951), 90-100.

892. Blunden, Edmund. "'The Gentleman's Magazine,' 1731-1907." VOTIVE TABLETS. STUDIES CHIEFLY APPRECIATIVE OF ENGLISH AUTHORS AND BOOKS. London: Cobden-Sanderson, 1931. Pp. 119-31.

893. Boswell, James. LIFE OF JOHNSON. Ed. George Birkbeck Hill, rev. by L.F. Powell. 6 vols. Oxford: Clarendon Press, 1950. I, 111-18, 501-12.

894. Burroughs, Sara A. "Biographies in the GENTLEMAN'S MAGAZINE, 1740's and 1790's." DAI, 31 (1971), 6004A.

895. Carlson, C. Lennart. THE FIRST MAGAZINE. A HISTORY OF THE GENTLEMAN'S MAGAZINE. Brown University Studies, vol. IV. Providence, R.I.: Brown University, 1938.

Reviewed in JEGP 38:637-39; MLN 55:305-6; MP 38:85-100.

896. "A Cibber 'Puff.'" N&Q, 201 (1956), 388-91.

In the GENTLEMAN'S MAGAZINE, 15:98-99.

897. Clemens, Will M. "The First Magazine." AUTHOR, 1 (1889), 177-79.

898. Cordasco, Francesco. "Gibbon and the 'Gentleman's Magazine.'" N&Q, 194 (1949), 254.

899. "Dippings into Old Magazines. The Gentleman's for 1731." CHAMBERS'S EDINBURGH JOURNAL, 4 (1835), 7-8.

900. "Dippings into Old Magazines: The Gentleman's for 1748." CHAMBERS'S EDINBURGH JOURNAL, 9 (1848), 249-51.

901. Eddy, Donald D. "John Hawkesworth: Book Reviewer in the GENTLEMAN'S MAGAZINE." PQ, 43 (1964), 223-38.

902. Farrar, R. Henry. AN INDEX TO THE BIOGRAPHICAL AND OBITU-

ARY NOTICES IN THE GENTLEMAN'S MAGAZINE, 1731-1780. London: British Record Society, 1891.

903. French, David P. "The Identity of C.M.P.G.N.S.T.N.S." JONATHAN SWIFT: TERCENTENARY ESSAYS. Ed. David P. French, et al. University of Tulsa Department of English Monograph Series, no. 3. Tulsa, Okla.: University of Tulsa, 1967. Pp. 1-9.

Identifies John Geree as the author of an article suggesting that Stella was Sir William Temple's daughter.

904. GENERAL INDEX TO THE GENTLEMAN'S MAGAZINE, FROM THE YEAR 1787 TO 1818. Ed. John Nichols. London: Nichols, 1821.

905. THE GENTLEMAN'S MAGAZINE LIBRARY; BEING A CLASSIFIED COLLECTION OF THE CHIEF CONTENTS OF THE GENTLEMAN'S FROM 1731 TO 1868. Ed. George Laurence Gomme. 29 vols. in 30. London: E. Stock, 1883-1905.

Most of these volumes are on topography. Volume IX, BIBLIOGRAPHICAL NOTES, edited by A.C. Bickley, contains several articles pertaining to the history of early newspapers.

906. "The Gentleman's Magazine, 1731-1907." TLS, 11 June 1931, pp. 453-54.

See also R.B. McKerrow in TLS, 18 June 1931, p. 487, and Edgar Whitaker in TLS, 25 June 1931, p. 510.

907. Greene, D.J. "Was Johnson Theatrical Critic of the GENTLEMAN'S MAGAZINE?" RES, 3 (1952), 158-61.

908. ______. "Some Notes on Johnson and the GENTLEMAN'S MAGAZINE." PMLA, 74 (1959), 75-84.

Concerned with attribution.

909. Griffin, Leland M. "Letter to the Press: 1778." QJS, 33 (1947), 148-50.

Concerns an anonymous contribution to the GENTLEMAN'S MAGAZINE on pulpit oratory.

910. H.,A.J. "The Gentleman's Magazine." N&Q, 166 (1934), 320.

Answer to question "When did it cease?"

911. H.,T. "Last Century Magazines." FRASER'S MAGAZINE, 1876, pp. 325-33; rpt. LIVING AGE, 131 (1876), 112-19.

912. Hart, Edward. "An Ingenious Editor: John Nichols and the GENTLEMAN'S MAGAZINE." BUCKNELL REVIEW, 10 (1962), 232-42.

913. Haverfield, F. "Extracts from the Gentleman's Magazine Relating to Oxford, 1731-1800." COLLECTANEA. SECOND SERIES. Ed. Montague Burrows. Oxford Historical Society Publications, vol. 16. Oxford: Oxford Historical Society, 1890. Pp. 417-48.

914. Hilles, Frederick R. "Johnson's Correspondence with Nichols: Some Facts and a Query." PQ, 48 (1969), 679-95.

One of the letters, the original of which cannot be found, was printed by Nichols in the GENTLEMAN'S MAGAZINE.

915. Hoover, Benjamin Beard. SAMUEL JOHNSON'S PARLIAMENTARY REPORTING: DEBATES IN THE SENATE OF LILLIPUT. Berkeley: University of California Press, 1953.

A study of Johnson's parliamentary reporting which appeared in the GENTLEMAN'S MAGAZINE, including a comparison with the reports in other periodicals of the time. Reviewed in MLQ, 17:75-76, and RES, 7:433-35.

916. Hope, Henry Gerald. "The 'Gentleman's Magazine.'" N&Q, 3 (1899), 144.

See also the material by John C. Francis, (pages 230-31, 291-93).

917. Hutton, Arthur Wollaston. "Dr. Johnson and the 'Gentleman's Magazine.'" ENGLISH ILLUSTRATED MAGAZINE, 1897; rpt. JOHNSON CLUB PAPERS. By Various Hands. London: T. Fisher Unwin, 1899. Pp. 95-113.

918. Jackson, William A. "The Curse of Ernulphus." HARVARD LIBRARY BULLETIN, 14 (1960), 392-94. 2 plates.

Evidence that Sterne used the version published in the GENTLEMAN'S MAGAZINE (September 1745).

919. Keesey, Donald Earl. "Dramatic Criticism in the GENTLEMAN'S MAGAZINE, 1747-1784." DA, 25 (1965), 6628.

920. Kolb, Gwin J. "More Attributions to Dr. Johnson." SEL, 1 (1961), 77-95.

Six of the attributions are from the GENTLEMAN'S MAGAZINE.

921. Kuist, James Marquis. "THE GENTLEMAN'S MAGAZINE, 1754-1800: A Study of Its Development as a Vehicle for the Discussion of Literature." DA, 26 (1965), 6045.

922. ______. THE WORKS OF JOHN NICHOLS: AN INTRODUCTION. New York: AMS and Kraus, 1968.

Includes a survey of Nichols' association with the GENTLEMAN'S MAGAZINE.

923. Leed, Jacob. "Samuel Johnson and the 'Gentleman's Magazine': An Adjustment of the Canon." N&Q, 202 (1957), 210-13.

Concerns the essay on the Duchess of Marlborough in the issue for March 1742.

924. ______. "Two New Pieces by Johnson in the GENTLEMAN'S MAGAZINE?" MP, 54 (1957), 221-29.

Attributes to Johnson two pieces signed "Pamphilus," which appeared in 1738. See also PQ, 37:340.

925. ______. "Two Notes on Johnson and 'The Gentleman's Magazine.'" PBSA, 54 (1960), 101-10.

Attribution of two passages in 1742.

926. ______. "Some Reprintings of the GENTLEMAN'S MAGAZINE." SB, 17 (1964), 210-14.

927. "A Literary Competition." TLS, 20 March 1930, p. 256.

On the GENTLEMAN'S MAGAZINE EXTRAORDINARY, 1735.

928. Lonsdale, Roger. "Christopher Smart's First Publication in English." RES, 12 (1961), 516-32.

"To Idleness" was printed in the GENTLEMAN'S MAGAZINE for May 1745.

929. McR.,A.T. "THE GENTLEMAN'S MAGAZINE and Scotland in 1749." N&Q, 1 (1932), 114-16.

Extracts and comment to show the kind of Scottish news contained in the GENTLEMAN'S MAGAZINE.

930. Meyerstein, E.H.W. "Rimbaud and the 'Gentleman's Magazine.'" TLS, 11 April 1935, p. 244.

931. N. "Royal Paper Copies of the 'Gentleman's Magazine.'" N&Q, 11 (1861), 349.

932. Powell, L.F. "An Addition to the Canon of Johnson's Writings." ESSAYS AND STUDIES BY MEMBERS OF THE ENGLISH ASSOCIATION, 28 (1942), 38-41.

Attribution of the preface to the first index (1735) of the GENTLEMAN'S MAGAZINE.

933. R. "THE GENTLEMAN'S MAGAZINE." N&Q, 192 (1947), 369.

934. Reade, Aleyn Lyell. "The Seatonian Prize at Cambridge." N&Q, 190 (1946), 68-69.

Concerns the relationship of the poetry prize instituted in 1738 to competitions in the GENTLEMAN'S MAGAZINE.

935. Roberts, S.C. "Johnson in Grub Street." CORNHILL MAGAZINE, 65 (1928), 440-51.

936. Roberts, W. "The History of 'The GENTLEMAN'S MAGAZINE.' I.--Its Predeccessors. II.--Its Founder and Number One. III.--Its Rivals. IV.--Its Publishers and Editors." BOOKWORM, 3 (1890), 97-101, 129-36, 281-87, 353-58.

937. Seguin, J.A.R. VOLTAIRE AND THE GENTLEMAN'S MAGAZINE, 1731-1868; AN INDEX COMPILED AND INDEXED WITH AN INTRODUCTION. Jersey City: R. Paxton, 1962.

938. Sherbo, Arthur. "Samuel Johnson and Certain Poems in the May 1747 GENTLEMAN'S MAGAZINE." RES, 17 (1966), 382-90.

939. Spectacles. "Literary Hoax." N&Q, 11 (1861), 191.

See also John Gough Nichols in N&Q, 11 (1861), 230.

940. "Swiftiana in 'The Gentleman's Magazine.'" BOOKWORM, 2 (1889), 39-42.

941. "Sylvanus Urban." TLS, 2 February 1906, p. 37.

942. Todd, William B. "A Bibliographical Account of THE GENTLEMAN'S MAGAZINE, 1731-1754." SB, 18 (1965), 81-109.

943. Walcott, Mackenzie E.C. "Army Lists." N&Q, 1 (1862), 75.

944. Yost, Calvin Daniel, Jr. "The Poetry of the Gentleman's Magazine. A Study in Eighteenth Century Literary Taste." Diss. University of Pennsylvania, 1936.

945. Zimmerman, Robert Lee. "Byron and THE GENTLEMAN'S MAGAZINE." N&Q, 204 (1959), 77.

GENTLEMAN'S MAGAZINE AND MONTHLY ORACLE (1736-38?)

See also No. 1286.

946. Roberts, William. "The 'Gentleman's Magazine' and Its Rivals." ATHENAEUM, no. 3235 (26 October 1889), p. 560.

GERM (1850)

947. Hosmon, Robert S. "THE GERM (1850) and THE OXFORD AND CAMBRIDGE MAGAZINE (1856)." VPN, 4 (1969), 36-47.

948. Jervis, H. "Carlyle and 'The Germ.'" TLS, 20 August 1938, p. 544.

GLASGOW MAGAZINE (1770)

949. Carnie, R.H. "'The Glasgow Magazine' 1770." BIBLIOTHECK, 5 (1968), 142-43.

Two numbers of this "first attempt to found a magazine in Glasgow," hitherto known only through references to it, have been discovered.

GLASGOW WEEKLY HISTORY (1743)

950. Austin, Roland. "'The Glasgow-Weekly-History.'" PROCEEDINGS OF THE WESLEY HISTORICAL SOCIETY, 13 (1922), 125-28.

951. C.,W.J. "The Earliest Scottish Religious Periodical." SN&Q, 11 (1933), 148.

952. Cone, Corson. "Rev. James Robe's Periodical." SN&Q, 6 (1905), 140, 174-75.

Also in this issue of SN&Q, see the material by James R. Anderson (page 159); in SN&Q, 7 (1905), 14, see Robert Adams.

GLOBE (1803-1900+)

953. Deering, Dorothy. "The London GLOBE of the 1840s and 1850s." VPN, 11 (1971), 28-29.

954. Roberts, David F. "Who Ran the London GLOBE in the 1830's, 1840's, and 1850's?" VPN, 12 (1971), 6-11.

955. Rosenberg, Shelia. "Some Further Notes on the History of the GLOBE: Its Editors, Managers, and Proprietors." VPN, 15 (1972), 40-47.

GORGON (1818-19)

956. F.,J.W. "THE GORGON." N&Q, 169 (1935), 370.

See also N&Q, 170 (1936), 11.

GOSSIP (1821)

957. Carolus. "THE GOSSIP and Its Authors." N&Q, 11 (1891), 209.

958. Ireland, Alex. "THE GOSSIP; A SERIES OF ORIGINAL ESSAYS AND LETTERS." N&Q, 3 (1875), 207.

GOWNSMAN (1829-30)

959. M.,J.M. "Rhymes on Timbuctoo: THE SNOB [1829] and THE GOWNSMAN." N&Q, 1 (1886), 492.

GRAND MAGAZINE OF MAGAZINES (1758-59)

See MAGAZINE OF MAGAZINES; OR, UNIVERSAL REGISTER.

GRAND MAGAZINE OF UNIVERSAL INTELLIGENCE (1758-60)

See also No. 2026.

960. Abhba. "'The Grand Magazine.'" N&Q, 9 (1866), 100.

961. Harlan, Robert D. "The Publishing of 'The Grand Magazine of Universal Intelligence and Monthly Chronicle of our Own Times.'" PBSA, 59 (1965), 429-36.

GRAY'S INN JOURNAL (1735-54)

See also MURPHY, ARTHUR (chapter 4).

962. Aycock, Roy Edwin. "A Study of Arthur Murphy's GRAY'S INN JOURNAL." DA, 21 (1961), 1936.

963. ______. "Shakespearean Criticism in the GRAY'S-INN JOURNAL." YES, 2 (1972), 68-72.

964. Murphy, Arthur. THE LIVES OF HENRY FIELDING AND SAMUEL JOHNSON, TOGETHER WITH ESSAYS FROM "THE GRAY'S-INN JOURNAL." Intro. Matthew Grace. Gainesville, Fla.: Scholars' Facsimiles & Reprints, 1968.

   The twenty-six essays from the JOURNAL (1752-54) are reproduced from the 1786 edition of Murphy's works.

GRUB-STREET JOURNAL (1730-37)

965. Crossley, James. "Grub Street Journal." N&Q, 7 (1853), 383.

   See also Alexander Andrews (page 486).

966. Goldgar, Bertrand A. "Fielding, Sir William Yonge, and the GRUB STREET JOURNAL." N&Q, 19 (1972), 226-27.

967. Hillhouse, James T. THE GRUB-STREET JOURNAL. Duke University Publications. Durham, N.C.: Duke University Press, 1928.

   Reviewed in MP, 26 (1929), 361-67.

968. Malahide, Talbot de. "The 'Grub Street Journal.'" ANTIQUARY, 2 (1880), 194-96, 236-38.

969. Roberts, W. "Grub Street and Its Journal. No. 2.--The Grub Street Journal." BOOKWORM, 1 (1888), 94-99.

970. Williamson, Raymond. "John Martyn and THE GRUB-STREET JOURNAL. With Particular Reference to His Attacks on Richard Bentley, Richard Bradley, and William Cheselden." MEDICAL HISTORY, 5 (1961), 361-74.

GRUMBLER (1715)

971. Joost, Nicholas T., Jr. "Burnet's 'Grumbler' and Ambrose Philips."

N&Q, 193 (1948), 340-42.

Concerns Philips' contributions.

GUARDIAN (1713)

See also ADDISON, JOSEPH; POPE, ALEXANDER; STEELE, RICHARD (all chapter 4); TATLER; SPECTATOR; and Nos. 181; 202; 302; 1859; 1985; and 2141.

972. Fineman, Daniel A. "The Motivation of Pope's GUARDIAN 40." MLN, 67 (1952), 24-28.

Argues that this essay was stimulated by a mocking reference to his pastorals in GUARDIAN, no. 30, rather than by a conspiracy of silence.

973. Furlong, E.J. "How Much of Steele's GUARDIAN, No. 39, Did Berkeley Write?" HERMATHENA, 89 (1957), 76-88.

Concludes that the second half of the paper was by Steele.

974. Graham, Walter. "Addison's Travel Letters in the TATLER and GUARDIAN." PQ, 15 (1936), 97-102.

975. Hall, Roland. "Did Hume Read Berkeley Unawares?" PHILOSOPHY, 42 (1967), 276-77.

Concerns a passage in GUARDIAN, no. 126.

976. Hopkins, Robert H. "The Issue of Anonymity and the Beginning of the Steele-Swift Controversy of 1713-14: A New Interpretation." ELN, 2 (1964), 15-21.

977. Kaufman, Paul. "Establishing Berkeley's Authorship of 'Guardian' Papers." PBSA, 54 (1960), 181-83.

See also No. 978.

978. Luce, A.A. "Berkeley's Essays in the GUARDIAN." MIND, 52 (1943), 247-63.

979. Lyttelton. "Notes from 'The Guardian.'" N&Q, 8 (1871), 166.

See also H.S.G. and E.C.F. (page 254).

980. Richardson, Charles. NOTICES AND EXTRACTS RELATING TO THE

LION'S HEAD, WHICH WAS ERECTED AT BUTTON'S COFFEE-HOUSE, IN THE YEAR 1713. London: Saunders and Otley, 1828.

981. Sharp, Robert L. "Lines in 'The Guardian.'" TLS, 8 March 1934, p. 162.

Source of verses in no. 15.

982. Stephens, John C., Jr. "Joseph Addison's 'Man Planter.'" N&Q, 203 (1958), 358-59.

In this reply to Templeman (No. 985), Stephens cites Bayle's DICTIONARY (1710 edition) as a source for an allusion in GUARDIAN (8 September 1713).

983. ______. "'Mr. Crab, the Librarian.'" N&Q, 201 (1956), 105-6.

Identifies a character in GUARDIAN, no. 60.

984. ______. "Steele Quotes Two Divines." N&Q, 201 (1956), 252-53.

Identifies quotations in the GUARDIAN from Tillotson and William Beveridge.

985. Templeman, William D. "Joseph Addison's 'Man-Planter.'" N&Q, 183 (1942), 311.

On the use of the term in GUARDIAN, no. 155. See also No. 982.

HALFPENNY JOURNAL (1861-66)

986. Summers, Montague. "The 'Black Band' Scandal." TLS, 17 February 1945, p. 84.

Concerns the novels of Braddon which appeared serially in the HALFPENNY JOURNAL and were attacked furiously in the ATHENAEUM.

HAVE AT YOU ALL; OR, THE DRURY LANE JOURNAL (1752)

987. D.,J.O. "The Drury Lane Journal." N&Q, 4 (1859), 68.

See also John Hawkins (page 97).

HEATHCOTE'S INTELLIGENCE (1718-?)

See ORIGINAL LONDON POST.

HERACLITUS RIDENS (1681-82)

988. C.,B.H. "'Heraclitus Ridens.'" N&Q, 5 (1864), 73.

See also W. Lee (page 469).

989. Newton, Theodore F.M. "The Mask of Heraclitus: A Problem in Restoration Journalism." HARVARD STUDIES AND NOTES IN PHILOLOGY AND LITERATURE, 16 (1934), 145-60.

Newton argues that this HERACLITUS RIDENS, the first periodical to introduce the dialogue method, was the work of a group of Tory writers, with Thomas Flatman as the probable author of the odes and Edward Rawlins in the chief role as the first journalist to act as "editor."

HEREFORD JOURNAL (1770-92)

See No. 298.

HIBERNIAN CHRONICLE (1768-1801)

990. C.,S.O. "Patrick Lord." "A Drogheda Printer." "A Loughrea Printer." "A Sligo Printer." IRISH BOOK LOVER, 17 (1929), 120.

Notes from issues of HIBERNIAN CHRONICLE for 1773 and 1785.

HIBERNIAN MAGAZINE (1786-1811)

991. Sparke, Archibald. "'The Hibernian Magazine.'" N&Q, 4 (1918), 197.

HOME AND FOREIGN REVIEW (1848-62)

See Nos. 57 and 1437.

HONEST GENTLEMAN (1718-19)

992. Bloom, Edward A., and Lillian D. Bloom. "Steele in 1719: Additions to the Canon." HLQ, 31 (1968), 123-51.

Includes a letter in the HONEST GENTLEMAN (no. 22) written against the Peerage Bill of 1719.

HOOD'S COMIC ANNUAL (1830-98)

See No. 330.

HOUSEHOLD WORDS (1850-59)

See also DICKENS, CHARLES (chapter 4).

993. Adrian, Arthur A. "Charles Dickens as Verse Editor." MP, 58 (1960), 99-107.

994. Buckler, W. "Dickens's Success with HOUSEHOLD WORDS." DICKENSIAN, 46 (1950), 197-203.

995. ______. "Dickens the Paymaster." PMLA, 64 (1951), 1177-80.

Based on the "Contributor's Book" kept by William Henry Wills, Dickens' subeditor.

996. ______. "HOUSEHOLD WORDS in America." PBSA, 45 (1951), 160-66.

997. CHARLES DICKENS' UNCOLLECTED WRITINGS FROM 'HOUSEHOLD WORDS.' Ed. Harry Stone. 2 vols. Bloomington: University of Indiana Press, 1968.

998. Clark, Harold F., Jr. "Dickensian Journalism: A Study of HOUSEHOLD WORDS." DA, 28 (1967), 1390A-91A.

999. Collins, Philip. "'Keep HOUSEHOLD WORDS Imaginative.'" DICKENSIAN, 52 (1956), 117-23.

1000. ______. "W.H. Wills' Plan for HOUSEHOLD WORDS." VPN, 8 (1970), 33-46.

1001. Easson, Angus. "Dickens, HOUSEHOLD WORDS, and a Double Standard." DICKENSIAN, 60 (1964), 104-14.

1002. Hopkins, Annette B. "Dickens and Mrs. Gaskell." HLQ, 9 (1946), 357-85.

Gaskell contributed to both HOUSEHOLD WORDS and ALL THE YEAR ROUND. Dickens's correspondence with her sheds light on his editorial methods.

1003. Lohrli, Anne. "Dickens's HOUSEHOLD WORDS on American English." AS, 37 (1962), 83-94.

1004. ______. "HOUSEHOLD WORDS and Its 'Office Book.'" PULC, 26 (1964), 27-47.

1005. ______. "Greek Slave Mystery." N&Q, 13 (1966), 58-60.

How did the poem by Elizabeth Barrett Browning come to be printed here?

1006. ______. "Coventry Patmore in HOUSEHOLD WORDS." VN, 31 (1967), 25-27.

1007. ______, comp. 'HOUSEHOLD WORDS'; A WEEKLY JOURNAL 1850-59, CONDUCTED BY CHARLES DICKENS. TABLE OF CONTENTS, LIST OF CONTRIBUTORS AND THEIR CONTRIBUTIONS. BASED ON THE 'HOUSEHOLD WORDS' OFFICE BOOK. Toronto: University of Toronto Press, 1973.

1008. Morley, M. "Plays from the Christmas Numbers of HOUSEHOLD WORDS." DICKENSIAN, 51 (1955), 127-32, 169-73.

1009. Ryan, J.S. "The Australian Materials in HOUSEHOLD WORDS." AULLA PROCEEDINGS, 1:57-59.

1010. Stone, Harry. "Dickens 'Conducts' HOUSEHOLD WORDS." DICKENSIAN, 64 (1968), 71-85.

HUMOURS OF A COFFEE HOUSE (1707-8)

See also No. 2231.

1011. Rockwell, Frederick S. "A Probable Source for 'Gulliver's Travels.'" N&Q, 169 (1935), 131-33.

HYPOCHONDRIACK

See LONDON MAGAZINE; OR, GENTLEMAN'S MONTHLY INTELLIGENCER.

IDLER (1758-60)

See also JOHNSON, SAMUEL (chapter 4) and Nos. 181, 203, 1429, and 1430.

1012. C[hapman]., R.W. "The Sale of Johnson's 'Idler.'" N&Q, 184 (1943), 256.

1013. Dubuque, Remi Gerard. "Samuel Johnson's IDLERS: A Study of Satire, Humor, and Irony." DA, 24 (1963), 2461.

1014. Green, Boylston. "Samuel Johnson's IDLER: A Critical Study." DA, 25 (1964), 3554.

1015. O'Flaherty, Patrick. "Johnson's IDLER: The Equipment of a Satirist." ELH, 37 (1970), 211-25.

1016. Rawson, C.J. "Frozen Words: A Note to IDLER, No. 46." N&Q, 17 (1970), 300.

1017. Rhodes, Rodman D. "IDLER No. 24 and Johnson's Epistomology." MP, 64 (1966), 10-21.

ILLUSTRATED LONDON NEWS (1842-1900+)

1018. Butterfield, Roger. "Pictures in the Papers." AH, 13 (June 1962), 32-55, 96-100.

A popular discussion of pictorial journalism.

1019. De Vries, Leonard, ed. PANORAMA 1842-1865: THE WORLD OF THE EARLY VICTORIANS AS SEEN THROUGH THE EYES OF THE ILLUSTRATED LONDON NEWS. Intro. W.H. Smith. London: Murray, 1969.

ILLUSTRATED TIMES (1855-72)

1020. Worth, George J. "'Popular Culture' and the Seminal Books of 1859." VN, 19 (1961), 24-27.

INDEPENDENT CHRONICLE (1769-70)

See No. 1860.

1021. Curran, John W. "Curran's Chronicle." ABC, 5 (1955), 12.

INDICATOR (1819-21)

1022. Tillett, Nettie S. "Elia and THE INDICATOR." SAQ, 33 (1934), 295-310.

INFALLIBLE ASTROLOGER (1700-1701)

1023. Eddy, William A. "Ned Ward and 'Lilliput.'" N&Q, 158 (1930), 148-49.

INFERNAL OBSERVATOR (1684)

1024. Lang, D.M. "Fontenelle and the 'Infernal Observator.'" MLR, 45 (1950), 222-25.

Concerns a 1684 translation of Fontenelle's NOUVEAUX DIALOGUES DES MORTS.

INQUIRER (1842-1900+)

1025. Tener, Robert H. "Hutton's Earliest Review of Arnold: An Attribution." ELN, 12 (1974), 102-9.

A review of Arnold's POEMS, which appeared in INQUIRER for 3 December 1853, is attributed to Hutton on the basis of internal evidence.

INQUISITOR (1808-9)

See No. 1057.

INTELLECTUAL REPOSITORY (1824-29)

See NEW CHURCH MAGAZINE.

INTELLIGENCER (1728)

1026. Gilmore, Thomas B., Jr. "A MODEST PROPOSAL and INTELLIGENCER Number XVIII." SCRIBLERIAN, 2, no. 1 (1969), 28-29.

JACKSON'S OXFORD JOURNAL (1753-1900+)

See OXFORD JOURNAL.

JACOBITE'S JOURNAL (1747-48)

See FIELDING, HENRY (chapter 4).

JOHN BULL MAGAZINE (1824?)

1027. Forward, Kenneth. "'Libellous Attack' on De Quincey." PMLA, 52 (1937), 244-60.

1028. Jones, Stanley. "Hazlitt and JOHN BULL: A Neglected Letter." RES, 17 (1966), 163-70.

JOURNAL DES SCAVANS (1665-1792)

See No. 1321.

JOVIAL MERCURY (1693)

1029. Piggot, John, Jr. "'The Jovial Mercury.'" N&Q, 10 (1872), 106-7.

JUDY (1867-1900+)

1030. Peyrouton, N.C. "Dickens and the JUDY Magazine." DICKENSIAN, 62 (1966), 14-20.

KENTISH GAZETTE (1768-1900+)

1031. Brade-Birks, S. Graham. "Jane Austen." TLS, 9 November 1962, p. 993.

Her belated obituary, 5 August 1817.

LADIES DIARY (1704-1840)

1032. Archibald, R.C. "English Mathematical Diaries." N&Q, 1 (1910), 147-48; 3 (1911), 252-53.

On the LADIES' DIARY and GENTLEMAN'S DIARY (above).

LADIES MERCURY (1693)

See also ATHENIAN GAZETTE.

1033. Stearns, Bertha-Monica. "The First English Periodical for Women." MP, 28 (1930), 45-49.

On the development of the LADIES MERCURY from the issues of the ATHENIAN GAZETTE designed for feminine readers.

LADIES POCKET MAGAZINE (1824-40)

See No. 290.

LADY'S MAGAZINE; OR, ENTERTAINING COMPANION FOR THE FAIR SEX (1770-1832)

1034. Dowling, John Nesbitt. "Wheble's 'Lady's Magazine.'" N&Q, 3 (1917), 453-54.

See also Edward Bensly (page 454).

1035. Roberts, W.J. "THE LADY'S MAGAZINE, 1819 and 1822." N&Q, 194 (1949), 105.

LADY'S MAGAZINE; OR, POLITE COMPANION FOR THE FAIR SEX (1760-63)

See also Nos. 290 and 2007.

1036. Friedman, Arthur. "An Essay by Goldsmith in the LADY'S MAGAZINE." MP, 30 (1933), 320-22.

1037. Mayo, Robert D. "How Long Was Gothic Fiction in Vogue?" MLN, 58 (1943), 58-64.

A study using the LADY'S MAGAZINE as a standard of popular taste.

1038. _____. "'To Our Correspondents.'" PERIODICAL POST-BOY, 12 (1952), 1-3.

Concerning reader-writer relationships in eighteenth-century magazines, especially the LADY'S MAGAZINE.

1039. Walker, Hilda A. "THE LADY'S MAGAZINE." N&Q, 159 (1930), 440.

Notes a copy dated 1759.

1040. Watson, Melvin R. "Mrs. Grey's Family." PERIODICAL POST-BOY, no. 14 (November 1953), pp. 2-5.

An account of "The Matron" in the LADY'S MAGAZINE.

LADY'S MUSEUM (1760-61)

See No. 2103.

LEEDS INTELLIGENCER (1754-1866)

1041. EXTRACTS FROM 'THE LEEDS INTELLIGENCER,' 1791-1796. Publications of the Thoresby Society, XLIV for 1955. Leeds: Thoresby Society, 1956.

1042. EXTRACTS FROM 'THE LEEDS INTELLIGENCER' AND 'THE LEEDS MERCURY,' 1777-1782. With an Introductory Account of THE LEEDS INTELLIGENCER, 1754-1786 [by Frank Beckwith]. Publications of the Thoresby Society, XL. Leeds: Thoresby Society, 1947-1955.

Reviewed in EHR, 71:165-66.

LEEDS MERCURY (1718-1900+)

See also No. 1042.

1043. "A Champion of Reform: The LEEDS MERCURY. The Baines Family. The Brontes' Paper." The Oldest Newspapers--IX. NEWSPAPER WORLD, no. 2159 (May 27, 1939), pp. 5, 12.

LEICESTER HERALD (1792-95)

See No. 2137.

LETTERS OF THE CRITICAL CLUB (1738)

See No. 1451.

LIBERAL (1822-23)

See also No. 2119.

1044. Bethel, George, Jr., et al. "THE LIBERAL: Leigh Hunt." N&Q, 7 (1889), 131-32; 9 (1890), 467; 10 (1890), 231.

1045. Bostetter, Edward E. "The New Romantic Criticism." SR, 69 (1961), 490-500.

A review article that includes a discussion of Marshal's BYRON, SHELLEY, HUNT, AND 'THE LIBERAL' (No. 1050).

1046. Dilke, Charles W. "THE LIBERAL." N&Q, 8 (1883), 392-93.

1047. _____. "THE LIBERAL." N&Q, 4 (1893), 10.

1048. Gates, Payson G. "A Leigh Hunt-Byron Letter." KSJ, 2 (1953), 11-18.

1049. Marshall, William Harvey. "THE LIBERAL: 1822-1823." DA, 16 (1956), 1684.

1050. _____. BYRON, SHELLEY, HUNT, AND 'THE LIBERAL.' Philadelphia: University of Pennsylvania Press, 1960.

See also 1045.

1051. _____. "A News Letter from Byron to John Hunt." N&Q, 203 (1958), 122-24.

1052. Mayer, S.R. Townshend. "THE LIBERAL." N&Q, 7 (1877), 388.

1053. Tillett, Nettie S. "The Unholy Alliance of Pisa--A Literary Episode." SAQ, 28 (1929), 27-44.

LIBRARY; OR, MORAL AND CRITICAL MAGAZINE, (1761-62)

See Nos. 1891 and 2025.

LILLIPUTIAN MAGAZINE (1751?)

1054. Botting, Roland B. "Christopher Smart and the LILLIPUTIAN MAGAZINE." ELH, 9 (1942), 286-87.

Not entered in the Crane & Kaye CENSUS (No. 32).

1055. Grey, Jill E. "The Lilliputian Magazine--A Pioneering Periodical?" JOURNAL OF LIBRARIANSHIP, 2 (1970), 107-15.

A mid-century children's publication, probably planned as a periodical. Christopher Smart was probably the author of most articles.

1056. Thoms, William T. "Christopher Smart's Lilliputian Magazine." N&Q, 3 (1857), 425-26.

LITERARY EXAMINER (1823)

1057. Stout, George D. "A Note on THE LITERARY EXAMINER and THE

INQUISITOR." TLS, 6 August 1925, p. 521.

LITERARY GAZETTE (1817-62)

1058. Duncan, Robert W. "William Jerdan and the LITERARY GAZETTE." DA, 15 (1955), 1396-97.

1059. ______. "Byron and the London LITERARY GAZETTE." BUSE, 2 (1956), 240-50.

1060. ______. "The London LITERARY GAZETTE and American Writers." PELL, 1 (1965), 153-66.

LITERARY MAGAZINE; OR, UNIVERSAL REVIEW (1756-58)

See also JOHNSON, SAMUEL (chapter 4) and No. 628.

1061. Golden, Morris. "Goldsmith Attributions in the 'Literary Magazine.'" N&Q, 201 (1956), 432-35, 489-93.

Attempts to restore several issues to the Goldsmith canon. Reviewed in PQ, 36:371-72.

1062. Greene, D.J. "Johnson's Contributions to the LITERARY MAGAZINE." RES, 7 (1956), 367-92.

1063. ______. "Dr. Johnson and 'An Authentic Account of the Present State of Lisbon.'" N&Q, 202 (1957), 351.

The piece in the LITERARY MAGAZINE (1756) is a reprint from the pamphlet, A SATIRICAL REVIEW.

1064. Seitz, R.W. "Goldsmith and the LITERARY MAGAZINE." RES, 5 (1929), 410-30.

1065. Sherbo, Arthur. "A Possible Addition to the Johnson Canon." RES, 6 (1955), 70-71.

Argues that a review of a travel book by Keysler which appeared in the LITERARY MAGAZINE (15 August-15 September 1756) is by Johnson.

LLOYD'S EVENING POST (1757-1818?)

See No. 2007.

LOITERER (1789-90)

See also No. 2293.

1066. Cope, Zachary. "Who Was Sophia Sentiment? Was She Jane Austen?" BC, 15 (1966), 143-51.

Suggests that a letter in LOITERER no. 9 (28 March 1789) is by Austen, then age 13.

1067. Litz, Walton. "THE LOITERER: A Reflection of Jane Austen's Early Environment." RES, 12 (1961), 251-61.

Her brother, James, founded the periodical.

LONDON CHRONICLE; OR, UNIVERSAL EVENING POST (1757-1823)

See also Nos. 275, 1864, and 2072.

1068. Aldridge, Alfred Owen. "Franklin's Deistical Indians." PROCEEDINGS OF THE AMERICAN PHILOSOPHICAL SOCIETY, 94 (1950), 398-410.

Concerned in part with "an ingenious hoax perpetrated by Franklin" in the LONDON CHRONICLE for June 1768.

1069. Emery, John P. "Murphy's Criticisms in the London CHRONICLE." PMLA, 54 (1939), 1099-104.

1070. Golden, Morris. "Lines Attributed to Charles Churchill." N&Q, 203 (1958), 443.

1071. Lindsay, Jack. "A Churchill Poem?" TLS, 25 April 1958, p. 225.

In the LONDON CHRONICLE (8-11 September 1764).

1072. P.,J. "Newspaper Variants." BODLEIAN QUARTERLY RECORD, 7 (1934), 517-19.

1073. Patterson, Alexander. "THE LONDON CHRONICLE." N&Q, 1 (1874), 187.

Also in this issue, see page 255.

LONDON DAILY ADVERTISER (1730-1803)

See DAILY ADVERTISER.

LONDON EVENING POST (1727-1806)

See also No. 275.

1074. Cranfield, G.A. "The LONDON EVENING POST, 1727-1744: A Study in the Development of the Political Press." HISTORICAL JOURNAL, 6 (1963), 20-37.

Concerns the excise crisis of 1733 and the fall of Walpole.

1075. ______. "The London Evening Post and the Jew Bill of 1753." HISTORICAL JOURNAL, 8 (1965), 16-30.

LONDON GAZETTE (1665-1900+)

See GAZETTE (OXFORD AND LONDON).

LONDON JOURNAL (1719-44)

1076. Joshi, L.L. "The London Journal, 1719-1738." JOURNAL OF THE UNIVERSITY OF BOMBAY, 9, ii (1940), 33-66.

Stresses relation to contemporaries and government; uses STATE PAPERS DOMESTIC and TREASURY BOOKS AND PAPERS.

1077. Realey, Charles Bechdolt. THE LONDON JOURNAL AND ITS AUTHORS, 1720-1723. Bulletin of the University of Kansas, Humanistic Studies, V, iii. Lawrence: University of Kansas, 1935.

LONDON JOURNAL (1834-35)

1078. Marchand, Leslie A. "Leigh Hunt's LONDON JOURNAL." JRUL, 6 (1943), 45-51.

LONDON MAGAZINE (1820-29)

See also No. 537.

1079. Bauer, Josephine. "Some Verse Fragments and Prose CHARACTERS by Samuel Butler Not Included in the COMPLETE WORKS." MP, 45 (1948), 160-68.

Reprints prose and verse from issues of the LONDON MAGAZINE (1825-26) which are now missing from the Butler MS in the British Museum.

1080. _____. THE LONDON MAGAZINE, 1820-29. Anglistica, vol. I. Copenhagen: Rosenkilde & Bagger, 1953.

An attempt "to analyse the contents of the magazine as it struck its contemporaries."

1081. Blunden, Edmund. "Clare on the 'Londoners.'" LONDON MERCURY, 7 (1923), 393-98.

1082. Brooks, Elmer L. "Studies in the LONDON MAGAZINE." Diss. Harvard University, 1954.

1083. _____. "Byron and the LONDON MAGAZINE." KSJ, 5 (1956), 49-67.

Criticism of and comments on Byron.

1084. Bulloch, John Malcolm. "John Scott of the LONDON MAGAZINE." N&Q, 170 (1936), 132.

1085. Butterworth, S. "The Old LONDON MAGAZINE." BOOKMAN, 63 (October 1922), 12-17.

1086. C.,J.D. "THE LONDON MAGAZINE." ATHENAEUM, no. 3104 (23 April 1887), p. 546.

1087. Gilmour, J.S.L. "Contemporary Collectors XXXI: A Freethought Collection and Its Predecessors." BC, 11 (1962), 184-96.

1088. Green, David Bonnell. "A Thomas De Quincey Letter." N&Q, 203 (1958), 392-93.

1089. House, Humphry. "A Famous Literary Periodical." LISTENER (BBC), 15 July 1954, pp. 100-101.

1090. Kimber, Sidney A. "The 'Relation of a Late Expedition to St. Augustine,' with Biographical and Bibliographical notes on Isaac and Edward Kimber." PBSA, 28 (1934), 81-96.

Contributions of the Kimbers to the LONDON MAGAZINE.

1091. King, R.W. "Charles Lamb, Cary, and the LONDON MAGAZINE." NC, 94 (1923), 363-69, 520-30.

1092. _____. "The LONDON MAGAZINE and the 'Londoners.'" PARSON PRIMROSE: THE LIFE, WORK, AND FRIENDSHIPS OF HENRY

FRANCIS CARY (1772-1844), TRANSLATOR OF DANTE. New York: George H. Doran, 1925. Pp. 124-77.

1093. "THE LONDON MAGAZINE and Its First Editor." TLS, 22 January 1920, pp. 41-42.

See also TLS, 29 January 1920, p. 69.

1094. Morgan, Peter F. "Taylor and Hessey: Aspects of their Conduct of the LONDON MAGAZINE." KSJ, 7 (1958), 61-68.

1095. Prance, C.A. "London Magazine, 1820-29." TLS, 16 March 1951, p. 165.

1096. ______. "A Forgotten Skit by Lamb." TLS, 9 February 1951, p. 92.

In the November 1823 issue.

1097. ______. "The London Magazine." CLSB, May 1951, pp. 3-5.

1098. Rees, J. Rogers. "The Lambs in Great Russell Street." N&Q, 8 (1907), 421-22.

Distinguishes between Gold's LONDON MAGAZINE (see below) and Baldwin's.

1099. Sikes, Herschel M. "Hazlitt, the LONDON MAGAZINE, and the 'Anonymous Reviewer.'" BNYPL, 65 (1961), 159-74.

1100. Tave, Stuart M. "THE LONDON MAGAZINE, 1820-29." MP, 52 (1954), 139-41.

A review of no. 718, with new materials.

1101. Zeitlin, Jacob. "The Editor of the LONDON MAGAZINE." JEGP, 20 (1921), 328-54.

LONDON MAGAZINE (Gold's, 1820-21)

See also No. 1098.

1102. Betteridge, H.T. "Howard's Ehrenhedachtnis." MLR, 47 (1952), 212-13.

LONDON MAGAZINE; OR, GENTLEMAN'S MONTHLY INTELLIGENCER (1732-85)

See also BOSWELL, JAMES (chapter 4) and Nos. 179, 911, and 2119.

1103. Bailey, Margery, ed. BOSWELL'S COLUMN: BEING HIS SEVENTY CONTRIBUTIONS TO THE LONDON MAGAZINE UNDER THE PSEUDONYM THE HYPOCHONDRIACK FROM 1777 to 1783. HERE FIRST PRINTED IN BOOK FORM IN ENGLAND. London: William Kimber, 1951.

A reprint, with minor revisions, of Bailey's 1928 Stanford University Press edition (No. 1109).

1104. Bauerle, R.F. "John Donne Redone and Undone." N&Q, 7 (1960), 386.

A revision of "Go and Catch a Falling Star" (June 1741).

1105. Dellbrook. "'The London Magazine.'" N&Q, 5 (1894), 109.

See also G.F.R.B., Daniel Hipwell, E[vard]. H[ome]. Coleman (page 193). Concerns first publication and files.

1106. "An Eighteenth Century Crowning." FR, 173 (1953), 363-69.

Reprints a letter describing coronation of George III which first appeared in the LONDON MAGAZINE for September 1761.

1107. Fabian, Bernhard, and Karen Kloth. "The Manuscript Background of James Beattie's 'Elements of Moral Science.'" BIBLIOTHECK, 5 (1969), 181-89.

A student provided the LONDON MAGAZINE with lecture notes.

1108. Garton, Charles. "Boswell's Favourite Lines from Horace." N&Q, 203 (1958), 306-7.

A passage from the HYPOCHONDRIACK, published in the LONDON MAGAZINE, also used as the title-page motto for the LIFE.

1109. THE HYPOCHONDRIACK. BEING THE SEVENTY ESSAYS BY THE CELEBRATED BIOGRAPHER, JAMES BOSWELL, APPEARING IN THE LONDON MAGAZINE, FROM NOVEMBER, 1777 TO AUGUST 1783, AND HERE FIRST REPRINTED. Ed. Margery Bailey. 2 vols. Stanford, Calif.: Stanford University Press, 1928.

See also No. 1103.

1110. Sambrook, A.J. "Another Early Version of Shenstone's PASTORAL BALLAD." RES, 18 (1967), 169-73.

The "earliest extant printed version" in the issue for December 1751.

1111. Tave, Stuart M. "Some Essays by James Beattie in the 'London Magazine.'" N&Q, 197 (1952), 534-37.

1112. Whiting, George W. "Mrs. M---- and M.M." N&Q, 202 (1957), 446-47.

A passage in the LONDON MAGAZINE is apparently by a Mrs. Madan; see also N&Q, 200:200-201.

LONDON MERCURY (1692)

See No. 1869.

LONDON REVIEW (1860-69)

See also No. 57.

1113. Brooks, Roger L. "Matthew Arnold and the LONDON REVIEW." PMLA, 76 (1961), 622-23.

LONDON SPY (1698-1700)

See also WARD, EDWARD (chapter 4) and No. 1868.

1114. Hayward, Arthur [L.]. "Ned Ward: The London Spy." BOOK-COLLECTOR'S QUARTERLY, no. XVI (October 1934), pp. 79-85.

1115. Kawai, Michio. "The 'Scurrilous' Language of THE LONDON SPY." ANGLICA (Publication of The Anglica Society of Kansai University, Osaka, Japan), 5 (1962), 20-35.

1116. Matthews, W. "The Character-Writings of Edward Ward." NEOPHILOLOGUS, 21 (1936), 116-34.

1117. Ward, Edward. THE LONDON SPY BY NED WARD. Ed., intro., and notes by Kenneth Fenwick. Contemporary Prints by Hogarth and Others. London: Folio Society, 1955.

1118. ______. THE LONDON SPY. THE VANITIES AND VICES OF THE TOWN EXPOSED TO VIEW. By Ned Ward. Ed., with notes, by

Arthur L. Hayward. London: Cassell, 1927.

A modernized reprint with no specific data on the original serialization.

1119. ______. THE LONDON SPY COMPLEAT, IN EIGHTEEN PARTS. Intro. Ralph Straus. London: Casanova Society, 1924.

LONGMAN'S MAGAZINE (1822-1900+)

1120. Blagden, Cyprian. "LONGMAN'S MAGAZINE." REL, 4, ii (1963), 9-22.

1121. Maurer, Oscar. "Andrew Lang and LONGMAN'S MAGAZINE, 1882-1905." UNIVERSITY OF TEXAS STUDIES IN ENGLISH, 34 (1955), 152-78.

LOOKER-ON (1792-94)

See also No. 181.

1122. Willey, Edward P. "The LOOKER-ON in America: Reception of a Latter-Day SPECTATOR." PBSA, 64 (1970), 431-48.

Subscription lists indicate that this journal, a publishing success in England, was also well received in America.

1123. ______. "A Study of the Essay-Journal the LOOKER-ON (1792-1793)." DA, 29 (1969), 4472A.

LOUNGER (1785-87)

See Nos. 181 and 2112.

LOVER (1714)

See also No. 2178.

1124. Blanchard, Rae. "Richard Steele's Maryland Story." AQ, 10 (1958), 78-82.

Primitivism in the story of an American Negro in the LOVER, no. 36.

LOYAL OBSERVATOR REVIV'D (1722-23)

1125. Limouze, A. Sanford. "Doctor Gaylard's LOYAL OBSERVATOR REVIV'D." MP, 48 (1950), 97-103.

The former printer of MIST'S WEEKLY JOURNAL published forty-seven numbers of his own paper (1722), with Tory and High Church sympathies. Limouze discusses Gaylard's career and his paper, and appends an index to all forty-seven numbers.

LOYAL POST (1705-?)

1126. Scouten, Arthur H. "An Early Printed Report on the Apparition of Mrs. Veal." RES, 6 (1955), 259-63.

Reprints a version of the ghost story found in the LOYAL POST, 24 December 1705.

1127. _____. "THE LOYAL POST: A Rare Queen Anne Newspaper and Daniel Defoe." BNYPL, 59 (1955), 195-97.

Describes fifty-five issues (23 November 1705 to 29 March 1706) in the New York Public Library. The issue for 24 December 1705 contains Bargrave's story in shorter form than that used by Defoe.

MACARONI AND THEATRICAL MAGAZINE (1772-73)

1128. Walford, E. "'The Macaroni Magazine.'" N&Q, 12 (1879), 247.

MACMILLAN'S MAGAZINE (1859-1900+)

See also No. 57.

1129. Gurr, A.J. "MACMILLAN'S MAGAZINE." REL, 6, pt. i (1965), 39-55.

1130. Morgan, Charles. THE HOUSE OF MACMILLAN. London: Macmillan, 1943.

MAGAZINE OF ART (1878-1900+)

1131. Rumbaugh, Liela M. "THE MAGAZINE OF ART." DAI, 30 (1970), 2979A.

MAGAZINE OF MAGAZINES (Limerick, 1751-61)

1132. Buckley, James. SOME ACCOUNT OF THE EARLIEST LIMERICK PRINTING. Cork: Guy, 1902.

Contains a note by E.R. McC. Dix on the MAGAZINE OF MAGAZINES.

MAGAZINE OF MAGAZINES; OR, UNIVERSAL REGISTER (1758-59)

See also No. 2024.

1133. Sutton, W.H. "'The Grand Magazine of Magazines.'" N&Q, 12 (1891), 227.

See further notes on pages 316-16 and see N&Q, 1 (1892), 93-94.

MANCHESTER GUARDIAN (1821-1900+)

1134. Drew, Fraser Bragg. "John Masefield and the MANCHESTER GUARDIAN." PQ, 37 (1958), 126-28.

MEDLEY (1710-12)

1135. Poston, M.L. "THE MEDLEYS of 1712." LIBRARY, 13 (1958), 205-7.

Distinguishes "three distinct series."

MEDUSA (1819-20)

1136. "The MEDUSA." N&Q, 5 (1888), 487.

See also N&Q, 6 (1888), 193.

MERCATOR (1713-14)

1137. Crossley, James. "Daniel Defoe and the 'Mercator.'" N&Q, 4 (1851), 388.

MERCURIUS ACADEMICUS (1648)

See No. 2293.

MERCURIUS AQUATICUS (1648)

See No. 2293.

MERCURIUS AULICUS (1643-45)

See also Nos. 2293 and 2294.

1138. F. "'Mercurius Aulicus': Battle of Newcastle Emlyn, 1645." N&Q, 12 (1873), 247.

1139. Homo, Ignotus. "A Birkenhead Newspaper in 1642!" MANCHESTER GUARDIAN, no. 8683 (15 June 1874), p. 6.

1140. Madan, Falconer. "A Description of a Complete Set of MERCURIUS AULICUS." TRANSACTIONS OF THE BIBLIOGRAPHICAL SOCIETY, 9 (1908), 111-12.

MERCURIUS BELLICUS (1643)

1141. Weber, Hilmar H. "The MERCURIUS BELLICUS of 1643." N&Q, 165 (1933), 345-46.

MERCURIUS BRITANNICUS (1643-46)

1142. F.,T.D. "The Mercurius Britannicus." N&Q, 1 (1874), 345.

MERCURIUS CALEDONIUS (1661)

1143. "The Earliest Scottish Newspaper." GOOD WORDS, 42 (1901), 58-63.

1144. "Two Extracts from 'The Mercurius Caledonius' of January 8th, 1661." CLARENDON HISTORICAL SOCIETY'S REPRINTS, ser. 1 (1882), 9-16.

MERCURIUS CIVICUS (1643)

1145. Plomer, Henry R. "An Analysis of the Civil War Newspaper 'Mercurius Civicus.'" LIBRARY, 6 (1905), 184-207.

MERCURIUS DOMESTICUS (1679)

1146. Burch, J.C. "Mercurius Domesticus, 1679." TLS, 13 October 1921, pp. 661-62.

1147. Newton, E.E. "'Mercurius Domesticus.'" N&Q, 154 (1928), 408-9.

See also, in this issue of N&Q, Fredk. A. Edwards (page 408) and J. Ardagh (page 409). In N&Q, 155 (1928), 12, see J.G. Muddiman. All of these notes expose this leaflet as a fraud.

MERCURIUS MELANCHOLICUS (1647-49)

1148. Frank, Joseph. "MERCURIUS MELANCHOLICUS." URLB, 13 (1957), 50-56.

1149. Williams, J.B. "A Royalist Cryptogram." N&Q, 11 (1915), 225-26.

MERCURIUS OXONIENSIS (1707)

See No. 2293.

MERCURIUS POETICUS (1660)

1150. Weber, Hilmar H. "The MERCURIUS POETICUS of 1660." N&Q, 169 (1935), 454-55.

MERCURIUS POLITICUS (1650-60)

See also No. 2118.

1151. Bond, Richmond P. "MERCURIUS POLITICUS." NEWBERRY LIBRARY BULLETIN,. 6 (1966), 216-21. Plates.

A description of the complete file of 515 issues acquired by the Newberry Library. MERCURIUS POLITICUS was the first periodical in England to last for nearly a decade.

1152. French, J. Milton. "Milton, Needham, and MERCURIUS POLITICUS." SP, 33 (1936), 236-52.

1153. Robbins, Alfred F. "Words from 'Mercurius Politicus.'" N&Q, 2 (1916), 147.

Cites appearances of two phrases predating earliest use according to OXFORD ENGLISH DICTIONARY.

1154. Weber, Hilmar H. "On a File of MERCURIUS POLITICUS in the Harvard College Library." N&Q, 164 (1933), 364-66.

MERCURIUS POLITICUS (1716-20)

See also No. 1926.

1155. Crossley, James. "Defoe: 'Mercurius Politicus': Mesnager's 'Negociations.'" N&Q, 3 (1869), 548-49.

Reprints a Defoe letter from the issue of July 1717.

MERCURIUS ROMANUS (1706-7)

1156. Sparke, Archibald. "Mercurius Romanus." N&Q, 150 (1926), 422.

MERCURIUS RUSTICUS; OR, THE COUNTRY'S COMPLAINT (1643-44)

See also No. 2293.

1157. Blaydes, F.A. "'Mercurius Rusticus.'" N&Q, 9 (1890), 288.

See also W.E. Buckley (pages 398-99).

1158. Ford, W.K. "The Date of Ryves' MERCURIUS RUSTICUS." N&Q, 4 (1957), 378.

METROPOLITAN MAGAZINE (1831-32)

1159. "'The Metropolitan Magazine' and Dickens's Early Work." DICKENSIAN, 33 (1937), 93-96.

MIDDLESEX JOURNAL (1769-1790?)

Title changes.

1160. Bryant, Donald C. "Rhetorical Criticism in THE MIDDLESEX JOURNAL, 1774." QJS, 50 (1964), 45-52.

MIDWIFE (1750-53)

See also SMART, CHRISTOPHER (chapter 4).

1161. M.,J. "Maxims: Newberry: Goldsmith." N&Q, 4 (1863), 229.

See also Jas. Crossley (page 254).

1162. Perreten, Peter F. "Satire in Christopher Smart's MIDWIFE." DAI, 33 (1972), 2902A.

MIRROR (1779-80)

See also Nos. 181 and 2112.

1163. Hudson, Randolph. "Henry Mackenzie, James Beattie et al., and the Edinburgh MIRROR." ELN, 1 (1963), 104-8.

Assignment of authorship based on a copy in the University of Wisconsin Library with annotations made in 1790.

1164. Rubinstein, E. "NORTHANGER ABBEY: The Elder Morlands and 'John Homespun.'" PLL, 5 (1969), 434-40.

Concerns an essay in the MIRROR (6 March 1779) recommended to Catherine by Morland.

1165. Walford, E. "The 'Mirror.'" N&Q, 12 (1879), 128.

See page 354 for replies.

MISCELLANY: GIVING AN ACCOUNT OF THE RELIGION, MORALITY, AND LEARNING OF THE PRESENT TIMES (1732-41)

See No. 2144.

MIST'S WEEKLY JOURNAL (1716-37)

See also No. 1926.

1166. Limouze, A. Sanford. "Burlesque Criticism of the Ballad in MIST'S WEEKLY JOURNAL." SP, 47 (1950), 607-18.

1167. Peterson, Spiro. "A Sonnet not Defoe's." N&Q, 202 (1957), 208-10.

Sonnet "Upon one who was bribed . . ." attributed to George Coningsby rather than to Defoe.

MODERATE (1648-49)

1168. Frank, Joseph. "England's First Newspaper Article on Flying." HLQ, 20 (1957), 185-89.

In the MODERATE for 12-19 December 1648.

MONITOR; OR, BRITISH FREEHOLDER (1755-65)

See also No. 1269.

1169. Peters, Marie. "The 'Monitor' on the Constitution, 1755-1765: New Light on the Ideological Origins of English Radicalism." EHR, 86 (1971), 706-27.

MONTH (1864-1900+)

1170. Martindale, C.C. "Newman and 'The Month.'" MONTH, 4 (December 1950), 365-74.

1171. Thomas, Alfred. "THE MONTH: Attribution of Articles." N&Q, 11 (1964), 235.

MONTHLY AMUSEMENT (1709)

1172. B.,G.F.R. "The 'Monthly Amusement.'" N&Q, 10 (1890), 249.

See reply on page 356.

MONTHLY CATALOGUE (1714-15)

See also No. 5.

1173. McKillop, Alan D. "Lintot's MONTHLY CATALOGUE." NEWBERRY LIBRARY BULLETIN, 6 (1963), 74-75.

MONTHLY CHRONICLE (1728-32)

1174. Cook, D.F. "'Register of Books,' 1732." BC, 16 (1967), 374-75.

Describes issues of the MONTHLY CHRONICLE (January-March 1732) among material presented to Liverpool University Library.

MONTHLY MAGAZINE AND BRITISH REGISTER (1796-1843)

See also Nos. 1963 and 2137.

1175. Carnall, Geoffrey. "A Hazlitt Contribution." TLS, 19 June 1954, p. 397.

In the issue for February 1809.

1176. _____. "The MONTHLY MAGAZINE." RES, 5 (1954), 158-64.

1177. Coldicutt, Dorothy. "Was Coleridge the Author of the 'Enquirer' Series in the MONTHLY MAGAZINE, 1796-9?" RES, 15 (1939), 45-60.

See also No. 1183.

1178. Cummins, Roger William. "The Monthly Magazine and Emerson (1841)." ATQ, 1 (1969), 64-75.

1179. Dowden, Wilfred S. "A Jacobin Journalist's View of Lord Byron." SP, 48 (1951), 56-66.

An account of the MONTHLY'S comments from 1818 to 1824.

1180. Erdman, David V. "Coleridge as Nehemiah Higginbottom." MLN, 73 (1958), 569-80.

Coleridge's hand in three burlesque sonnets.

1181. McGuire, Richard L. "The MONTHLY MAGAZINE (1796-1843): Politics and Literature in Transition." DA, 29 (1968), 1542A.

1182. N.,F. "The 'Monthly Magazine.'" N&Q, 7 (1889), 327.

Concerned with location of copy belonging to Griffiths. See page 457 for replies.

1183. Patton, Lewis. "Coleridge and the 'Enquirer' Series." RES, 16 (1940), 188-89.

In this reply to Coldicutt (No. 1177), Patton claims that Rev. William Enfield, not Coleridge, wrote the 'Enquirer' series, 1796-99.

1184. Piggot, John, Jr. "The 'Monthly Magazine.'" N&Q, 5 (1870), 434.

1185. Pollin, Burton R. "Mary Hays on Women's Rights in the MONTHLY MAGAZINE." EA, 24 (1971), 271-82.

1186. Rule, Fredk. "Sir Richard Phillips and the 'Monthly Magazine.'" N&Q, 2 (1874), 316.

MONTHLY MELODY (1760)

See also No. 2072.

1187. Hazen, A[llen]. T. "Unlocated British Newspapers." N&Q, 168 (1935), 250.

MONTHLY MERCURY (Irregularly from 1693)

1188. Blagden, Cyprian. "Henry Rhodes and the MONTHLY MERCURY, 1702 to 1720." BC, 5 (1956), 343-53.

MONTHLY MISCELLANY; OR, MEMOIRS FOR THE CURIOUS (1707-10)

1189. Adams, Percy G. "Benjamin Franklin's Defense of the De Fonte Hoax." PULC, 22 (1961), 133-40.

Concerns "one of the most influential hoaxes of the eighteenth century"; the purported letter from Admiral Bartholomew de Fonte appeared in the MONTHLY MISCELLANY in 1708. See also No. 1191.

1190. Ardagh, J. "THE MONTHLY MISCELLANY, OR MEMOIRS FOR THE CURIOUS." N&Q, 158 (1930), 134.

Holdings of the British Museum.

1191. Williams, G. "An Eighteenth-Century Spanish Investigation into the Apocryphal Voyage of Admiral Fonte." PACIFIC HISTORICAL REVIEW, 30 (1961), 319-27.

See also No. 1189.

MONTHLY REPOSITORY (1806-38)

1192. Barnett, George L. "A Disquisition on Punch and Judy Attributed to Charles Lamb." HLQ, 25 (1962), 225-47.

Reprints with commentary an 1837 essay from the MONTHLY REPOSITORY.

1193. Mineka, Francis E. THE DISSIDENCE OF DISSENT: 'THE MONTHLY REPOSITORY,' 1806-1838, UNDER THE EDITORSHIP OF ROBERT ASPLAND, W.J. FOX, R.H. HORNE, AND LEIGH HUNT. Chapel Hill: University of North Carolina Press, 1944.

1194. Smith, F.B. "R.H. Horne's Attributions of Authorship in the MONTHLY REPOSITORY." VPN, (1972), 26-28.

MONTHLY REVIEW (1749-1845)

See also Nos. 2025 and 2128.

1195. Fama. "'Monthly Review': Thomas Marryat: Samuel Badcock." N&Q, 2 (1886), 123-24.

Reprints a manuscript letter from Marryat concerning the founding of the MONTHLY REVIEW.

1196. Hawkins, Aubrey. "Some Writers on THE MONTHLY REVIEW." RES, 7 (1931), 168-81.

1197. Hopkins, Robert H. "'The Vicar of Wakefield,' A Puzzler to the Critic." N&Q, 203 (1958), 113-14.

Southey's response to the MONTHLY REVIEW (1766).

1198. Knapp, Lewis M. "Griffiths's 'Monthly Review' as Printed by Strahan." N&Q, 203 (1958), 216-17.

Information from Strahan's account books about the number of copies printed.

1199. Lonsdale, Roger. "William Bewley and THE MONTHLY REVIEW: A Problem of Attribution." PBSA, 55 (1961), 309-18.

Rejects attributions assigned by Nangle (see No. 1202).

1200. _____. "Dr. Burney and the MONTHLY REVIEW." RES, 14 (1963), 346-58; 15 (1964), 27-37.

1201. "The 'Monthly Review.'" TLS, 5 April 1934, p. 248.

A tribute to the MONTHLY'S founder, Ralph Griffiths.

1202. Nangle, Benjamin Christie. THE MONTHLY REVIEW, FIRST SERIES, 1749-1789. INDEXES OF CONTRIBUTORS AND ARTICLES. Oxford: Clarendon Press, 1934.

See also No. 1199.

1203. _____. "Charles Burney, Critic." THE AGE OF JOHNSON: ESSAYS PRESENTED TO CHAUNCEY BREWSTER TINKER. New Haven, Conn.: Yale University Press, 1949. Pp. 99-109.

Concerns Burney's articles for the MONTHLY REVIEW.

1204. _____. THE MONTHLY REVIEW, SECOND SERIES, 1790-1815: INDEXES OF CONTRIBUTORS AND ARTICLES. Oxford: Clarendon Press, 1955.

Reviewed in PQ 35:265-66; LIBRARY 10:224-25; MLR 51:308; RES 7:320-21.

1205. Oakes, Norman Edwin. "Ralph Griffiths and THE MONTHLY REVIEW." DA, 22 (1961), 1160-61.

1206. Riley, Henry T. "Colonel Cleland, Griffiths, Will Honeycomb." N&Q, 2 (1856), 351.

Also in this issue, see G.D. (pages 376-77) and D.S. (page 458).

1207. Seguin, J.A.R. VOLTAIRE AND THE 'MONTHLY REVIEW,' 1749-1778: A DESCRIPTIVE AND BIBLIOGRAPHICAL INDEX. Jersey City: R. Paxton, 1963.

1208. Spector, Robert Donald. "The MONTHLY and its Rival." BNYPL, 64 (1960), 159-61.

1209. Symonds, Emily Morse. "The 'Monthly Review' in the Eighteenth Century." MONTHLY REVIEW, 8, ii (1902), 123-37.

Reprinted in SIDE-LIGHTS ON THE GEORGIAN PERIOD, 1903.

MONTHLY VISITOR (1797-1804)

1210. Sarason, Bertram D. "A Sketch of Burke by Single-Speech Hamilton." BURKE NEWSLETTER, 5 (1964), 327-31.

MORNING CHRONICLE (1769-1862)

See also Nos. 1288 and 1963.

1211. Carlton, W. "'The Story Without a Beginning': An Unrecorded Contribution by Boz to the MORNING CHRONICLE." DICKENSIAN, 47 (1951), 67-70.

1212. Cline, C.L. "Thackeray and the 'Morning Chronicle.'" TLS, 19 December 1942, p. 619.

1213. Dexter, Walter. "Dickens and the MORNING CHRONICLE: Some Hitherto Unpublished Letters." FR, 136 (1934), 591-98.

1214. "Dickens' First Contributions to 'The Morning Chronicle.'" DICKENSIAN, 31 (1935), 5-10.

1215. Erdman, David V. "Byron's Mock Review of Rosa Matilda's Epic on the Prince Regent--A New Attribution." KSJ, 19 (1970), 101-17.

1216. Glasheen, Adaline E. "Shelley's First Published Review of Mandeville.'" MLN, 59 (1944), 172-73.

1217. "One Hundred Years Ago Dickens Leaves 'The Chronicle.'" DICKENSIAN, 32 (1936), 275-80.

1218. Pollin, Burton R. "Southey's 'Battle of Blenheim' Parodied in the MORNING CHRONICLE--A Whig Attack on the Battle of Copenhagen." BNYPL, 72 (1968), 507-19.

1219. Price, Cecil. "The Text of the First Performance of 'The Duenna.'" PBSA, 53 (1959), 268-70.

MORNING CHRONICLE review (22 November 1775) as basis for reconstruction.

1220. Ray, Gordon N., ed. WILLIAM MAKEPEACE THACKERAY'S CONTRIBUTIONS TO THE MORNING CHRONICLE. Urbana: University of Illinois Press, 1955.

The development of Thackeray's views of fiction shown through thirty-five reviews.

MORNING POST AND DAILY ADVERTISER (1772-1900+)

See also BELL, JOHN (chapter 4) and Nos. 1857, 1904, and 2099.

1221. Bourne, H.R. Fox. "Coleridge Among the Journalists." GENTLEMAN'S MAGAZINE, 263 (1887), 472-87.

1222. "Coleridge and the MORNING POST." MORNING POST, 21 October 1922; rpt. LIVING AGE, 316 (1923), 282-84.

1223. Colmer, John A. "Coleridge on Addington's Administration." MLR, 54 (1959), 69-72.

Attributes one essay to Coleridge.

1224. Erdman, David V. "The Case for Internal Evidence (6): The Signature of Style." BNYPL, 63 (1959), 88-109.

Concerns Coleridge's contributions and the identification of them.

1225. ______. "Coleridge as Editorial Writer." POWER AND CONSCIOUSNESS. Eds. Conor Cruise O'Brien and William Dean Vanech. New York: New York University Press, 1969. Pp. 183-201.

His prose contributions, 1798-1803.

1226. Glickfield, Charlotte Woods. "Coleridge's Prose Contributions to the MORNING POST." PMLA, 69 (1954), 681-85.

1227. Hindle, Wilfred. THE MORNING POST, 1772-1737: PORTRAIT OF A NEWSPAPER. London: Routledge, 1937.

Many romantic poets contributed to this periodical during the nineteenth century.

1228. Landon, Carol. "Wordsworth, Coleridge, and the MORNING POST: An Early Version of 'The Seven Sisters.'" RES, 11 (1960), 392-402.

1229. McElderry, B.R., Jr. "Southey and Wordsworth's 'The Idiot Boy.'" N&Q, 200 (1955), 490-91.

1230. Terrett, Dulaney. "Coleridge's Politics, 1789-1810." SUMMARIES OF DOCTORAL DISSERTATIONS, NORTHWESTERN UNIVERSITY, 9 (1941), 29-33.

MUSES MERCURY (1707-8)

1231. McCutcheon, Roger Philip. "Addison and the MUSES MERCURY." SP, 20 (1923), 17-28.

MUSEUM; OR, THE LITERARY AND HISTORICAL REGISTER (1746-47)

See also Nos. 1986 and 2137.

1232. Cunningham, Peter. "Dr. Akenside." GENTLEMAN'S MAGAZINE, 39 (1853), 157-58.

Agreement with Dodsley for editing the MUSEUM.

1233. Roberts, W. "THE MUSEUM, a Periodical." N&Q, 2 (1886), 409-10.

See also pages 458-59 in this issue of N&Q.

1234. Tierney, James E. "A Study of THE MUSEUM; OR, LITERARY AND HISTORICAL REGISTER." DAI, 30 (1970), 3438A.

1235. Z.,X.Y. "THE MUSEUM." N&Q, 161 (1931), 208.

For replies, see pages 251, 340, 355-56. See also N&Q, 162 (1932), 47-48.

MY OWN MAGAZINE (1899-?)

1236. Scott, John William Robertson. "WE" AND ME: MEMOIRS OF OUR EMINENT EDITORS I WORKED WITH, A DISCUSSION BY EDITORS OF THE FUTURE OF EDITING, AND A CANDID ACCOUNT OF THE FOUNDING AND EDITING, FOR TWENTY-ONE YEARS, OF 'MY OWN MAGAZINE.' London: W.H. Allen, 1956.

NATIONAL JOURNAL (1746)

1237. Bullock, J.M. "'The National Journal,' 1746." N&Q, 10 (1908), 49.

On the arrest of George Gordon for his treasonable article in no. 35.

NATIONAL REVIEW (1883-1900+)

See also Nos. 57 and 2052.

1238. Christian, Robert Murray. "Leo Maxse and the NATIONAL REVIEW: A Study of the Periodical Press and British Foreign Policy, 1893-1914." Diss. University of Virginia, 1940.

1239. Tener, Robert H. "Bagehot and Tennyson." TLS, 21 August 1959, p. 483.

Argues that Bagehot wrote the REVIEW article (October 1859) on Tennyson's IDYLLS.

NEW ANNUAL REGISTER (1781-1826)

1240. Forsey, C.A. "THE NEW ANNUAL REGISTER." N&Q, 154 (1928), 284-85.

Also in this issue of N&Q, see pages 188 and 213.

1241. Marken, Jack W. "William Godwin's Writing for the NEW ANNUAL REGISTER." MLN, 68 (1953), 477-79.

NEWCASTLE CHRONICLE (1764-1864)

1242. Pollard, Graham. "Novels in Newspapers: Some Unpublished Letters of Captain Mayne Reid." RES, 18 (1942), 72-85.

Letters to the editor concerning the publishing of novels by syndication.

NEWCASTLE JOURNAL (1739-76?)

1243. Berman, David. "A New Letter by Berkeley on Tar-water." HERMATHENA, 107 (1968), 45-48.

Appeared 10 November 1744.

NEW CHURCH MAGAZINE (1824-29)

1244. Higham, Charles. "Centenary of a Swedenborgian Magazine." N&Q, 5 (1912), 84-85.

NEW LADY'S MAGAZINE (1786-95)

1245. Tillotson, Geoffrey. "The NEW LADY'S MAGAZINE of 1786." LONDON MERCURY, 24 (1931), 545-51.

Reprinted in his ESSAYS IN CRITICISM AND RESEARCH (Cambridge: 1942).

NEW MAGAZINE (Strabane, 1800)

1246. Campbell, A.A. "'The Strabane Magazine.'" IRISH BOOK LOVER, 3 (1912), 144-45.

NEW MONTHLY MAGAZINE (1814-36)

1247. Grill, Neil G. "The NEW MONTHLY MAGAZINE: 1814-1820." DAI, 31 (1971), 6607A-8A.

1248. Heide, John A. "THE NEW MONTHLY MAGAZINE." N&Q, 196 (1951), 414.

1249. Jones, Linda B. "The NEW MONTHLY MAGAZINE, 1821-1830." DAI, 32 (1971), 969A.

1250. Jones, Stanley. "Isabella Bridgwater: A Charade by Hazlitt?" REL, 8, no. 3 (1967), 91-95.

1251. Mayer, S.R. Townshend. "Leigh Hunt and the NEW MONTHLY MAGAZINE." N&Q, 7 (1877), 265-66.

1252. Rollins, Hyder E. "Letters of Horace Smith to His Publisher Colburn." HARVARD LIBRARY BULLETIN, 3 (1949), 359-70.

1253. Sikes, Herschel M. "'The Infernal Hazlitt,' THE NEW MONTHLY MAGAZINE, and the Conversations of James Northcote, R.A." ESSAYS IN HISTORY AND LITERATURE: PRESENTED BY FELLOWS OF THE NEWBERRY LIBRARY TO STANLEY PARGELLIS. Ed. Heinz Bluhm. Chicago: 1965. Pp. 179-91.

1254. Taplin, Gardner. "An Early Poem by Mrs. Browning." N&Q, 195 (1950), 252-53.

In 1821, apparently her first periodical contribution.

1255. Urban. "NEW MONTHLY MAGAZINE." N&Q, 2 (1886), 388.

Concerns Thomas Noon Talfourd. See also N&Q, 3 (1887), 18.

NEW QUARTERLY MAGAZINE (1873-80)

See No. 57.

NEWS FROM ABROAD (1722)

1256. Wiles, R.M. "Manchester's First Newspaper 'News from Abroad,' 1722." ManR, 11 (1968), 161-66.

NEWS FROM PARNASSUS (1681)

See No. 180.

NEWS OF THE WORLD (1843-1900+)

See No. 1857.

NEW WEEKLY CHRONICLE (1758-67?)

See OWEN'S WEEKLY CHRONICLE.

NINETEENTH CENTURY (1877-1900+)

See Nos. 57 and 642.

NONSENSE OF COMMON SENSE (1737-38)

1257. Ransom, Harry H. "Mary Wortley Montagu's Newspaper." STUDIES IN

ENGLISH, DEPARTMENT OF ENGLISH, THE UNIVERSITY OF TEXAS, 1947 (Austin: 1947), pp. 84-89.

NORTHAMPTON MISCELLANY (1721)

1258. "'The Northampton Miscellany.'" N&Q, 3 (1890), 211-12.

NORTHAMPTONSHIRE JOURNAL (1741?)

1259. Taylor, John. "The 'Northamptonshire Journal.'" N&Q, 12 (1885), 30.

NORTH BRITISH REVIEW (1814)

See also No. 57.

1260. "The Story of the 'North British Review.'" SCOTTISH REVIEW, 3 January, 1907.

NORTH BRITON (1762-63)

See also WILKES, JOHN (chapter 4) and No. 1860.

1261. A.,F.S. "Who Were the Writers in the North Briton?" N&Q 3 (1851), 409.

1262. Beatty, Joseph M., Jr. "The Political Satires of Charles Churchill." SP, 16 (1919), 303-33.

1263. ______. "Notes on the Authorship of THE NORTH BRITON." MLN, 36 (1921), 442.

1264. Bleackley, Horace. "'The North Briton'; 'No. 45.'" LIFE OF JOHN WILKES. London: John Lane, 1917. Pp. 71-109.

1265. Cappon, Alexander P. "Chapters in the Struggle for Liberty." UNIVERSITY OF KANSAS CITY REVIEW, 22 (1955), 159-60.

1266. Cordasco, Francesco. "Junius as the Author of 'The North Briton': A Note on the Rev. Allen's 'Junius Unmasked' (1828)." N&Q, 196 (1951), 413.

1267. THE CORRESPONDENCE OF JOHN WILKES AND CHARLES CHURCHILL.

Ed., with intro., Edward H. Weatherly. New York: Columbia University Press, 1954.

The "Introduction" includes a discussion of the collaboration between Wilkes and Churchill in the writing of the NORTH BRITON, 1762-63.

1268. Halsband, I.R. "The Poet of the NORTH BRITON." PQ, 17 (1938), 389-95.

1269. Needham, Francis. "A Strawberry Hill 'North Briton.'" TLS, 27 November 1930, p. 1014.

See also John C. Fox, TLS, 11 December 1930, p. 1066. For more on this number of the NORTH BRITON, see A.T. Hazen's BIBLIOGRAPHY OF THE STRAWBERRY HILL PRESS (New Haven: Yale University Press, 1942, pages 270-72).

1270. Nobbe, George. THE NORTH BRITON. A STUDY IN POLITICAL PROPAGANDA. Columbia University Studies in English and Comparative Literature, no. 140. New York: Columbia University Press, 1939.

1271. Rhodon. "Wilkes and the NORTH BRITON." N&Q, 161 (1931), 165-66.

Also in this issue of N&Q, see J.F.M. (pages 211-12) and E.G.B. (page 268).

1272. _____. "The NORTH BRITON and the Journeymen Printers." N&Q, 166 (1934), 137.

1273. Treloar, William Purdie. "'The North Briton,' No. 45." WILKES AND THE CITY. London: John Murray, 1917. Pp. 13-41.

1274. Y.,J.T. "The Third Volume of Wilkes's Reprint of the 'North Briton.'" N&Q, 8 (1889), 101-2.

1275. _____. "Bibliography of the 'North Briton.'" N&Q, 9 (1890), 104-6.

NORTHERN STAR (1792-97)

See No. 2282.

NORWICH MERCURY (1725-1900+)

See No. 1912.

NOTES & QUERIES (1844-1900+)

1276. Algar, F., and Wilfred H. Holden. "W.J. Thoms: Our First Editor." N&Q, 198 (1953), 125, 223.

OBSERVATOR IN QUESTION AND ANSWER (1681-87)

1277. Aarts, Jan. "The 'Colloquial Style' and Sir Roger L'Estrange's OBSERVATOR." NEOPHILOLOGUS, 53 (1969), 302-7.

1278. Faulkner, Thomas C. "A Selected Edition of Sir Roger L'Estrange's OBSERVATOR." DAI, 33 (1972), 24A.

1279. Jordain, Violet. "Mission in the Market Place: Sir Roger L'Estrange's OBSERVATOR IN DIALOGUE as an Instrument for Teaching and Delighting the Common Londoner, 1681-1687." DAI, 30 (1969), 686A.

1280. L'Estrange, Sir Roger. SELECTIONS FROM THE OBSERVATOR (1681-1687). Intro. Violet Jordain. Augustan Reprint Society Publication no. 141. Los Angeles: Clark Memorial Library, 1970.

1281. McCutcheon, Roger P. "The Observator and Increase Mather: A Note on Seventeenth Century Book-Reviewing." PUBLICATIONS OF THE COLONIAL SOCIETY OF MASSACHUSETTS: TRANSACTIONS, 1920-1922, 24 (1923), 313-17.

OBSERVER (1791-1900+)

1282. Miliband, Marion. THE 'OBSERVER' OF THE NINETEENTH CENTURY, 1791-1901: A SELECTION. Intro. Asa Briggs. London: Longmans, 1966.

1283. Waller, John O. "Edward Dicey and the American Negro in 1862: An English Working Journalist's View." BNYPL, 66 (1962), 31-45.

Dicey, editor from 1870-89, was also associated with the DAILY TELEGRAPH and the London DAILY NEWS. His articles on America also appeared in the SPECTATOR and MACMILLAN'S MAGAZINE.

OLD ENGLAND (1743-53)

See Nos. 275 and 660.

OLLA PODRIDA (1787-88)

See also No. 2293.

1284. Walford, E. "The 'Olla Podrida' and its Author." N&Q, 2 (1886), 407.

For replies, see pages 449-50.

ONCE A WEEK (1859-80)

1285. Buckler, William E. "ONCE A WEEK under Samuel Lucas, 1859-65." PMLA, 67 (1952), 924-41.

1286. _____. "Edward Walford: A Distressed Editor." N&Q, 198 (1953), 536-38.

Walford's difficulties as editor of ONCE A WEEK (1865-67) and the GENTLEMAN'S MAGAZINE (1866-68).

1287. _____. "E.S. Dallas's Appointment as Editor of 'Once a Week.'" N&Q, 195 (1950), 279-80.

ORIGINAL LONDON POST (1718-?)

See No. 1317.

ORIGINAL WEEKLY JOURNAL (1715?-36?)

See APPLEBEE'S ORIGINAL WEEKLY JOURNAL.

OWEN'S WEEKLY CHRONICLE (1758-67?)

1288. Gove, Philip B. "Early Numbers of THE MORNING CHRONICLE and OWEN'S WEEKLY CHRONICLE." LIBRARY, 20 (1940), 412-24.

1289. _____. "No. I of OWEN'S WEEKLY CHRONICLE." LIBRARY, 21 (1940), 95.

OXFORD AND CAMBRIDGE MAGAZINE (1856)

See also GERM and No. 57.

1290. Gordon, Walter K. "A Critical Selected Edition of William Morris's

'Oxford and Cambridge Magazine' (1856)." Diss. University of Pennsylvania, 1960.

1291. _____. "Pre-Raphaelitism and the OXFORD AND CAMBRIDGE MAGAZINE." JRUL, 29 (1966), 42-51.

1292. Kegel, Charles H. "An Undergraduate Magazine, 1856 Style." BASIC COLLEGE QUARTERLY, Winter 1956, pp. 27-32.

1293. Paden, W.D. "A Few Annotations by Swinburne." N&Q, 8 (1961), 469-70.

In a copy for 1856.

OXFORD GAZETTE (1665-1900+)

See GAZETTE (OXFORD AND LONDON).

OXFORD JOURNAL (1753-1900+)

1294. Brooking, Cecil. "JACKSON'S OXFORD JOURNAL." N&Q, 178 (1940), 157.

1295. Davies, Eileen C. "JACKSON'S OXFORD JOURNAL." N&Q, 208 (1963), 428.

1296. _____. "An Epigram of Boswell." N&Q, 212 (1967), 182.

The epigram appeared in the issue for 8 September 1787.

1297. Gove, Philip B. "JACKSON'S OXFORD JOURNAL." N&Q, 178 (1940), 98.

See also No. 1294.

1298. Marshall, Ed. "CAMBRIDGE CHRONICLE: OXFORD JOURNAL." N&Q, 1 (1886), 392.

1299. Mordaunt, Edward A.B., comp. INDEX TO OBITUARY AND BIOGRAPHICAL NOTICES IN JACKSON'S OXFORD JOURNAL (NEWSPAPER) 1753-1853. Volume I (1753-1754-1755). London: 1904.

1300. Townsend, James. NEWS OF A COUNTRY TOWN; BEING EXTRACTS FROM 'JACKSON'S OXFORD JOURNAL' RELATING TO ABINGDON, 1753-1853. London: Milford, 1914.

OXFORD MAGAZINE; OR, UNIVERSITY MUSEUM (1768-76)

See also No. 2293.

1301. Meyerstein, E.H.W. "Chatterton and the Oxford Magazine." TLS, 31 May 1923, pp. 371-72.

1302. Pickford, John. "The 'Oxford Magazine.'" N&Q, 3 (1881), 329.
See also the reply on page 373.

OXFORD QUARTERLY MAGAZINE (1825)

1303. Inglis, R. "OXFORD QUARTERLY MAGAZINE." N&Q, 1 (1880), 256.

PALL MALL GAZETTE (1865-1900+)

1304. Baylen, Joseph O. "Matthew Arnold and the PALL MALL GAZETTE: Some Unpublished Letters, 1884-1887." SAQ, 68 (1969), 543-55.

1305. _____. "Swinburne and the PALL MALL GAZETTE." RS, 36 (1968), 325-34.

1306. Beer, Gillian. "Meredith's Contribution to THE PALL MALL GAZETTE." MLR, 61 (1966), 395-400.

1307. Bevington, Merle M. "Three Letters of Robert Browning to the Editor of the PALL MALL GAZETTE." MLN, 75 (1960), 304-9.

1308. Booth, Bradford A. "Trollope and the PALL MALL GAZETTE." NCF, 4 (1949), 51-69, 137-58.

1309. Neiman, Fraser. "Some Newly Attributed Contributions of Matthew Arnold to the PALL MALL GAZETTE." MP, 55 (1957), 84-92.

1310. Scott, J.W. Robertson. THE STORY OF THE PALL MALL GAZETTE, OF ITS FIRST EDITOR, FREDERICK GREENWOOD, AND OF ITS FOUNDER, GEORGE MURRAY SMITH. New York: Oxford University Press, 1950.

1311. _____. THE LIFE AND DEATH OF A NEWSPAPER: AN ACCOUNT OF THE TEMPERAMENTS, PERTUBATIONS AND ACHIEVEMENTS OF

JOHN MORLEY, W.T. STEAD, E.T. COOK, HARRY CUST, J.L. GARVIN, AND THREE OTHER EDITORS OF THE PALL MALL GAZETTE. London: Methuen, 1952.

1312. Sharps, John Geoffrey. "Articles on Mrs. Gaskell in THE PALL MALL GAZETTE (1865)." N&Q, 12 (1965), 301-2.

PARTHENON (1825-26)

1313. Forsythe, Robert S. "THE PARTHENON." N&Q, 170 (1936), 7, 50, 121, 213, 265.

PASQUIN (1722-24)

See No. 2022.

PENNY MAGAZINE (1832-45)

1314. Feldberg, Michael. "Knight's PENNY MAGAZINE and CHAMBER'S EDINBURGH JOURNAL: A Problem in Writing Cultural History." VPN, 3 (1968), 13-16.

1315. Tomlinson, C. "Penny Cyclopedia." N&Q, 6 (1894), 469-70; 7 (1895), 149-50, 197.

1316. Washington, William D. "The PENNY MAGAZINE: A Study of the Genesis and Utilitarian Application of the Popular Miscellany." DA, 28 (1968), 5030A-31A.

PENNY POST (1725?)

1317. Torriano, Col. "Sir Peter Parravicini." N&Q, 9 (1890), 30.

See also W.E. Buckley (page 152). References to an unidentifiable PENNY POST (by Heathcote, 1725), and the ORIGINAL LONDON POST, OR HEATHCOTE'S INTELLIGENCE (1719), in which ROBINSON CRUSOE was originally published.

PHILOSOPHICAL MAGAZINE (1798-1840)

Title varies.

1318. "THE PHILOSOPHICAL MAGAZINE." ENDEAVOR, 8 (1949), 1-2.

PHILOSOPHICAL TRANSACTIONS OF THE ROYAL SOCIETY (1665-1900+)

1319. Doxey, William S. "William Blake, James Basire, and the PHILOSOPHICAL TRANSACTIONS: An Unexplored Source of Blake's Scientific Thought." BNYPL, 72 (1968), 252-60.

1320. Lloyd, L.S. "Musical Theory in the early PHILOSOPHICAL TRANSACTIONS." NOTES AND RECORDS OF THE ROYAL SOCIETY OF LONDON, 3 (1941), 149-59.

1321. McCutcheon, Roger Philip. "The JOURNAL DES SCAVANS and the PHILOSOPHICAL TRANSACTIONS OF THE ROYAL SOCIETY." SP, 21 (1934), 626-28.

1322. Olson, R.C. "Swift's Use of the PHILOSOPHICAL TRANSACTIONS in Section V of A TALE OF A TUB." SP, 49 (1952), 459-67.

Argues convincingly that at least two items in Swift's ludicrous list of modern achievements are drawn from materials which appeared in the PHILOSOPHICAL TRANSACTIONS OF THE ROYAL SOCIETY.

1323. Pedersen, Olaf. "Master John Perks and His Mechanical Curves." CENTAURUS, 8 (1963), 1-18.

Perks contributed papers on mathematics in 1699, 1706, and 1715.

1324. Potter, George Reuben. "The Significance to the History of English Natural Science of John Hill's 'Review of the Works of the Royal Society.'" ESSAYS AND STUDIES BY MEMBERS OF THE DEPARTMENT OF ENGLISH. University of California Publications in English, XIV. Berkeley: University of California Press, 1943. Pp. 157-80.

Hill's REVIEW was an attack on the TRANSACTIONS.

1325. Thomson, Thomas. HISTORY OF THE ROYAL SOCIETY, FROM ITS INSTITUTION TO THE END OF THE EIGHTEENTH CENTURY. London: Robert Baldwin, 1812.

Largely an elucidation of the TRANSACTIONS.

1326. Webster, C.M. "Swift and the Royal Society's PHILOSOPHICAL TRANSACTIONS." N&Q, 161 (1931), 99-100.

1327. Weld, Charles Richard. A HISTORY OF THE ROYAL SOCIETY, WITH MEMOIRS OF THE PRESIDENTS. COMPILED FROM AUTHENTIC DOCUMENTS. 2 vols. London: John W. Parker, 1848.

PHRENOLOGICAL JOURNAL (1823-37)

1328. McDonald, W.U., Jr. "Scottish Phrenologists and Scott's Novels." N&Q, 207 (1962), 415-17.

PLAIN DEALER (1724-25)

See also Nos. 2040 and 2144.

1329. Love, Alice Louisa. "A Study of the PLAIN DEALER." DA, 21 (1961), 1940-41.

1330. McKillop, Alan Dugald. "Peter the Great in Thompson's WINTER." MLN, 67 (1952), 28-31.

The chief source for the passage is Aaron Hill's PLAIN DEALER, no. 106.

1331. Stout, George D. "Leigh Hunt and THE PLAIN DEALER." MLN, 42 (1927), 383-85.

POCKET MAGAZINE (1794-95)

See No. 290.

POLITICAL HERALD AND REVIEW (1785-86)

1332. Marken, Jack W. "William Godwin and the POLITICAL HERALD AND REVIEW." BNYPL, 65 (1961), 517-33.

POLITICAL MAGAZINE AND PARLIAMENTARY, NAVAL, MILITARY, AND LITERARY JOURNAL (1780-1891)

1333. Tuck, W. "'The Political Magazine.'" N&Q, 7 (1865), 301.

POLITICAL REGISTER AND IMPARTIAL REVIEW OF NEW BOOKS (1767-72)

1334. Birrell, T.A. "The POLITICAL REGISTER: Cobbett and English Literature." ES, 45 (1964), Supp., pp. 213-19.

1335. Hawkins, Edward. "'Political Register.'" N&Q, 10 (1854), 492.

Also in this issue, see P.R. (page 492); see C. Ross in N&Q, 11 (1855), 35.

1336. Rea, Robert R. "The Impact of Party Journalism in the POLITICAL REGISTER." HISTORIAN, 17 (1954), 1-17.

A description of the political background of the periodical started by John Almon, May 1767.

1337. Solly, Edward. "The 'Political Register,' 1767." N&Q, 11 (1885), 346; 12 (1885), 57-58.

PORTFOLIO (1830?)

1338. Thomas, Gillian. "Dickens and THE PORTFOLIO." DICKENSIAN, 68 (1972), 167-72.

PORTSMOUTH AND GOSPORT GAZETTE (1750?)

1339. Wiles, R.M. "The Earliest Hampshire Newspaper." N&Q, 211 (1966), 219-22.

POST BOY (1695-1735)

See No. 1990.

POST-MAN (1694-1730)

See No. 1930.

PRECEPTOR (1809)

1340. McCutcheon, Roger P. "Johnson and Dodsley's PRECEPTOR, 1748." TULANE STUDIES IN ENGLISH, 3 (1952), 125-32.

1341. Randall, Dale. "Dodsley's PRECEPTOR--A Window into the Nineteenth Century." JRUL, 22 (1958), 10-22.

PROMPTER (1734-36)

See also Nos. 164, 2040, and 2144.

1342. Burnim, Kalman A. "Aaron Hill's THE PROMPTER: An Eighteenth-Century Theatrical Paper." EDUCATIONAL THEATRE JOURNAL, 13 (1961), 73-81.

Concerns theatrical politics.

1343. Hill, Aaron, and William Popple. THE PROMPTER, A THEATRICAL PAPER (1734-1736). Sel. and ed. William W. Appleton and Kalman A. Burnim. New York: Benjamin Blom, 1966.

1344. Hummert, Paul A. "THE PROMPTER: An Intimate Mirror and the Theatre in 1789." RECTR, 3 (1964), 37-46.

1345. Sutherland, W.O.S., Jr. "Polonius, Hamlet, and Lear in Aaron Hill's PROMPTER." SP, 49 (1952), 605-18.

Examples of "character criticism" of Shakespeare.

PROTESTANT MAGAZINE (1780?)

1346. Sedgwick, Daniel. "'Protestant Magazine.'" N&Q, 11 (1861), 29.

Not entered in the Crane & Kaye CENSUS (No. 24).

PUBLIC ADVERTISER(1752-94)

See also No. 2223.

1347. Ryskamp, Charles. "Cowper's Ambition: Two Documents." YALE UNIVERSITY LIBRARY GAZETTE, 34 (1960), 152-62.

Two 1786 letters (15 and 16 May) defending his translation of Homer.

PUBLIC LEDGER (1760-1900+)

See also GOLDSMITH, OLIVER (chapter 4) and No. 33.

1348. Abbot, Sister M. John V., S.S.N.D. "Irony in Oliver Goldsmith's THE CITIZEN OF THE WORLD." DA, 28 (1968), 3134A-35A.

1349. Demsbolton, John. "Definition of 'Berserk.'" N&Q, 203 (1958), 127.

Cites, among other works, Goldsmith's CITIZEN OF THE WORLD, which originally appeared in the PUBLIC LEDGER.

1350. Kolb, Gwin J. "Dr. Johnson and the PUBLIC LEDGER: A Small Addition to the Canon." SB, 11 (1958), 252-55.

A notice in the UNIVERSAL CHRONICLE (5-12 January 1760) concerning the PUBLIC LEDGER.

1351. Levine, Philip. "A Critical and Historical Study of Oliver Goldsmith's

THE CITIZEN OF THE WORLD." DAI, 31 (1971), 6558A-59A.

The CITIZEN essays originally appeared in the PUBLIC LEDGER.

1352. McAdam, E.L., Jr. "New Essays by Dr. Johnson." RES, 18 (1942), 197-207.

Three papers from the PUBLIC LEDGER, 1760--the second one attributed to Goldsmith--are claimed for Johnson.

1353. Patrick, Michael D. "Oliver Goldsmith's CITIZEN OF THE WORLD: A Rational Accommodation of Human Existence." ENLIGHTENMENT ESSAYS, 2 (1971), 82-90.

1354. Ponthieu, Judy F.S. "Oliver Goldsmith as Social Critic in THE CITIZEN OF THE WORLD." DAI, 32 (1971), 2651A.

1355. Weatherly, Edward H. "Beau Tibbs and Colonel Sellers." MLN, 59 (1944), 310-13.

Unconvincing argument for parallels between the CITIZEN OF THE WORLD and Mark Twain's GILDED AGE.

PUBLIC REGISTER; OR, FREEMAN'S JOURNAL (1763-1900+)

1356. Francis, John Collins. "'The Freeman's Journal,' 1763-1913." N&Q, 8 (1913), 321-22, 344-45, 363-65, 383-84.

PUBLISHER (1745)

1357. Chapman, R.W. "Johnson's Works: A Lost Piece and a Forgotten Piece." LONDON MERCURY, 21 (1930), 438-44.

The "lost piece" is "Proposals for Printing Every Fortnight, The Publisher . . ." which Chapman suggests may be ascribed to Johnson.

PUNCH (1841-1900+)

See also No. 197.

1358. Adrian, Arthur A. MARK LEMON, FIRST EDITOR OF 'PUNCH.' London and New York: Oxford University Press, 1966.

1359. Darwin, Bernard. "Christmas and Mr. Punch." NR, 135 (1950), 495-98.

Christmas cartoons from c. 1864-1900.

1360. Falconer, J.W. "A Hundred Years of PUNCH." DALHOUSIE REVIEW, 21 (1941), 170-76.

1361. Hambourg, Daria. RICHARD DOYLE: HIS LIFE AND WORK. London: Art and Technics, 1948; New York: Pellegrini and Cudahy, 1949.

Doyle was an illustrator for PUNCH.

1362. Horton-Smith, L.G.H. "PUNCH: Have You a Complete Set?" N&Q, 192 (1947), 36.

See also page 84.

1363. Kelly, Richard. "The Hangman Hanged: PUNCH and the Death Penalty." SNL, 9 (1972), 121-27.

1364. Nadelhaft, Janice R. "PUNCH Among the Aesthetes: A Chapter in Victorian Criticism." DAI, 31 (1971), 6019A.

1365. Price, R.G.G. A HISTORY OF PUNCH. London: Collins, 1957.

1366. Ray, Gordon N. "Thackeray and PUNCH." TLS, 1 January 1949, p. 16.

Identifies forty-four of Thackeray's contributions, 1848-54.

1367. Williams, R.W., ed. A CENTURY OF 'PUNCH.' London: Heinemann, 1956.

QUARTERLY REVIEW (1809-1900+)

See also Nos. 57, 549, and 2154.

1368. Bennett, Scott. "Catholic Emancipation, the QUARTERLY REVIEW, and Britain's Constitutional Revolution." VS, 12 (1969), 283-304.

1369. Brightfield, Myron F. "Lockhart's QUARTERLY Contributors." PMLA, 59 (1944), 491-512.

1370. Brown, Simon. "Ebenezer Elliott and Robert Southey: Southey's Break with THE QUARTERLY REVIEW." RES, 22 (1971), 307-11.

1371. "Centenary of the London QUARTERLY REVIEW." REVIEW OF REVIEWS,

39 (1909), 730-31.

1372. "The Centenary of THE QUARTERLY REVIEW." QR, 210 (1909), 731-84; 211 (1909), 279-34.

1373. Cook, D. "Murray's Mysterious Contributor: Unpublished Letters of Sir Walter Scott." NC, 101 (1927), 605-13.

1374. "Croker on Tennyson." COLOPHON, 1 no. 4 (1941), 95-96.

Identifies Croker as the author of an anonymous review of Tennyson's POEMS (1833).

1375. Elwin, Malcolm. "The Founder of the 'Quarterly Review'--John Murray II." QR, no. 557 (1943), pp. 1-15.

1376. Fahney, David M. "Southey's Review of Hallam." N&Q, 13 (1966), 178-79.

In QUARTERLY REVIEW (January 1828); concerns Southey's collaborator, Mr. Edwards.

1377. Fetter, Frank Whitson. "The Economic Articles in the QUARTERLY REVIEW and Their Authors." JPE, 66 (1958), 47-64, 154-70.

1378. Flanagan, Cabell. "Robert Southey and Thomas Adams." N&Q, 197 (1952), 554-55.

1379. Graham, Walter. TORY CRITICISM IN THE 'QUARTERLY REVIEW.' New York: Columbia University Press, 1921.

1380. ______. "Scott and Mr. Reitzel." PMLA, 44 (1929), 309-10.

Attributes to Scott the famous review of Jane Austen's EMMA, but see also Nos. 1381 and 1400.

1381. Hogan, Charles B. "Sir Walter Scott and EMMA." PMLA, 45 (1930), 1264-66.

Follows Graham, No. 1380, in arguing that Scott wrote the Jane Austen review, but see also No. 1400.

1382. Jenks, Mary H. "Literary Criticism in the QUARTERLY REVIEW, 1809-1824." Diss. University of Tennessee, 1958.

1383. "John Murray, 1778-1843. The Anax of Publishers." TLS, 26 June

1943, p. 308.

A tribute to the founder of the QUARTERLY REVIEW.

1384. Johnson, R.V. "Pater and the Victorian Anti-Romantics." EC, 4 (1954), 42-57.

The QUARTERLY versus Pater on romantic poets, about 1876.

1385. Kaderley, Nat Lewis. "Southey and the QUARTERLY REVIEW." MLN, 70 (1955), 261-63.

1386. Kern, John D., Elisabeth Schneider, and Irwin Griggs. "Lockhart to Croker on the QUARTERLY." PMLA, 60 (1945), 175-98.

Concerns the authorship of over 300 reviews in the QUARTERLY.

1387. ______. "An Unidentified Review, Possibly by Scott." MLQ, 6 (1945), 327-28.

1388. Lockhead, Marion. "Lockhart, the QUARTERLY, and the Tractarians." QR, 291 (1953), 196-209.

1389. ______. "Miss Rigby and THE QUARTERLY REVIEW." QR, 298 (1960), 59-69.

1390. "Memorabilia." N&Q, 185 (1943), 61-62.

1391. "Musings without Method: THE QUARTERLY REVIEW--Its Origins--The Slashing Article--The Reigns of Gifford and Lockhart." BLACKWOOD'S MAGAZINE, 173 (1903), 100-117.

1392. Neiman, Fraser. "Matthew Arnold's Review of the LETTERS ET OPUSCULES INEDITS by Joseph de Maistre." MLN, 74 (1959), 492-94.

Evidence for Arnold's authorship of an article in the October 1879 issue. See also No. 1309.

1393. Nickerson, Charles C. "Disraeli, Lockhart, and Murray: An Episode in the History of the Quarterly Review." VS, 15 (1972), 279-306.

1394. Parker, W.M. "Lockhart's OBITER DICTA." TLS, 5 February 1944, p. 72; 12 February 1944, p. 72; 12 February 1944, p. 84.

1395. ______. "Dean Milman and THE QUARTERLY REVIEW." QR, 293 (1955), 30-43.

1396. ______. "Gladstone as a QUARTERLY REVIEW Contributor." QR, 293 (1955), 464-76.

1397. Pfeiffer, Karl G. "The Authorship of Certain Articles in the QUARTERLY REVIEW." PQ, 11 (1932), 97-108.

1398. "THE QUARTERLY." LIVING AGE, 261 (1909), 733-37.

1399. "The QUARTERLY Centenary." NATION, 88 (1909), 528-30.

1400. Reitzel, William. "Sir Walter Scott's Review of Jane Austen's EMMA." PMLA, 43 (1928), 487-93.

Attributes the review of EMMA in the QUARTERLY REVIEW to Archbishop Whateley, but see also Nos. 1380 and 1381.

1401. "Retrospect: Nos. 1-500." QR, 253 (1929), 1-17.

1402. Robbins, Alfred. "Keats's Death and the QUARTERLY REVIEW." N&Q, 10 (1922), 221.

1403. "Scott and Lockhart: The Editorship of the QUARTERLY." TLS, 21 October 1915, p. 369.

Also in this issue of TLS, see pages 369 and 381.

1404. Shine, Hill, and Helen Chadwick Shine. THE QUARTERLY REVIEW UNDER GIFFORD: IDENTIFICATION OF CONTRIBUTORS, 1809-1824. Chapel Hill: University of North Carolina Press, 1949.

1405. Strout, Alan Lang. "Some Unpublished Letters of John Gibson Lockhart to John Wilson Croker." N&Q, 185 (1943), 152-57, 186-92, 217-22.

QUERIST (1735-37, 1750)

1406. Johnston, Joseph. BERKELEY'S 'QUERIST' IN HISTORICAL PERSPECTIVE. Dundalk, Ireland: Dundalgan Press, 1970.

The QUERIST reprinted (pages 124-204).

RAMBLER (1750-52)

See also JOHNSON, SAMUEL (chapter 4) and Nos. 181, 203, and 1539.

1407. Bate, W[alter]. J[ackson]. ed. ESSAYS FROM THE 'RAMBLER,' 'ADVENTURER,' AND 'IDLER.' New Haven, Conn.: Yale University Press, 1968.

1408. Bradford, C.B. "The Edinburgh 'Ramblers.'" MLR, 34 (1939), 241-44.

1409. ______. "Johnson's Review of THE RAMBLER." RES, 15 (1939), 302-14.

1410. Cone, Corson. "Johnson's 'Rambler.'" SN&Q, 7 (1906), 140.

Pertains to the Edinburgh edition. See also the material signed S. in this issue of SN&Q (page 159).

1411. Corder, Jim W. "Ethical Argument and RAMBLER No. 154." QJS, 54 (1968), 352-56.

1412. Elder, A.T. "Irony and Humour in the RAMBLER." UTQ, 30 (1960), 57-71.

1413. Fleeman, J.D. "The Reprint of RAMBLER No. 1." LIBRARY, 18 (1963), 288-94.

1414. ______. "Johnson's 'Rambler.'" TLS, 21 May 1971, p. 594.

1415. Fox, Robert C. "The Imaginery Submarines of Dr. Johnson and Richard Owen Cambridge." PQ, 40 (1961), 112-19.

Background for RAMBLER no. 105 and SCRIBLERIAD, bk. IV.

1416. Graham, W.H. "Dr. Johnson's 'The Rambler.'" ConR, 184 (1953), 50-53.

1417. Greany, Helen T. "Johnson and the Institutes." N&Q, 5 (1958), 445.

Echoes of Quintilian in RAMBLER essays.

1418. Hamilton, Harlan W. "Boswell's Suppression of a Paragraph in RAMBLER 60." MLN, 76 (1961), 218-20.

Johnson's criticism of Racan, biographer of Malherbe.

1419. Hopper, Cl. "'The Rambler.'" N&Q, 5 (1858), 168.

1420. Johnson, Samuel. THE RAMBLER. Ed. W[alter]. J[ackson]. Bate and Albrecht B. Strauss. The Yale Edition of the Works of Samuel Johnson,

vols. III, IV, and V. New Haven, Conn.: Yale University Press, 1969.
Reviewed in PQ 49:358-59; MLR 66:870-72; RES 22:348-52; ECS 4:231-35.

1421. "Johnson's RAMBLER." TLS, 19 March 1971, pp. 323-24.
See also Paul J. Korshin in TLS, 9 April 1971, p. 423.

1422. Leed, Jacob. "Patronage in the RAMBLER." SBHT, 14 (1972), 5-21.

1423. Leyburn, Ellen Douglas. "The Translations of the Mottoes and Quotations in the RAMBLER." RES, 16 (1940), 169-76.

1424. Murphy, Mallie J. "THE RAMBLER, No. 191." PMLA, 50 (1940), 926-28.

1425. O'Flaherty, Patrick. "The Rambler's Rebuff to Juvenal: Johnson's Pessimism Reconsidered." ES, 51 (1971), 517-27.

1426. Rewa, Michael. "Aspects of Rhetoric in Johnson's 'Professedly Serious' RAMBLER ESSAYS." QJS, 56 (1970), 75-84.

1427. Sherbo, Arthur. "The Making of RAMBLERS 186 and 187." PMLA, 67 (1952), 575-80.

1428. _____. "The Translations of Mottoes and Quotations in Johnson's 'Rambler.'" N&Q, 197 (1952), 278-79.

1429. Smith, D. Nichol. "Johnson's Revision of his Publications, Especially THE RAMBLER, RASSELAS, and THE IDLER. A Paper Read before the Johnson Club, 17 March 1926." JOHNSON & BOSWELL REVISED BY THEMSELVES AND OTHERS. Oxford: Clarendon Press, 1928. Pp. 7-18.

1430. _____. "The Contributors to THE RAMBLER and THE IDLER." BODLEIAN QUARTERLY RECORD, 7 (1934), 508-9.

1431. Strauss, Albrecht B., and Clarence Tracy. "On Editing Johnson." ECS, 6 (1972), 99-105.
A FORUM debate on the textual policy of the Yale Johnson, occasioned by Tracy's criticism of the RAMBLER volume (ECS, 4 [1970], 231-35).

1432. 'THE VANITY OF HUMAN WISHES' (1749) AND TWO 'RAMBLER'

PAPERS (1750). Intro. Bertrand H. Bronson. Augustan Reprint Society Publication no. 22. Los Angeles: Clark Memorial Library, 1950.

1433. Wiles, Roy McKeen. "The Contemporary Distribution of Johnson's RAMBLER." ECS, 2 (1968), 155-71.

Concerns reprinting in provincial papers.

1434. Wimsatt, W.K., Jr. PHILOSOPHIC WORDS: A STUDY OF STYLE AND MEANING IN THE 'RAMBLER' AND 'DICTIONARY' OF SAMUEL JOHNSON. New Haven, Conn.: Yale University Press, 1948.

Reviewed in PQ, 28:393-95.

1435. ______. "A Philadelphian Meets Dr. Johnson." TLS, 1 January 1960, p. 7.

1436. Worden, John L. "The Themes and Techniques of Johnson's RAMBLER." DAI, 32 (1971), 939A.

RAMBLER (1848-62)

See also HOME AND FOREIGN REVIEW and No. 57.

1437. Altholz, Josef L. "Bibliographical Note on the RAMBLER." PBSA, 56 (1962), 113-14.

A leading Catholic magazine edited by, among others, John Henry Newman and Lord Acton. There was a brief title change to HOME AND FOREIGN REVIEW in the spring of 1862.

1438. Blehl, Vincent F. "Newman, the Bishops and THE RAMBLER." DownR, 90 (1972), 20-40.

1439. Houghton, Esther Rhoads. "Reviewer of Browning's MEN AND WOMEN in the RAMBLER Identified." VN, 33 (Spring 1968), 46.

1440. McElrath, Damian. "Richard Simpson and Count de Montalembert, the RAMBLER and the CORRESPONDENT." DownR, 84 (1966), 150-70.

1441. ______. "Richard Simpson and John Henry Newman: the RAMBLER, Laymen, and Theology." CATHOLIC HISTORICAL REVIEW, 52 (1967), 509-33.

1442. Pratt, Willis Winslow. "Leigh Hunt and THF RAMBLER." UNIVERSITY

OF TEXAS STUDIES IN ENGLISH, 1938, pp. 67-84.

RAMBLER'S MAGAZINE (1783)

1443. Waters, Arthur W. "The Earliest Mention of an Aerial Post." N&Q, 8 (1913), 347.

RAMBLER'S MAGAZINE (1822-23)

1444. Luke, Hugh J., Jr. "An Overlooked Obituary Notice of Shelley." PLL, 2 (1966), 38-46.

In the issue for September 1822.

READER (1714)

See also No. 2178.

1445. Snyder, Henry L. "Arthur Maynwaring, Richard Steele, and THE LIVES OF TWO ILLUSTRIOUS GENERALS." SB, 24 (1971), 152-62.

Concludes that "The History of the Duke of Marlborough" announced by Steele in the READER (3 May 1714) was not published separately.

READER (1863-67)

See also No. 2052.

1446. Byrne, John Francis. "The READER: A Review of Literature, Science and the Arts, 1863-1867." DA, 25 (1965), 6618.

1447. ______. "THE READER: A Review of Literature, Science and the Arts, 1863-67." VPN, 4 (1969), 47-50; 5-6 (1969), 19-28.

READING MERCURY (1723-24?)

See No. 2166.

RED REPUBLICAN (1850-51)

1448. 'THE RED REPUBLICAN' AND 'THE FRIEND OF THE PEOPLE,' 1850-1851. Intro. John Saville. 2 vols. London: Merlin Press, 1966.

Facsimiles of Chartist journals.

REFLECTOR (1810-11)

1449. Kendall, Kenneth Everett. "Leigh Hunt's REFLECTOR." DA, 26 (1966), 6697.

1450. ______. LEIGH HUNT'S 'REFLECTOR.' Studies in English Literature, no. 59. The Hague: Mouton, 1971.

REVEUR (1737-38)

1451. "Notice of Two Old Periodical Works." CHAMBERS'S EDINBURGH JOURNAL, 4 (1845), 34-37.

On the REVEUR and the LETTERS OF THE CRITICAL CLUB.

REVIEW (Defoe's, 1704-13)

See also DEFOE, DANIEL (chapter 4) and Nos. 368, 807, 1655, and 1854.

1452. Arber, Edward. AN ENGLISH GARNER. LATER STUART TRACTS. Intro. George A. Aitken. New York: Dutton, [1903].

Reprints prefaces to first eight volumes of the REVIEW and several issues.

1453. Burch, Charles Eaton. "Notes on the Contemporary Popularity of Defoe's REVIEW." PQ, 16 (1937), 210-13.

1454. Curry, Frank. "Defoe's 'Weekly Review.'" N&Q, 7 (1913), 448-49.

Corrections of statements in Lowndes' BIBLIOGRAPHER'S MANUAL.

1455. Davis, Andrew McFarland. "A Bibliographical Puzzle." PUBLICATIONS OF THE COLONIAL SOCIETY OF MASSACHUSETTS: TRANSACTIONS, 1910-1911, 13 (1912), 2-15.

1456. DEFOE'S REVIEW. Reproduced from the Original Editions, with an Introduction and Bibliographical Notes by Arthur Wellesley Secord. 22 vols. Facsimile Text Society, Publication no. 44. New York: Columbia University Press, 1938.

See also No. 1469.

1457. Fletcher, Edward G. "Defoe and the Theatre." PQ, 13 (1934), 382-89.

1458. _____. "The London and Edinburgh Printings of Defoe's REVIEW, Volume VI." UNIVERSITY OF TEXAS STUDIES IN ENGLISH, no. 14 (1934), pp. 50-58.

1459. _____. "Some Notes on Defoe's REVIEW." N&Q, 166 (1934), 218-21.

1460. _____. "Defoe on Milton." MLN, 50 (1935), 31-32.

1461. Greenough, Chester N[oyes]. "Defoe in Boston." PUBLICATIONS OF THE COLONIAL SOCIETY OF MASSACHUSETTS: TRANSACTIONS, 1930-1933, 28 (1935), 461-93.

1462. _____. "Defoe's Review." TLS, 15 February 1934, p. 108.

See also A[rthur]. W[ellesley]. Secord, TLS, 11 June 1938, p. 408, and TLS, 30 July 1938, p. 508; H. Bergholz, TLS, 18 June 1938, p. 424. A query for the location of volume IX, number 81.

1463. Healey, George H. "Defoe's Handwriting." TLS, 19 December 1952, p. 837.

Argues that the MS of REVIEW, 31 December 1709, is not in Defoe's hand.

1464. Hendley, William C., Jr. "Factional Journalism in the Age of Queen Anne: Defoe's REVIEW and Its Rivals." DAI, 32 (1972), 3953A.

1465. Lindsay, W.B. "Defoe's Review--Forerunner of Modern Journalism." ENGLISH JOURNAL, 16 (1927), 359-63.

1466. Meier, Tom K. "Defoe and the Defense of Commerce." DAI, 32 (1971), 3316A.

1467. Moore, John Robert. "Daniel Defoe and Modern Economic Theory." INDIANA UNIVERSITY STUDIES, 21, no. 104 (1934), 1-28.

1468. Morgan, William Thomas. "Defoe's REVIEW as a Historical Source." JMH, 12 (1940), 221-32.

1469. Payne, William L. INDEX TO DEFOE'S REVIEW. New York: Columbia University Press, 1948.

Essential adjunct to use of the Facsimile Text Society edition of the REVIEW (No. 1456). Reviewed in PQ 28:387-88; SAQ 25:322-38.

1470. ______, ed. THE BEST OF DEFOE'S 'REVIEW': AN ANTHOLOGY. New York: Columbia University Press, 1951.

The first and only significant effort to present the REVIEW in condensed form. Reviewed in PQ 31:264-65.

1471. Ross, John F. SWIFT AND DEFOE: A STUDY IN RELATIONSHIP. University of California Publications in English, vol. XI. Berkeley and Los Angeles: University of California Press, 1941.

See pages 56-70 for a discussion of the relationship of the REVIEW and the EXAMINER.

REVIEW OF REVIEWS (1890-1900+)

1472. De Ternant, Andrew. "REVIEW OF REVIEWS." N&Q, 161 (1931), 191.

ROYAL MAGAZINE; OR, GENTLEMAN'S MONTHLY COMPANION (1759-71)

See also No. 2007.

1473. Salmon, H. "The 'Royal Magazine.'" N&Q, 10 (1890), 267.

See also replies on page 357.

RUGBY MAGAZINE (1835-37)

1474. P., O., and G.A.F.M.C. "Matthew Arnold and the RUGBY MAGAZINE, 1837." N&Q, 187 (1942), 137, 178.

1475. Scott, P.G. "A Second Edition of THE RUGBY MAGAZINE, Number One." BC, 20 (1971), 386-87.

ST. JAMES'S CHRONICLE (1761-1866)

1476. Abrahams, Aleck, et. al. "ST. JAMES'S CHRONICLE." N&Q, 2 (1910), 481-82.

1477. Bond, Richmond P., and Marjorie N. Bond. "The Minute Books of the ST. JAMES'S CHRONICLE." SB, 28 (1975), 17-40.

ST. JAMES'S GAZETTE (dates unknown)

1478. Green, Roger Lancelyn. "Lewis Carroll and the ST. JAMES'S GA-

ZETTE." N&Q, 190 (1945), 134-35.

ST. JAMES'S JOURNAL (1722-23)

1479. Griffith, R.H. "Pope's Reading." N&Q, 195 (1950), 363-64.

Concerns the date at which Pope read the first printing of his Atticus lines in the ST. JAMES'S JOURNAL.

1480. Smith, M.E. "Four Hitherto Unidentified Letters by Alexander Pope." PMLA, 39 (1914), 236-55.

SATIRIST; OR, MONTHLY METEOR (1808-14)

1481. Zall, P.M. "Sam Spitfire: or, Coleridge in THE SATIRIST." BNYPL, 71 (1967), 239-44.

SATURDAY REVIEW (1855-1900+)

See also No. 157.

1482. Bevington, Merle Mowbray. THE SATURDAY REVIEW, 1855-1868: REPRESENTATIVE EDUCATED OPINION IN VICTORIAN ENGLAND. Columbia University Studies in English and Comparative Literature, no. 154. New York: Columbia University Press, 1941.

1483. Jump, J.D. "Matthew Arnold and the SATURDAY REVIEW." RES, 22 (1946), 322-24.

1484. Popkin, Henry. "Shaw to Beerbohm." (New York) TIMES BOOK REVIEW, 21 October 1951, p. 49.

Concerning these two as drama editors of the SATURDAY REVIEW.

SAVOY (1896)

1485. Garbaty, Thomas J. "THE SAVOY, 1896; A Re-Edition of Representative Prose and Verse, with a Critical Introduction, and Biographical and Critical Notes." DA, 17 (1957), 3014-15.

1486. _____. "The French Coterie of the SAVOY, 1896." PMLA, 75 (1960), 609-15.

1487. Weintraub, Stanley, ed. 'THE SAVOY': NINETIES EXPERIMENT.

University Park: Pennsylvania State University Press, 1966.

SCIENTIFIC RECEPTACLE (1824-?)

1488. Green, David Bonnell. "John Clare, John Savage, and THE SCIENTIFIC RECEPTACLE." REL, 7 (1966), 87-98.
Clare contributed eight poems; Savage was an editor.

SCOTS COURANT (1709-20)

See EDINBURGH COURANT.

SCOTS MAGAZINE (1739-1833)

See also Nos. 727, 728, and 911.

1489. Anderson, Iain F. "The Scots Magazine and the '45." SCOTS MAGAZINE, 14 (1931), 328-38.

1490. Cook, Davidson. "Burns and 'The Scots Magazine.' The Version of 'Highland Mary'; 'A Tragic Fragment'; 'The Poet's Punch-Bowl.'" SCOTS MAGAZINE, 20 (1934), 255-63, 361-69, 453-61.

1491. D.,C. "The SCOTS MAGAZINE." SN&Q, 9 (1931), 219-20.
See also pages 36, 140, and 200.

1492. Elliott, Robert C. "The Early SCOTS MAGAZINE." MLQ, 11 (1950), 189-96.
An account of "the first and most vigorous of the magazines published in Edinburgh during the eighteenth century" on the theory that it provides, "in a limited sense, an index to the culture of the period."

1493. Fawcett, J.W. "Editors of the Scots Magazine." SN&Q, 9 (1931), 140.
See also, in this issue of SN&Q, the material by C.D. (pages 160, 219-21).

1494. Grime. "Army List." N&Q, 11 (1861), 449.

1495. Imrie, D.S.M. "The Story of 'The Scots Magazine.' I.--Beginnings: 1739-1784. II.--The Missed Opportunity (1785-1816). III.--The Final

Struggle (1817-1826). IV.--Contributors (1739-74). V.--Contributors (1781-1826). VI.--Editors, Printers and Publishers (1739-1826)." SCOTS MAGAZINE, 30 (1939), 269-74, 341-49, 445-52; 31 (1939), 51-58, 141-50, 218-26.

1496. "Looking Backward. From the Scots Magazine, Vol. I, No. 10, October, 1739; Vol. I, No. 11, November, 1739." SCOTS MAGAZINE, VI (1962). In the unnumbered advertising pages.

1497. Niven, G.W. "Bibliography of Edinburgh Periodical Literature: The 'Scots Magazine.'" SN&Q, 11 (1898), 146.

1498. ______. "The Bibliography of THE SCOTS MAGAZINE." LIBRARY, 10 (1898), 310.

Concerns stoppage in 1826.

1499. ______. "The Bibliographies of the SCOTS MAGAZINE and BLACKWOOD'S MAGAZINE." N&Q, 1 (1898), 265.

1500. "Ourselves 150 Years Ago; Extracts From the Scots Magazine [1777-1788]." SCOTS MAGAZINE, 7 (1927)--30 (1938).

A monthly feature.

1501. "Ourselves 200 Years Ago; Extracts from the Scots Magazine [1739-40]." SCOTS MAGAZINE, 30 (1939)--32 (1940).

A monthly feature.

SCOTSMAN; OR, EDINBURGH POLITICAL AND LITERARY JOURNAL (1817-55)

1502. Jones, Stanley. "Hazlitt in Edinburgh: An Evening with Mr. Ritchie of THE SCOTSMAN." EA, 17 (1964), 9-20, 113-27.

SCOTTISH REVIEW (1882-1900)

See No. 57.

SNOB (1829)

See GOWNSMAN.

SPECTATOR (1711-13, 1714)

See also ADDISON, JOSEPH and STEELE, RICHARD (chapter 4), TATLER, and Nos. 181, 202, 302, 1868, 1985, 2117, 2141, and 2211.

1503. Addison, Joseph. CRITICISMS ON PARADISE LOST. Ed., intro., notes by Albert S. Cook. New York: G.E. Stechert, 1926.

1504. Atkinson, A.D. "'The Spectator' No. 543." N&Q, 195 (1950), 275.

Addison's debt to Newton's OPTICKS.

1505. B.,G.F.R. "Westminster School." N&Q, 7 (1895), 48.

Attempt to identify the characters of the story in SPECTATOR no. 313.

1506. Bates, William. "Inkle and Yarico." N&Q, 9 (1866), 341-42.

1507. Bede, Cuthbert. "Addison's 'Sir Roger de Coverley.'" N&Q, 3 (1857), 46.

1508. ______. "The 'Sir Andrew Freeport' of the 'Spectator.'" N&Q, 6 (1858), 324-25.

See also N&Q, 1 (1856), 238-39.

1509. Beta. "The 'Spectator,' No. 66." N&Q, 7 (1877), 289.

See also Mab (page 415).

1510. Bond, Donald F. "Pope's Contributions to the SPECTATOR." MLQ, 5 (1944), 69-78.

1511. ______. "The First Printing of the SPECTATOR." MP, 47 (1950), 164-77.

Because of large circulation, the original 555 numbers were printed in two shops, those of Buckley and Tonson, to avoid duplicate settings of type. For nos. 1-432 the shops worked in daily alternation; after no. 432 they alternated in groups of three. After no. 162, Tonson usually printed Addison's papers and Buckley, Steele's. Important article.

1512. ______. "The Spectator." NEWBERRY LIBRARY BULLETIN, 8 (1952), 239-41.

1513. ______. "The Text of the SPECTATOR." SB, 5 (1952-53), 109-28.

A study of textual differences in the three earliest editions, with a collation of all variants, as a preliminary to his critical edition (No. 1597).

1514. _____, ed. CRITICAL ESSAYS FROM 'THE SPECTATOR.' Oxford: At the University Press, 1970.

Some sixty essays, including four on drama by Steele, in a modernized text.

1515. Bond, Richmond P. "The SPECTATOR: Two Notes." SP, 42 (1945), 578-80.

1516. _____. QUEEN ANNE'S AMERICAN KINGS. Oxford: Clarendon Press, 1952.

Includes allusions in the SPECTATOR to the visit in 1710 of four American Indian sachems or "kings" to London.

1517. _____. "The Business of the SPECTATOR." UNIVERSITY OF NORTH CAROLINA EXTENSION BULLETIN (Lectures in the Humanities, Eighth Series), 32 (January 1953), 7-19.

A discussion of advertising revenues, printing costs, circulation problems, and other matters concerned with the SPECTATOR as a business venture.

1518. _____. "A Letter to Steele on the SPECTATOR." MLQ, 18 (1957), 303-4.

From an employee of the East India Co. in Sumatra.

1519. Bouchier, Jonathan. "Error in the 'Spectator.'" N&Q, 3 (1899), 104.

1520. _____. "'The Spectator': 'Bulfinch.'" N&Q, 3 (1899), 347.

Identification of Bulfinch in no. 188.

1521. _____. "Literary Parallel: Addison--Tennyson." N&Q, 6 (1900), 45.

On SPECTATOR no. 265 and THE LAST TOURNAMENT, lines 225-35.

1522. _____. "The 'Spectator.'" N&Q, 6 (1900), 29.

On the authorship of nos. 250, 262, 622. See also the material by Richard Welford in this issue of N&Q (page 97).

1523. Campbell, Hilbert H. "Addison's 'Cartesian' Passage and Nicholas Malebranche." PQ, 46 (1967), 408-12.

Concerns no. 417.

1524. Campbell, J.D. "Joseph Addison and the 'Spectator.'" N&Q, 4

(1863), 146, 507.

1525. Capper, J.B. "The Spectator." TLS, 20 October 1932, p. 768.

See also Sydney A. Mudie and C.J. Hindle in TLS, 27 October 1932, page 796.

1526. Carroll, John J. "Henry Fielding and the 'Trunk-Maker.'" N&Q, 204 (1959), 213.

SPECTATOR, no. 235 and TOM JONES, IV, 6.

1527. Casson, T.E. "Wordsworth and the SPECTATOR." RES, 3 (1927), 157-61.

1528. Chambers, Robert D. "Addison at Work on the SPECTATOR." MP, 56 (1959), 145-53.

Concerns a Bodleian MS of twenty-four essays by Addison "in the hand of an amanuensis," all of which he reworked for the SPECTATOR.

1529. Charlton, H.B. "Buckingham's Adaptation of 'Julius Caesar' and a Note in the 'Spectator.'" MLR, 16 (1921), 171-72.

On SPECTATOR no. 300.

1530. Child, Mary. "Mr. Spectator and Shakespeare." LIBRARY, 6 (1905), 360-79.

1531. Clarry. "Lecky's 'History of Morals': Addison." N&Q, 4 (1869), 9.

On SPECTATOR no. 116.

1532. Crossley, James. "Volume Ninth of the 'Spectator.'" N&Q, 6 (1852), 381-82.

1533. D.,C. de. "Sir Roger de Coverley." N&Q, 5 (1852), 467.

1534. D.,R. "Addison and Johnson." N&Q, 12 (1861), 85.

On SPECTATOR no. 417.

1535. Davis, Kathryn. "A Note on the SPECTATOR 459." MLN, 60 (1945), 274.

Addison quotes from Swift's "Thoughts on Various Subjects."

1536. Dobson, Austin. "The Story of the 'Spectator.'" SIDE-WALK STUDIES. London: Chatto & Windus, 1902. Pp. 208-29.

Reprinted from the Gregory Smith edition of the SPECTATOR (1897-98); appeared also in Dobson's EIGHTEENTH CENTURY STUDIES (1914).

1537. E.,G. "Addison and Erasmus." N&Q, 1 (1856), 146-47.

On the "Vision of Mirzah."

1538. Eirionnach. "Addison's Essays." N&Q, 6 (1864), 363-64.

See also page 445.

1539. Elder, A.T. "A Johnson Borrowing from Addison?" N&Q, 206 (1961), 53-54.

An anecdote which appears in SPECTATOR no. 221 and in RAMBLER no. 10.

1540. Evans, G. Blackmore. "Addison's Early Knowledge of Milton." JEGP, 49 (1950), 204-7.

Hypothesizes that "The change of attitude towards Milton in the SPECTATOR . . . was in some part the result of a comparatively recently acquired firsthand knowledge of PARADISE LOST and the consequent breaking of earlier misconceptions."

1541. Fraser, Sir James George. "More Spectator Papers." NINETEENTH CENTURY AND AFTER, 89 (1921), 812-18.

Two descriptions of meetings of the Spectator Club "from the papers at Coverley Hall."

1542. _____. THE GORGON'S HEAD AND OTHER LITERARY PIECES. London: Macmillan, 1927.

A reissue, with additions, of SIR ROGER DE COVERLEY AND OTHER LITERARY PIECES (1920).

1543. Friedman, Albert B. "Addison's Ballad Papers and the Reaction to Metaphysical Wit." CompLit, 12 (1960), 1-13.

"Relates the ballad papers to the papers on wit in the SPECTATOR and places them in the context of the continental uses of popular poetry as a stick to beat 'Gothic' (metaphysical or baroque) taste" (PQ, 40:365.

1544. Furtwangler, Albert J. "Joseph Addison and the SPECTATOR: A Study of the Longer Essay Series." DA, 29 (1969), 4455A.

1545. Gay, Peter. "The Spectator as Actor: Addison in Perspective." ENCOUNTER, 29, vi (1960), 27-32.

1546. Green, David Bonnell. "Keats and 'The Spectator.'" N&Q, 200 (1955), 124.

References to names from Addison.

1547. Havens, Raymond D. "The Origin of the SPECTATOR." NATION, 42 (1911), 422.

Corrects the misunderstanding that Steele was more responsible than Addison for the machinery of the journal and the character of Sir Roger.

1548. Henderson, W.A. "Addison's Knowledge of Shakespeare." N&Q, 4 (1893), 146-47.

See also F.C. Holland, E.H. Marshall, and Constance Russell (page 210). Refutation of De Quincey's assertion that Shakespeare criticism in the SPECTATOR occurs in papers not by Addison.

1549. Hodgart, M.J.C. "The Eighth Volume of the SPECTATOR." RES, 5 (1954), 367-87.

This valuable study identifies contributors, discloses that Thomas Tickell was "sole acting editor during the last months of the SPECTATOR," and prints important new MS materials.

1550. Holland, F.C. "Bishop Berkeley." N&Q, 1 (1892), 167.

On whether Berkeley was the author of the Philonous letter in SPECTATOR no. 234.

1551. Hopkins, Robert H. "'The Good Old Cause' in Pope, Addison, and Steele." RES, 19 (1966), 62-68.

Includes comments on Sir Roger.

1552. Hugill, J.S. "Sir Roger de Coverley and the SPECTATOR." BOOKWORM, 3 (1890), 321-26.

1553. Ito, Hiroyuki. "The Language of THE SPECTATOR--Chiefly Concerning the Aspect of Double Meaning." ANGLICA (publication of The Anglica Society of Kansai University, Osaka, Japan), 5 (1962), 36-62.

1554. _____. "The Uses of Word[s] in THE SPECTATOR with Special Reference to Semantic Deviation." ERA (Bulletin of the English Research Association of Hiroshima), 6 (October 1969), 2-35.

1555. Kay, Donald. SHORT FICTION IN THE 'SPECTATOR.' University of Alabama Studies in the Humanities, vol. 8. University: University of Alabama Press, 1975.

Devises "viable major categories" for the one hundred short stories which the author finds in the 555 issues of the original SPECTATOR.

1556. Kay, Wayne D. "'After Smoke the Light': The Short Story in the SPECTATOR." DA, 28 (1967), 2211A.

1557. Keightley, Thomas. "Chaucer and Addison." N&Q, 12 (1861), 434.

On SPECTATOR no. 73.

1558. Kenney, William. "The Morality of 'The Spectator.'" N&Q, 202 (1957), 37-38.

1559. Kinsley, William. "Meaning and Format; Mr. Spectator and His Folio Half-Sheets." ELH, 34 (1967), 482-94.

Suggests that Addison and Steele were the first to fully exploit their format, which in turn determined their artistic use of anonymity and their relationship to their audience.

1560. Knight, Charles. "The First Newspaper Stamp." ONCE UPON A TIME. 2 vols. London: John Murray, 1854. II, 1-5.

An imaginary conversation between Addison, Steele, and their printer Buckley the night before the Stamp Act goes into effect.

1561. Law, Alice. "Addison in 'The Spectator.'" FR, 89 (1911), 629-40.

1562. Legouis, Pierre. "Marvell and Addison: A Note to No. 89 of THE SPECTATOR." RES, 10 (1934), 447-50.

1563. Lewis, Lawrence. THE ADVERTISEMENTS OF THE SPECTATOR. BEING A STUDY OF THE LITERATURE, HISTORY AND MANNERS OF QUEEN ANNE'S ENGLAND AS THEY ARE REFLECTED THEREIN, AS WELL AS AN ILLUSTRATION OF THE ORIGINS OF THE ART OF ADVERTISING. WITH APPENDIX OF REPRESENTATIVE ADVERTISEMENTS NOW FOR THE FIRST TIME REPRINTED, AND AN INTRODUCTORY NOTE BY GEORGE LYMAN KITTREDGE. Boston and New York: Houghton Mifflin, 1909.

Selections appeared as "The 'Spectator' as an Advertising Medium," ATLANTIC MONTHLY, 103 (1909), 605-15.

1564. Lonsdale, Roger. "Dr. Burney, John Weaver, and the SPECTATOR." BNYPL, 64 (1960), 286-88.

Weaver's authorship of nos. 67, 334, 370.

1565. Lovett, Robert W. "Mr. Spectator in BLEAK HOUSE." DICKENSIAN, 59 (1963), 124.

The SPECTATOR as source for two of Dicken's details.

1566. Lysons, Samuel. "Sir Roger de Coverley." N&Q, 3 (1863), 54-55.

1567. McCarthy, Justin. "The 'Spectator.'" THE REIGN OF QUEEN ANNE. 2 vols. New York: Harper, 1902. II, 142-64.

1568. Mackenzie, Donald A. "Sir Roger de Coverley's Portrait Gallery." N&Q, 1 (1910), 204.

On SPECTATOR no. 109.

1569. Markland, J.H. "Addison and his Hymns." N&Q, 5 (1852), 513-14.

Also in this issue of N&Q, see James Crossley (page 548) and Joseph A. Kidd (page 597). In N&Q, 9 (1854), 424, see J.H. Markland.

1570. Marshall, Ed. "Bridge in the Visions of Mirza." N&Q, 7 (1883), 344-45.

A passage from St. Anselm's MEDITATIONS "which may be placed in connexion with the vision in the SPECTATOR No. 159."

1571. Martindale, Colin. "A Note on an Eighteenth Century Anticipation of Freud's Theory of Dreams." JOURNAL OF THE HISTORY OF BEHAVIORAL SCIENCES, 6 (1970), 362-64.

A series of essays in the SPECTATOR (1714) by John Byrom asserts that dreams constitute wish-fulfillments.

1572. Mount, C.B. "Addison on the Copernican System." N&Q, 12 (1891), 26-27.

Discussion of a hymn in SPECTATOR no. 465. See replies on page 94.

1573. Mudie, Sydney A. "The Spectator." TLS, 27 October 1932, p. 796.

On volumes VIII and IX of the SPECTATOR, answering the query of J.B. Capper in TLS, 20 October 1932 (page 768). See also the note by C.J. Hindle, TLS, 27 October 1932 (page 796).

1574. P.,O. "Hilpa and Schallum." N&Q, 7 (1865), 37.

On SPECTATOR nos. 584 and 585.

1575. Peterson, H. "Notes on the Influence of Addison's SPECTATOR and Marivaux's SPECTATEUR FRANCAIS upon EL PENSADOR." HISPANIC REVIEW, 4 (1936), 256-63.

1576. Philomot. "The SPECTATOR: Preheminence: Spencer." N&Q, 168 (1940), 425.

See also Harriet Sampson in N&Q, 169 (1940), 159.

1577. Powell, L.F. "The SPECTATOR, 1775 and 1789." N&Q, 156 (1929), 9.

1578. Price, Lawrence Marsden. INKLE AND YARICO ALBUM. Berkeley: University of California Press, 1937.

On the numerous English and Continental treatments of the story in SPECTATOR no. 11.

1579. Ramsey, Roger. "The Ambivalent Spectator." PLL, 9 (1973), 81-84.

A discussion of some aspects of the putative author. Reviewed in SCRIBLERIAN, 6 (1973), 20-21.

1580. Reichert, John F. "'Gronger Hill': Its Origin and Development." PLL, 5 (1969), 123-29.

Suggests Addison's first two essays on the imagination as a source.

1581. Robertson, J.G. "The Beginnings of a New Aesthetics in England: Addison." STUDIES IN THE GENESIS OF ROMANTIC THEORY IN THE EIGHTEENTH CENTURY. Cambridge: At the University Press, 1923. Pp. 235-49.

1582. Robinson, W.H. "Anne's Lane and Sir Roger de Coverley." N&Q, 7 (1877), 185.

On the location of the street referred to in SPECTATOR no. 125. See also Edward Solly (page 238-39) and C.A. Ward (page 374).

1583. Rogal, Samuel J. "Addison's SPECTATOR Hymns." NEMLA, 2, i (1971), 8-13.

1584. S.,W. "Addison's 'Spectator.'" N&Q, 10 (1922), 235.

A note on the date of the edition published by J. and R. Tonson and S. Draper. See also Archibald Sparke (page 235).

1585. Sabine, Waldo. "The SPECTATOR, Vol. IX." N&Q, 151 (1926), 177.

Quotes from Chalmers' BRITISH ESSAYISTS on the authorship of this volume.

1586. Saer, H.A. "Notes on the Use of Themes Taken from the 'Spectator' in Eighteenth-Century French Plays." MODERN LANGUAGES, 21 (1939), 5-16, 55-61.

1587. Salisbury, E.E. [Letter of 19 October 1871 on the SPECTATOR.] PROCEEDINGS OF THE AMERICAN ANTIQUARIAN SOCIETY (annual meeting, held in Worcester, October 21, 1871), 1872, pp. 14-17.

1588. Sallé, Jean-Claude. "A Source of Sterne's Conception of Time." RES, 6 (1955), 180-82.

The suggested source is SPECTATOR, no. 94.

1589. Salmon, David. "'The Spectator.'" N&Q, 7 (1920), 158.

On the signatures of contributors. See also A.G. Kealy (pages 174-75), W.S. (page 175), and S. (pages 196-97).

1590. Scanland, Sylvia I.B. "The Place of Addison in Neo-Classical Criticism of Milton's PARADISE LOST." DAI, 31 (1971), 4135A.

1591. Scott, R. McNair. "An Aspect of Addison & Steele." LONDON MERCURY, 27 (1933), 524-29.

1592. Simpson, Donald Roberts. "The SPECTATOR Reconsidered." DA, 23 (1963), 3891.

1593. "Sir Roger de Coverley." QR, 90 (1852), 285-311.

1594. "'The Spectator.' 1 March 1711." TLS, 3 March 1911, pp. 81-82.

1595. THE SPECTATOR. Intro. and notes by George A. Aitken. 8 vols. London: John C. Nimmo, 1898.

1596. THE SPECTATOR. Ed. and annotated by G. Gregory Smith. Intro. essay by [Henry] Austin Dobson. 8 vols. London: J.M. Dent, 1897-98.

Reprinted, without the Dobson essay, as no. 164 in Everyman's Library.

1597. THE SPECTATOR. Ed., intro., and notes by Donald F. Bond. 5 vols. Oxford: Clarendon Press, 1965.

Reviewed in PQ 45:585-86; TLS 26 May 66, p. 474; ANGLIA 84:456-59.

1598. Stephens, John C., Jr. "Addison and Steele's 'Spectator.'" TLS, 15 December 1950, p. 801.

1599. Streatfield, G.S. THE MIND OF THE SPECTATOR UNDER THE EDITORSHIP OF ADDISON & STEELE. New York: Holt, 1923.

1600. Thorpe, Clarence De Witt. "Addison and Hutcheson on the Imagination." ELH, 2 (1935), 215-34.

1601. _____. "Addison's Theory of the Imagination as 'Perceptive Response.'" PAPERS OF THE MICHIGAN ACADEMY OF SCIENCE, ARTS AND LETTERS, 21 (1935), 509-30.

1602. Turner, Margaret. "The Influence of La Bruyère on the 'Tatler' and the 'Spectator.'" MLR, 48 (1953), 10-16.

Argues that methods of characterization and occasional use of CARACTÈRES in quotation and reference show the influence of La Bruyère on the contributors to the TATLER and the SPECTATOR.

1603. W. "Roger de Coverley." N&Q, 1 (1849), 49.

On the dance tune of that name. See also Edward F. Rimbault (page 118).

1604. Wagner, John C. "The Making of an Authority: Evolving Attitudes Among Eighteenth-Century Commentators Toward Addison's Essays on PARADISE LOST." DAI, 33 (1972), 1746A-47A.

1605. Watson, Melvin R. "The SPECTATOR Tradition and the Development of the Familiar Essay." ELH, 13 (1946), 189-215.

1606. Welker, John J. "The Spectator's Notable Jew." SP, 28 (1931), 519-21.

1607. Wheeler, William. THE SPECTATOR; A DIGEST-INDEX. London: George Routledge and Sons, 1892.

Notations are to pages in Morley's one-volume edition; thus the references are practically unusable for other editions. Reissued as A CONCORDANCE TO THE SPECTATOR (1897).

1608. Wiatt, William H. "A Note on Addison's Upholsterer." N&Q, 197 (1952), 236.

1609. Wills, W. Henry, ed. SIR ROGER DE COVERLEY. London: Longman, 1850.

1610. Wood, H.T.W. THE RECIPROCAL INFLUENCE OF ENGLISH AND FRENCH LITERATURE IN THE EIGHTEENTH CENTURY. London: Macmillan, 1870. Pp. 16-22.

1611. Woodruff, James F. "Dr. Johnson's Advertisement for THE SPECTATOR, 1776, and the Source of Our Information About Johnson's Receipts from IRENE: Two Notes on a Volume of Johnsoniana Once Belonging to Isaac Reed." N&Q, 18 (1971), 61-62.

1612. Yardley, E. "Mistake in Addison's 'Spectator.'" N&Q, 7 (1889), 426.

Concerns quotation incorrectly assigned in no. 275, first folio edition. See replies on page 498.

SPECTATOR (1716)

See also No. 1515.

1613. Yeowell, J. "'The Spectator,' No. 1, June 13, 1716." N&Q, 6 (1852), 387.

SPECTATOR (1828-1900+)

See also No. 2051.

1614. "The Centenary of the SPECTATOR." SPECTATOR, 141 (3 November 1928), supp., pp. 1-48.

1615. Colby, Robert A. "'How It Strikes a Contemporary': The SPECTATOR as Critic." NCF, 11 (1956), 182-206.

1616. Jump, J.D. "Matthew Arnold and the SPECTATOR." RES, 25 (1949), 61-64.

1617. "One Hundred Years of the SPECTATOR." LIVING AGE, 335 (1929), 369.

1618. Paden, W.D. "Swinburne, the SPECTATOR in 1862, and Walter Bagehot." SIX STUDIES IN NINETEENTH-CENTURY ENGLISH LITERATURE AND THOUGHT. Ed. Harold Orel and George J. Worth. University of Kansas Political History Series, XXXV. Lawrence: University of Kansas Press, 1962. Pp. 91-115.

1619. Skilton, David. "The SPECTATOR's Attack on Trollope's PRIME MINISTER: A Mistaken Attribution." N&Q, 15 (1968), 420-21.

1620. "THE SPECTATOR." NATION, 127 (1928), 704.

1621. THE SPECTATOR. 125th Anniversary Number. 15 May 1953.

1622. Tener, Robert H. "Swinburne as Reviewer." TLS, 25 December 1959, p. 755.

Concerns his contributions to the SPECTATOR.

1623. _____. "The SPECTATOR Records, 1874-1897." VN, no. 17 (1960), pp. 33-36.

1624. _____. "An Arnold Quotation as a Clue to R.H. Hutton's SPECTATOR Articles." N&Q, 18 (1971), 100-101.

1625. Thomas, William Beach. THE STORY OF 'THE SPECTATOR,' 1828-1928. London: Methuen, 1928.

SPECULATOR (dates unknown)

1626. J.,R. "Dr. Edward Ash and 'The Speculator.'" N&Q, 12 (1855), 167.

SPORTING MAGAZINE (1792-1870)

1627. INDEX OF ENGRAVINGS WITH THE NAMES OF THE ARTISTS IN THE SPORTING MAGAZINE FROM THE YEAR 1792 TO 1870. London: Published for Walter Gilbey by Vinton & Co., 1892.

Contains "History of the SPORTING MAGAZINE," by Francis

Lawley (pages 3-18).

SPY (1810-11)

1628. Bushnell, George Herbert. "The SPY: James Hogg's Adventure in Journalism." SCOTS MAGAZINE, 36 (1941), 197-205.

1629. Strout, Alan Lang. "James Hogg's THE SPY, 1810-11." N&Q, 180 (1941), 272-76.

STAR (1788-1831)

1630. Werkmeister, Lucyle. "Some Account of Robert Burns and the London Newspapers. With Special Reference to the Spurious STAR (1789)." BNYPL, 65 (1961), 483-504.

1631. _____. "An Early Version of Burns's Song, 'Their Groves of Sweet Myrtle.'" N&Q, 207 (1962), 460.

Appeared in the London STAR, 22 December 1796.

STRABANE MAGAZINE (1800)

1632. Campbell, A. Albert. "THE STRABANE MAGAZINE." IRISH BOOK LOVER, 3 (1912), 144-45.

STRATFORD, SHIPSTON, AND AULCESTER JOURNAL (1750-?)

1633. Morgan, Paul. "The Earliest Stratford Newspaper." N&Q, 195 (1950), 52.

A weekly begun in 1750.

STUDENT (1821?)

See also No. 2293.

1634. Gray, G.J. "Cambridge University Periodicals." CAMBRIDGE REVIEW, 7 (1886), 258-59.

TATLER (1709-11)

See also ADDISON, JOSEPH and STEELE, RICHARD (chapter 4), SPECTATOR, and Nos. 164, 181, 202, 302, 974, 1990, and 2211.

1635. Aitken, G.A. "Steele, and Some English Grammars of His Time." WALFORD'S ANTIQUARIAN, 8 (1885), 166-70.

TATLER no. 234 is the point of departure for a discussion of the "Grammars" which appeared in 1710-12 and which were advertised in the periodicals of the time.

1636. _____. "Swift's Church Pamphlets." ATHENAEUM, 17 December 1898, p. 867.

On the authorship of TATLER no. 220.

1637. Allen, Robert J. "Contemporary Allusions in THE TATLER." MLN, 55 (1940), 292-94.

1638. Aubin, Robert A. "Behind Steele's Satire on Undertakers." PMLA, 64 (1949), 1008-26.

Article includes discussion of the "upholder" passages in the TATLER, "though it is rather more concerned with the beginnings of the 'death business' than with Steele" (PQ, 29:298-99).

1639. Bateson, F.W. "The Errata in THE TATLER." RES, 5 (1929), 155-66.

1640. Betz, Siegmund A.E. "The Operatic Criticism of the TATLER and SPECTATOR." MUSICAL QUARTERLY, 31 (1945), 318-30.

1641. Blanchard, Rae. "Steele's CHRISTIAN HERO and the Errata in THE TATLER." RES, 6 (1930), 183-85.

1642. Bond, Donald F. "Armand de la Chapelle and the First French Version of the TATLER." RESTORATION AND EIGHTEENTH-CENTURY LITERATURE. ESSAYS IN HONOR OF ALAN DUGALD MCKILLOP. Ed. Carroll Camden. Chicago: University of Chicago Press for William Marsh Rice University, 1963. Pp. 161-84.

1643. Bond, Richmond P., ed. NEW LETTERS TO THE 'TATLER' AND 'SPECTATOR.' Austin: University of Texas Press, 1959.

Ninety-six hitherto unpublished letters. Reviewed in PQ 39: 958-59; MP 57:126-27; TLS 15 May 1959, p. 283.

1644. _____. "Isaac Dickerstaff, Esq." RESTORATION AND EIGHTEENTH-CENTURY LITERATURE. ESSAYS IN HONOR OF ALAN DUGALD MCKILLOP. Ed. Carroll Camden. Chicago: University of Chicago Press for William Marsh Rice University, 1963. Pp. 103-24.

1645. ______. "The Pirate and the TATLER." LIBRARY, 18 (1963), 257-74; rpt. London: The Bibliographical Society, 1965.

Concerns Henry Hills, the "foremost pirate of the age," who in 1709 reprinted the TATLER "in a partial edition and thus prompted the first authorized reprint."

1646. ______. "Mr. Bickerstaff and Mr. Wortley." CLASSICAL, MEDIAEVAL AND RENAISSANCE STUDIES IN HONOR OF BERTHOLD LOUIS ULLMAN. Ed. Charles Henderson, Jr. Rome: Edizioni di Storia e Letteratura, 1964. Pp. 491-504.

Concerns editorial methods.

1647. ______. THE TATLER: THE MAKING OF A LITERARY JOURNAL. Cambridge, Mass.: Harvard University Press, 1971.

Reviewed in PQ 51:768-69; SCRIBLERIAN 4, no. 2:83-84.

1648. [Channing, E.T.] "Periodical Essays of the Age of Anne." NORTH AMERICAN REVIEW, 46 (1838), 341-66.

1649. Dixon, P. "Pope and Steele." N&Q, 210 (1965), 451.

Concerns a paraphrase of a portion of TATLER no. 214 in a letter by Pope.

1650. Durham, W.H. "Some Forerunners of the TATLER and the SPECTATOR." MLN, 33 (1918), 95-101.

1651. Elliott, Robert C. "Swift's 'Little' Harrison, Poet and Continuator of the TATLER." SP, 44 (1949), 544-59.

1652. Garrison, Fielding H. "Medicine in the TATLER, SPECTATOR and GUARDIAN." BULLETIN OF THE INSTITUTE OF THE HISTORY OF MEDICINE, 2 (1934), 477-503.

1653. Gibson, George H., and Judith C. Gibson. "The Influence of the TATLER and the SPECTATOR on the 'Monitor.'" FURMAN STUDIES, 14, i (1966), 12-23.

1654. Graham, Walter. "Some Predecessors of the TATLER." JEGP, 24 (1952), 548-54.

1655. ______. "Defoe's REVIEW and Steele's TATLER--the Question of Influence." JEGP, 33 (1934), 250-54.

1656. Greenough, C[hester]. N[oyes]. "The Development of the TATLER, Particularly in Regard to News." PMLA, 31 (1916), 633-63.

1657. Hendrix, W.S. "Quevedo, Guevara, Lesage, and the TATLER." MP, 19 (1921), 177-86.

1658. Jackson, R. Wyse. "An Unrecorded TATLER." TLS, 7 December 1946, p. 603.

Concerns an unrecorded Dublin edition of three numbers.

1659. Koster, Patricia. "'Monoculus' and Party Satire." PQ, 49 (1970), 259-62.

See also No. 1663.

1660. League, James Benjamin, Jr. "Addison and Steele as Educational Realists in the TATLER, the SPECTATOR, and the GUARDIAN." DA, 26 (1965), 2035.

1661. McDonald, Daniel, ed. JOSEPH ADDISON AND RICHARD STEELE: SELECTED ESSAYS FROM 'THE TATLER,' 'THE SPECTATOR,' AND 'THE GUARDIAN.' New York: Bobbs-Merrill, 1973.

Reviewed in SCRIBLERIAN, 6 (1973), 37.

1662. Neumann, Joshua H. "Shakespearean Criticisms in the TATLER and the SPECTATOR." PMLA, 39 (1924), 612-23.

1663. Snyder, Henry L. "The Identity of Monoculus in THE TATLER." PQ, 48 (1960), 20-26.

See also No. 1659.

1664. THE TATLER. Ed., intro., and notes by George A. Aitken. 4 vols. London: Duckworth, 1898-99.

1665. Todd, William B. "Early Editions of THE TATLER." SB, 15 (1962), 121-33.

A study of textual variants.

1666. Walford, E. "Bickerstaffe." N&Q, 12 (1891), 408.

For replies, see pages 496-97.

1667. Webster, Ernest R. "The Evolving Critical Reputation of Richard Steele's Role in the TATLER." DAI, 31 (1971), 5378A.

1668. Wheatley, Katherine E. "Addison's Portrait of the Neo-Classical Critic (the TATLER, No. 165)." RES, 1 (1950), 245-47.

1669. White, Robert B., Jr. "A 'New' Continuation of the 'Tatler.'" N&Q, 201 (1956), 104-5.

Concerns a single half-sheet in the Yale University Library.

1670. ______. "Character of the Tatler." PQ, 45 (1966), 450-54.

The sheet so entitled, published by B. Bragge, probably should be dated between 17 October and 4 November, 1709.

1671. Winton, Calhoun. "Steele, the Junto and THE TATLER, No. 4." MLN, 72 (1957), 178-82.

TATLER, BY DONALD MACSTAFF OF THE NORTH (1711)

See also No. 2301.

1672. White, Robert B., Jr. "The Hepburn 'Tatler,' Edinburgh, 1711." N&Q, 200 (1955), 344-45.

Establishes the correct date and numbering for the termination of this imitation of Steele's TATLER.

TATLER REVIVED (1750)

1673. Resupinus. "'The Tatler Revived.'" N&Q, 4 (1857), 435.

TEMPLE BAR MAGAZINE (1860-1900+)

See also No. 512.

1674. De Baun, Vincent C[laud]. "TEMPLE BAR: Index of Victorian Middle-Class Thought." JRUL, 19 (1956), 6-16.

1675. ______. "TEMPLE BAR: Index of Victorian Middle Class Thought." DA, 17 (1957), 2607-8.

TERRAE FILIUS (1721)

See No. 2293.

THEATRE (1720)

1676. Loftis, John. "'Sir John Falstaffe's' THEATRE." JEGP, 48 (1949), 252-58.

An account of a periodical published anonymously and purporting to be a continuation of Steele's THEATRE but in fact a continuation of "Falstaffe's" ANTI-THEATRE, written in opposition to Steele.

1677. ______. "Sir John Falstaffe's THEATRE, a Correction." JEGP, 53 (1954), 141.

1678. ______, ed. RICHARD STEELE'S THE THEATRE, 1720. Oxford: Clarendon Press, 1962.

Reviewed in PQ (briefly) 42:373; MLR 58:102; RES 14:413-15; JEGP 62:658-88; LIBRARY 18:248-49.

1679. SIR JOHN FALSTAFFE, THE THEATRE (1720. Intro. John Loftis. Augustine Reprint Society, Series IV: Men, Manners, and Critics, no. 1. Los Angeles: Clark Memorial Library, 1948.

A continuation of Steele's THE THEATRE by an unknown author using the pseudonym of Sir John Falstaffe.

THEATRICAL INQUISITOR (1812-21)

See No. 290.

THEATRICAL RECORDER (1805-6)

1680. Holcroft, Thomas. THE THEATRICAL RECORDER. New York: Burt Franklin, 1968.

A reprint of this 1805 periodical.

THEATRIC TOURIST (1805)

1681. Cunningham, John E. "The Origin of the THEATRIC TOURIST." TN, 4 (1950), 38-40.

1682. Highfill, Philip H., Jr. "Folger Manuscripts Relating to THE THEATRIC TOURIST." TN, (1966), 121-26.

Describes four MS notebooks in the hand of James Winston.

1683. Hogan, Charles Beecher. "The Manuscript of Winston's THEATRIC

TOURIST." TN, 1 (1947), 86-90.

1684. Irvin, Eric. "More Drawings for Winston's THEATRIC TOURIST." TN, 19 (1964-65), 64-66.

1685. Nelson, Alfred L. "The Periodicity of THE THEATRIC TOURIST." TN, 21 (1966-67), 59-62.

1686. ______. "James Winston's THEATRIC TOURIST: A Critical Edition with a Biography and a Census of Winston Material." DA, 29 (1968), 573A-74A.

1687. R.,S. "The Winston MS. and Theatre Design." TN, 1 (1947), 93-95.

THEOLOGICAL INQUIRER (1815)

1688. Boas, Louise Schutz. "'Erasmus Perkins' and Shelley." MLN, 70 (1955), 408-13.

"Perkins" was George Cannon, the editor.

THESPIAN TELEGRAPH (1796)

1689. Abrahams, Aleck. "THE THESPIAN TELEGRAPH." N&Q, 4 (1911), 149.

THISTLE (1734-36)

1690. M.,J. "Ancient Alliance of the Scots with France: The Rebel Marquis of Tullibardine: 'The Thistle,' 1734-6." N&Q, 10 (1872), 161.

TIMES (1788-1900+)

See also No. 2289.

1691. Andrews, W.L. "The TIMES Review that Made Charlotte Brontë Cry." TRANSACTIONS OF THE BRONTE SOCIETY, 11 (1950), 359-69.

The review of SHIRLEY.

1692. Baker, John M. HENRY CRABB ROBINSON OF BURY, JENA, THE 'TIMES,' AND RUSSELL SQUARE. London: Allen & Unwin, 1937.

1693. Bond, W.H. "Henry Hallam, THE TIMES Newspaper, and the Halliwell

Case." LIBRARY, 18 (1963), 133-40.

1694. Furneaux, Howard. THE FIRST WAR CORRESPONDENT, WILLIAM HOWARD RUSSELL, OF 'THE TIMES.' London: Cassell, 1945.

1695. Ganzel, Carol H. "THE TIMES Correspondent and THE WARDEN." NCF, 21 (1967), 325-36.

1696. Hamilton, Harlan W. DOCTOR SYNTAX: A SILHOUETTE OF WILLIAM COMBE, ESQ. (1742-1823). Kent, Ohio: Kent State University Press, 1969.

Reviewed in PQ 49:334-35. According to Hamilton, Combe was "editor of THE TIMES when not in prison for debt."

1697. Hudson, Derek. THOMAS BARNES OF 'THE TIMES,' WITH SELECTIONS FROM HIS CRITICAL ESSAYS NEVER BEFORE REPRINTED. Ed. Harold Child. New York: Macmillan, 1944.

1698. Schwartz, Lewis M. "A New Review of Coleridge's CHRISTABEL." SIR, 9 (1970), 115-24.

Identifies Lamb as the author of the review in the TIMES (20 May 1816) and the COURIER (4 June 1816).

1699. Whitley, Alvin. "Thomas Hood and THE TIMES." TLS, 17 May 1957, p. 309.

See also P[eter]. F. Morgan, TLS, 7 June 1957, page 349.

1700. Williams, T.L. "Matthew Arnold and the TIMES." N&Q, 16 (1969), 211-12.

TOWN AND COUNTRY MAGAZINE (1769-96)

1701. Bleachley, Horace. "Tête-à-Tête Portraits in THE TOWN AND COUNTRY MAGAZINE." N&Q, 4 (1905), 241-42, 342-44, 462-64, 522-23.

1702. Xi. "'Town and Country Magazine.'" N&Q, 6 (1858), 190.

See also T.C. (page 337).

1703. Lee, Chung Nan. "A Study of the TOWN AND COUNTRY MAGAZINE." DA, 25 (1964), 479.

1704. M.,J. "'Town and Country Magazine.'" N&Q, 10 (1866), 187.

1705. Mitchell, Eleanor J. "The Tête-à-Têtes and Other Biography in the TOWN AND COUNTRY MAGAZINE, 1769-1796." DA, 28 (1968), 3644A.

1706. Osborne. "Tête-à-Tête Portraits of the 'Town and Country Magazine.'" N&Q, 5 (1888), 488.

For replies, see N&Q, 6 (1888), 10, 136, 175.

1707. Peacock, Edward. "The 'Town and Country Magazine.'" N&Q 2 (1886), 287.

See additional notes on page 419.

1708. Solomons, Israel. "'The Insect and the Reptile.'" N&Q, 12 (1915), 221.

TOWN-TALK IN A LETTER TO A LADY IN THE COUNTRY (1715-16)

See Nos. 2178 and 2188.

TRUE BRITON (1723-24)

1709. Benjamin, Lewis S. [Lewis Melville]. THE LIFE AND WRITINGS OF PHILIP DUKE OF WHARTON. London: Lane, 1913.

Chapter IX deals with the TRUE BRITON.

TRUE BRITON (1751-53)

1710. "English Periodicals: 'The True Briton.'" N&Q, 2 (1880), 243-44.

See also the note on page 317.

TRUE PATRIOT (1745-46)

See also FIELDING, HENRY (chapter 4).

1711. French, Robert D. "THE TRUE PATRIOT by Henry Fielding." DAI, 33 (1972), 1140A.

1712. Jones, Claude E. "Fielding's 'True Patriot' and the Henderson Murder." MLR, 52 (1957), 498-503.

TRUE SUN (1832-37)

1713. Stam, David H. "Leigh Hunt and THE TRUE SUN: A List of Reviews, August 1833- to February 1834." BNYPL, 77 (1974), 436-53.

1714. Vivian, Charles H. "Dickens, the TRUE SUN, and Samuel Laman Blanchard." NCF, 4 (1950), 328-30.

UNIVERSAL CHRONICLE (1758-60)

See also IDLER and Nos. 1350, 2065, and 2072.

1715. Green, Boylston. "Possible Additions to the Johnson Canon." YALE UNIVERSITY LIBRARY GAZETTE, 16 (1942), 70-79.

1716. Kolb, Gwin J. "John Newberry, Projector of the UNIVERSAL CHRONICLE: A Study of the Advertisements." SB, 11 (1958), 249-51.

UNIVERSAL MAGAZINE OF KNOWLEDGE AND PLEASURE (1747-1815)

1717. Clarke, A. "Essex in the Universal Magazine, 1750." ESSEX REVIEW, 24 (1915), 19-22.

1718. Dandridge, Edmund P., Jr. "An Eighteenth Century Theft of Chaucer's PURSE." MLN, 68 (1953), 237-38.

An imitation of Chaucer's poem published in the UNIVERSAL MAGAZINE OF KNOWLEDGE AND PLEASURE for June 1747.

1719. Friedman, Arthur. "Goldsmith's 'Essay on Friendship': Its First Publication and the Problem of Authorship." PQ, 35 (1956), 346-49.

1720. Pickford, John. "'The Universal Magazine.'" N&Q, 12 (1879), 328.

For replies, see pages 455 and 497.

UNIVERSAL MUSEUM AND COMPLETE MAGAZINE (1764)

1721. Golden, Morris. "Goldsmith and 'The Universal Museum and Complete Magazine.'" N&Q, 202 (1957), 339-48.

1722. ______. "A Goldsmith Essay in the 'Complete Magazine.'" N&Q, 203 (1958), 465-66.

1723. Sherbo, Arthur. "The Case for Internal Evidence (5): The Uses and Abuses of Internal Evidence." BNYPL, 58 (1959), 5-22.

Claims a 1767 "Essay on Elegies" for Johnson.

UNIVERSAL SPECTATOR (1728-46)

See also Nos. 1856 and 1926.

1724. Bond, Richmond P. "A Fragment by Addison." RES, 5 (1929), 203-5.

UNIVERSAL VISITOR (1756)

See also SMART, CHRISTOPHER (chapter 4).

1725. Botting, Roland B. "Johnson, Smart, and the UNIVERSAL VISITER." MP, 36 (1939), 293-300.

On manuscript notes in a copy of the UNIVERSAL VISITER in the British Museum.

1726. Jones, Claude. "Christopher Smart, Richard Rolt, and THE UNIVERSAL VISITER." LIBRARY, 18 (1937), 212-14.

1727. Piggott, Stuart. "New Light on Christopher Smart." TLS, 13 June 1929, p. 474.

On the contract with Rolt for writing contributions.

1728. Sherbo, Arthur. "Christopher Smart and THE UNIVERSAL VISITER." LIBRARY, 10 (1955), 203-5.

1729. ______. "Fielding and Chaucer--and Smart." N&Q, 203 (1958), 441-42.

Attributes to Smart articles on Chaucer and Spenser in the UNIVERSAL VISITER and "A Pleasunt Balade" in the COVENT-GARDEN JOURNAL, no. 50.

VISIONS OF SIR HEISTER RYLEY (1710-11)

1730. Partington, E. "'The Visions of Sir Heister Ryley.'" N&Q, 9 (1890), 326.

See also G[eorge]. A. Aitken (pages 411-12).

1731. Walford, Cornelius. "Periodical Publications." N&Q, 7 (1883), 306-7.

See also Edward Solly (page 354).

WATCHMAN (1796)

1732. Beer, J.B. "Coleridge's WATCHMAN." N&Q, 206 (1961), 217.

1733. Campbell, James D. "The Prospectus of Coleridge's WATCHMAN." ATHENAEUM, no. 3450 (9 December 1893), pp. 808-9.

1734. Gibbs, Warren E. "An Autobiographical Note of Coleridge's in the WATCHMAN." N&Q, 160 (1931), 99-100.

1735. Johnson, S.F. "Coleridge's THE WATCHMAN: Decline and Fall." RES, 4 (1953), 147-48.

1736. Patton, Lewis. "Coleridge's THE WATCHMAN." TLS, 8 October 1931, p. 778.

1737. Priestly, Mary Ellen. "English Syntax in the Early Prose of Samuel Taylor Coleridge: A New Reading of THE WATCHMAN, 1796." DA, 28 (1968), 319A.

1738. Wordsworth, Jonathan. "Some Unpublished Coleridge Marginalia." TLS, 14 June 1957, p. 369.

WEEKLY AMUSEMENT (1763-67)

1739. Price, Cecil. "An Early Publication of One of Chesterfield's Letters to His Son." NEUPHILOLOGISCHE MITTEILUNGEN, 67 (1966), 401-11.

In the WEEKLY AMUSEMENT (2 November 1765), pages 696-99.

WEEKLY COMEDY (1707-8)

See also No. 2231.

1740. McCue, G.S. "A Seventeenth-Century Gulliver." N&Q, 50 (1935), 32-34.

WEEKLY JOURNAL; OR, SATURDAY'S POST (1716-37)

See also No. 1926.

1741. Aitken, G.A. "Defoe and Mist's 'Weekly Journal.'" ATHENAEUM, 26 August 1893, pp. 287-88.

1742. J.,F. "Mist's and Fog's Journal." N&Q, 3 (1957), 387.

See also S.H.H. in N&Q, 5 (1858), 424.

1743. M.,S.N. "Stray Notes on Edmund Curll, His Life, and Publications. No. 6--Curll's Controversy with Mist, &c." N&Q, 2 (1856), 421-24.

1744. McCutcheon, Roger P. "Another Burlesque of Addison's Ballad Criticism." SP, 23 (1926), 451-56.

A letter by Hypercriticus in no. 144 (2 September 1721).

1745. Novak, Maxmillian E. "'Simon Forecastle's Weekly Journal': Some Notes on Defoe's Conscious Artistry." TEXAS STUDIES IN LANGUAGE AND LITERATURE, 6 (1965), 433-40.

1746. Robbins, Alfred F. "'Jonathan Wild the Great': Its Germ." N&Q, 2 (1910), 261-63; 3 (1917), 388-93.

A controversy on the probability of Fielding's authorship of two articles in the issues for 12 and 19 June 1725. The first reference reprints the two articles. See also Paul de Castro in N&Q, 2 (1916), 442-43; 3 (1917), 74.

WEEKLY MAGAZINE; OR, EDINBURGH AMUSEMENT (1768-84)

1747. Fergusson, Robert. SCOTS POEMS, FAITHFULLY RE-PRINTED FROM THE WEEKLY MAGAZINE AND THE EDITIONS OF 1773 AND 1779. Edinburgh: Porpoise Press, 1925.

1748. Friedman, Arthur. "Goldsmith and the WEEKLY MAGAZINE." MP, 32 (1935), 281-99.

1749. Golden, Morris. "Goldsmith Attributions in the 'Weekly Magazine.'" N&Q, 201 (1956), 350-51.

1750. Walker, Ian C. "Scottish Verse in THE WEEKLY MAGAZINE." SSL, 5 (1967), 3-13.

1751. ______. "Dr. Johnson and THE WEEKLY MAGAZINE." RES, 19 (1968), 14-24.

Describes the anti-Johnson campaign in this journal from 1769 on.

WEEKLY MEMORIALS (1682-83)

1752. Frazer, W. "'Weekly Memorials for the Ingenious.'" N&Q, 2 (1881), 267.

See page 397 for replies.

1753. James, T.E. "The Earliest Weekly Journal of Science." N&Q, 5 (1894), 11.

See also H.S. Pearson (pages 250-51).

WEEKLY MISCELLANY (1732-41)

See No. 2144.

WEEKLY MISCELLANY; OR, INSTRUCTIVE ENTERTAINER (1773-82)

1754. H.,W.S.B. "'The Weekly Miscellany,' 1775 and 1776." N&Q, 8 (1921), 11.

Also in this issue, see M. (page 56). See J. Paul de Castro in this issue (pages 132-33) and N&Q, 10 (1922), 134.

WEEKLY PACKET (1712-21)

See also No. 2022.

1755. Rimbault, Edward F. "A Bundle of Old Newspapers." N&Q, 5 (1870), 1-3.

See also W. Lee (page 45).

WEEKLY REGISTER; OR, UNIVERSAL JOURNAL (1730-34?)

See No. 179.

WEEKLY REVIEW OF THE AFFAIRS OF FRANCE

See REVIEW (Defoe's).

WESTMINSTER JOURNAL AND OLD BRITISH SPY (1794-1812)

1756. Vidler, Leopold A. "WESTMINSTER JOURNAL AND OLD BRITISH SPY." N&Q, 169 (1935), 298.

WESTMINSTER REVIEW (1824-1900+)

See also Nos. 197 and 802.

1757. Coss, John Jacob, ed. AUTOBIOGRAPHY OF JOHN STUART MILL. New York: Columbia University Press, 1924.

See especially pages 63-70, 90-92, 139-40.

1758. Daniels, Elizabeth A., and Emilia Ashurst Hawkes. "Collaboration of Mazzini on an Article in the WESTMINSTER REVIEW." BNYPL, 65 (1961), 577-82.

1759. Fetter, Frank W. "Economic Articles in the WESTMINSTER REVIEW and Their Authors, 1824-1851." JPE, 70 (1962), 570-96.

1760. Fraiberg, Louis. "The WESTMINSTER REVIEW and American Literature, 1824-1885." AL, 24 (1952), 310-20.

1761. Haight, Gordon S. "George Meredith and the WESTMINSTER REVIEW." MLR, 53 (1958), 1-16.

1762. Lease, Benjamin. "John Neale's Quarrel with the WESTMINSTER REVIEW." AL, 26 (1954), 86-88.

1763. Morgan, Peter F. "Francis Place's Copy of the WESTMINSTER REVIEW." N&Q, 13 (1966), 330-32.

1764. Nesbitt, George Lyman. BENTHAMITE REVIEWING: THE FIRST TWELVE YEARS OF THE 'WESTMINSTER REVIEW,' 1824-36. New York: Columbia University Press, 1934.

1765. Race, Sydney. "Dr. John Chapman, Editor of the WESTMINSTER REVIEW." N&Q, 198 (1953), 211-13.

1766. Van Arsdel, Rosemary Thorstenson. "The WESTMINSTER REVIEW, 1824-1857: With Special Emphasis on Literary Attitudes." DA, 22 (1961), 251.

1767. ______. "The WESTMINSTER REVIEW: Change of Editorship, 1840." SB, 25 (1972), 191-204.

WESTMORLAND GAZETTE (1818-1900+)

1768. Bailey-Kempling, W. "De Quincey's Editorship of the 'Westmorland

Gazette.'" N&Q, 2 (1904), 101.

1769. Strout, Alan Lang. "De Quincey and Wordsworth." N&Q, 174 (1938), 423.

WHIG EXAMINER (1710)

1770. E.,T.W. "'The Whig Examiner.'" N&Q, 12 (1855), 47.

See also E.W.O. (page 194).

WHIGG (1718)

1771. Blanchard, Rae. "XVIII-Century Periodical: THE WHIGG." N&Q, 184 (1943), 200.

WHITE DWARF (1817-18)

1772. Povey, K. "THE WHITE DWARF." TLS, 24 May 1928, p. 396.

WHITEHALL EVENING POST (1746-1801)

See No. 1926.

WINDSOR AND ETON EXPRESS AND GENERAL ADVERTISER (1812-1900+)

1773. Bebbington, W.G. "The Most Remarkable Man of His Age: Byron in THE WINDSOR AND ETON EXPRESS AND GENERAL ADVERTISER." KSMB, 7 (1956), 27-31.

1774. _____. "Charles Knight and Shelley." KSJ, 6 (1957), 75-85.

Knight's views on Shelley appeared in this periodical and in the GUARDIAN.

1775. Scott, Noel. "Byron and the Stage." QR, 294 (1955), 496-503.

WIT'S MAGAZINE (1784)

1776. Samuel, Wilfred S. "Isaac D'Israeli: First Published Writings." N&Q, 194 (1949), 192-93.

Evidence for his authorship of two papers in WIT'S MAGAZINE (1784).

WORKS OF THE LEARNED (1691-92)

1777. Parks, Stephen. "John Dunton and THE WORKS OF THE LEARNED." LIBRARY, 23 (1968), 13-24.

WORLD (1753-56)

See also Nos. 164, 181, 378, and 2120.

1778. Todd, William B. "Bibliography and the Editorial Problem in the Eighteenth Century." SB, 4 (1951), 41-55.

Text of the WORLD illustrates certain bibliographical problems which developed after 1695.

1779. ______. "The First Edition of THE WORLD." LIBRARY, 11 (1956), 283-84.

1780. Tucker, Susie I. "Visitation, Guetre: Two Pre-Datings." N&Q, 205 (1960), 343.

Early usages in the WORLD, 1754 and 1756.

1781. Weinbrot, Howard D. "Johnson's DICTIONARY and THE WORLD: The Papers of Lord Chesterfield and Richard Owen Cambridge." PQ, 50 (1971), 663-69.

Suggests that a reading of papers in the WORLD by Chesterfield and Cambridge explains the celebrated letter from Johnson to Chesterfield.

1782. Werkmeister, Lucyle. "The First Publication of Chatterton's Verses 'To Miss C./ on Hearing Her Play on the Harpsichord." N&Q, 207 (1962), 270-71.

YELLOW BOOK (1894-97)

1783. Brisau, A. "THE YELLOW BOOK and Its Place in the Eighteen-Nineties." SGG, 8 (1966), 135-72.

1784. Huntley, John. "Aline and Henry Harland, Aubrey Beardsley, and THE YELLOW BOOK: A Verification of Some Evidence." N&Q, 9 (1962), 107-8.

1785. Townsend, J. Benjamin. "THE YELLOW BOOK." PULC, 16 (1955), 101-3.

1786. Weintraub, Stanley. "THE YELLOW BOOK: A Reappraisal." JGE, 16 (1964), 136-52.

1787. _____, ed. THE YELLOW BOOK: QUINTESSENCE OF THE NINETIES. Garden City, N.Y.: Doubleday, 1964.

1788. White, Terence De Vere, ed. A LEAF FROM 'THE YELLOW BOOK': THE CORRESPONDENCE OF GEORGE EGERTON. London: Richards Press, 1958.

Egerton was the pseudonym of Mary Dunne Bright.

YELLOW DWARF (1818)

1789. Marshall, William H. "An Addition to the Hazlitt Canon: Arguments from External and Internal Evidence." PBSA, 55 (1961), 347-70.

The case for Hazlitt's authorship of an essay on "Pulpit Oratory" in the YELLOW DWARF.

YORK COURANT (1725-1848)

See No. 2202.

YORK GAZETTEER (dates unknown)

See No. 2202.

YOUDE'S BILLPOSTING JOURNAL (1897)

1790. Smyth, A.L. "Youde's Billposting Journal." ManR, 10 (1963), 47-50.

YOUNG FOLKS (1879-84)

1791. McCleary, G.F. "Stevenson in YOUNG FOLKS." FR, 165 (February 1949), 125-30.

Chapter 4
PERSONS

ACTON, LORD [JOHN DALBERG-ACTON, 1ST BARON]

See also No. 1437.

1792. Hill, Roland. "Lord Acton and the Catholic Reviews." BLACKFRIARS, 36 (1955), 469-82.

Acton's connection with several "liberal" Catholic newspapers.

ADAMS, THOMAS

See No. 1378.

ADDISON, JOSEPH

See also FREEHOLDER, GUARDIAN, SPECTATOR, and TATLER (all chapter 3), STEELE, RICHARD (below), and Nos. 390, 1231, 1724, 1744, 1868, 2079, 2186, and 2206.

1793. Abernethy, Cecil. "Addison and Swift: A Note on Style and Manners." ESSAYS IN HONOR OF RICHEBOURG GAILLARD MCWILLIAMS. Ed. with pref. by Howard Creed. Birmingham, Ala.: Birmingham-Southern College Press, 1970. Pp. 1-8.

1794. Aikin, Lucy. THE LIFE OF JOSEPH ADDISON. 2 vols. London: Longman, Brown, Green, and Longmans, 1843.

Reviewed in NORTH AMERICAN REVIEW, 64:314-72.

1795. Baldwin, Edward Chauncey. "La Bruyère's Influence upon Addison." PMLA, 19 (1904), 479-95.

1796. Battersby, James. "The SERINO Biography of Joseph Addison." PBSA,

65 (1971), 67-69.

1797. Beljame, Alexandre. MEN OF LETTERS AND THE ENGLISH PUBLIC IN THE EIGHTEENTH CENTURY, 1660-1744: DRYDEN, ADDISON, POPE. Ed., intro., notes by Bonamy Dobrée. London: Kegan Paul, 1948.

The first English translation of this important work.

1798. Bloom, Edward A., and Lillian D. Bloom. "Addison's 'Enquiry After Truth': The Moral Assumptions of his Proof for Divine Existence." PMLA, 65 (1950), 198-220.

1799. ______. "Joseph Addison and Eighteenth-Century 'Liberalism.'" JHI, 12 (1951), 560-83.

1800. ______. "Addison on 'Moral Habits of the Mind.'" JHI, 21 (1960), 409-27.

1801. ______. JOSEPH ADDISON'S SOCIABLE ANIMAL: IN THE MARKET PLACE, ON THE HUSTINGS, IN THE PULPIT. Providence, R.I.: Brown University Press, 1971.

Reviewed in PQ, 51:636-37.

1802. Bloom, Lillian D. "Addison as Translator: A Problem in Neo-Classical Scholarship." SP, 46 (1949), 31-53.

1803. Bond, Donald F. "Addison in Perspective." MP, 54 (1956), 124-28.

A review-article concerning Peter Smithers' LIFE OF JOSEPH ADDISON (see no. 1841).

1804. Broadus, Edmund K. "Addison's Influence on the Development of Interest in Folk-Poetry in the Eighteenth Century." MP, 8 (1910), 123-34.

1805. Brown, F. Andrew. "Addison's 'Imagination' and the 'Gessellschaft der Mahlern.'" MLQ, 15 (1954), 57-66.

Although the Swiss critics Bodmer and Breitinger were influenced by Addison's SPECTATOR papers on "The Pleasures of the Imagination," they nevertheless rejected his conclusions whenever he deviated from Locke.

1806. Cameron, Ruth A. "The Prose Style of Addison and Steele in the Periodical Essay." DAI, 33 (1972), 1705A.

1807. Campbell, Hilbert H. "The Sale Catalogue of Addison's Library." ELN, 4 (1967), 269-73.

1808. ______. "The Intellectual Position of Joseph Addison in Philosophy, Religion, and Science." DAI, 30 (1969), 2015A.

1809. Carter, Charlotte A. "Personae and Characters in the Essays of Addison, Steele, Fielding, Johnson, Goldsmith." DAI, 30 (1970), 4938A.

1810. Cooke, Arthur L. "Addison vs. Steele, 1708." PMLA, 68 (1953), 313-20.

1811. Courthope, W.J. ADDISON. English Men of Letters. London: Macmillan, 1884. Frequently reprinted.

1812. Crum, M.C. "A Manuscript of Essays by Joseph Addison." BODLEIAN LIBRARY RECORD, 5 (1954), 98-103.

Concerning a MS containing twenty-four essays by Addison (with corrections in Addison's hand), all but one of which appeared in some form in the SPECTATOR.

1813. Dobrée, Bonamy. "The First Victorian." ESSAYS IN BIOGRAPHY. Oxford: Oxford University Press, 1925. Pp. 201-345.

1814. Dust, Alvin I. "An Aspect of the Addison-Steele Literary Relationship." ELN, 1 (1964), 196-200.

1815. Elioseff, Lee Andrew. 'The Cultural Milieu of Addison's Literary Criticism." DA, 21 (1960), 187-88; rpt. in book form. Austin: University of Texas Press, 1963.

Reviewed unfavorably in PQ, 43:337-38.

1816. Freeman, Phyllis. "Who Was Sir Roger de Coverley?" QR, 285 (1947), 592-604.

Argues for William Walsh as the prototype, whereas the traditional identification was Sir John Packington. Reviewed in PQ, 27:137-38.

1817. Hadow, G.E., ed. ESSAYS ON ADDISON BY MACAULAY AND THACKERAY. WITH TWELVE ESSAYS BY ADDISON. Oxford: Clarendon Press, 1907.

1818. Hamm, Victor M. "Addison and the Pleasures of the Imagination." MLN, 52 (1937), 498-50.

1819. Hansen, David A. "Addison on Ornament and Poetic Style." STUDIES IN CRITICISM AND AESTHETICS, 1660-1800: ESSAYS IN HONOR OF SAMUEL HOLT MONK. Ed. Howard Anderson and John S. Shea. Minneapolis: University of Minnesota Press, 1967. Pp. 94-127.

1820. Hinnant, Charles H. "Joseph Addison and Mixed Satire." DA, 27 (1967), 3841A.

1821. Jackson, Wallace. "Addison: Empiricist of the Moral Consciousness." PQ, 45 (1966), 455-59.

1822. "Joseph Addison." TLS, 20 June 1919, 329-30.

1823. Kenney, William. "Addison, Johnson, and the 'Energetick' Style." STUDIA NEOPHILOLOGICA, 33 (1961), 103-14.

1824. Lannering, J. STUDIES IN THE PROSE STYLE OF JOSEPH ADDISON. Essays and Studies on English Language and Literature, vol. 9. Uppsala: Lundequistska, 1951.

1825. Lewis, C.S. "Addison." ESSAYS ON THE EIGHTEENTH CENTURY PRESENTED TO DAVID NICHOL SMITH IN HONOUR OF HIS SEVENTIETH BIRTHDAY. Oxford: Clarendon Press, 1945. Pp. 1-14; rpt. EIGHTEENTH-CENTURY ENGLISH LITERATURE: MODERN ESSAYS IN CRITICISM. Ed. James L. Clifford. New York: Oxford University Press, 1959. Pp. 144-57.

1826. Macaulay, Thomas Babington. "The Life and Writings of Addison." WORKS OF LORD MACAULAY. Ed. by his sister, Lady Trevelyan. 8 vols. New York: Longmans, Green 1897. VII, 52-122.

Originally appeared as a review of Aikin's work (No. 1794) in EDINBURGH REVIEW, July 1843.

1827. McDonald, Daniel Lamont. "An Examination of the Intellectual Premises Underlying the Religious, Political, and Social Criticism of Joseph Addison." DA, 21 (1961), 3092.

1828. Mahoney, John L. "Addison and Akenside: The Impact of Psychological Criticism on Early English Romantic Poetry." BRITISH JOURNAL OF AESTHETICS, 6 (1966), 365-74.

1829. Marcus, Mitchell. "Joseph Addison as Literary Critic." ABSTRACTS OF DISSERTATIONS, STANFORD UNIVERSITY, 26 (1951), 135-37.

1830. Morris, Robert Lee. "Joseph Addison's Literary Criticism." UNIVER-

SITY OF IOWA DOCTORAL DISSERTATIONS: ABSTRACTS AND REFERENCES (1900-1937), 1 (1940), 154-60.

1831. ______. "Addison's MIXT WIT." MLN, 57 (1942), 666-68.

1832. Ogle, Nathaniel. THE LIFE OF ADDISON. London: Thomas Davison, 1826.

1833. Oliphant, M.O.W. "Addison, the Humorist." HISTORICAL CHARACTERS OF THE REIGN OF QUEEN ANNE. New York: Century, 1894. Pp. 167-207.

1834. Paul, D.A. ADDISON'S INFLUENCE ON THE SOCIAL REFORM OF THE AGE. Hohere Burgerschule zu Hamburg, Progr. no. 573. Hamburg: Meissner, 1876.

1835. Perry, Thomas Sergeant. ENGLISH LITERATURE IN THE EIGHTEENTH CENTURY. New York: Harper, 1883.

1836. Reed, Edward Bliss. "Two Notes on Addison." MP, 6 (1908), 181-89.

On Addison's textual revisions, especially in the SPECTATOR, and the relation of his ballad papers to the satirical tract A COMMENT ON THE HISTORY OF TOM THUMB (1711).

1837. Rogal, Samuel J. "Joseph Addison (1672-1719): A Check List of Works and Major Scholarship." BNYPL, 77 (1974), 236-50.

Reviewed unfavorably in SCRIBLERIAN, 7:23-24.

1838. Salter, C.H. "Dryden and Addison." MLR, 69 (1974), 29-39.

"Annoying, important, and possibly fallacious . . . wearying, pedestrian . . . [and] irksome" (SCRIBLERIAN 6, no. 2:83-84).

1839. SELECTIONS FROM THE WRITINGS OF JOSEPH ADDISON. Ed., intro., notes by Barrett Wendell and Chester Noyes Greenough. Athenaeum Press Series. Boston: Ginn, 1905.

1840. Shawcross, I. "Addison as a Social Reformer." ConR, 153 (1938), 585-91.

1841. Smithers, Peter. THE LIFE OF JOSEPH ADDISON. Oxford: Clarendon Press, 1954.

A biography of Addison which emphasizes his performance as a statesman and administrator rather than as a man of letters. Reviewed in PQ, 34:267-69; MP 54:124-28; ANGLIA 75:116-18.

1842. Stephens, John C., Jr. "Addison as Social Critic." EUQ, 21 (1965), 157-72.

1843. Stevick, Philip. "Familiarity in the Addisonian Familiar Essay." COLLEGE COMPOSITION AND COMMUNICATION, 16 (1965), 169-73.

1844. Summers, Silas E. "Addison's Conception of Tragedy." COLLEGE ENGLISH, 8 (1947), 245-48.

1845. Thackeray, William Makepeace. "Congreve and Addison." THE ENGLISH HUMOURISTS OF THE EIGHTEENTH CENTURY. The Complete Work. New York: Crowell, [1904]. XXIII, 44-82.

1846. Thorpe, Clarence D. "Addison's Contribution to Criticism." THE SEVENTEENTH CENTURY: STUDIES IN THE HISTORY OF ENGLISH THOUGHT AND LITERATURE FROM BACON TO POPE, BY RICHARD FOSTER JONES AND OTHERS WRITING IN HIS HONOR. Stanford: Stanford University Press, 1951. Pp. 316-29.

Sees Addison as a critic whose views anticipate later criticism, rather than as a synthesizer as was Pope.

1847. Timmerman, John. "Divinity and Creativity: The Aesthetic Framework of Joseph Addison." UDR, 8, ii (1971), 17-28.

1848. Tucker, William John. "Two Great Essayists." CATHOLIC WORLD, 150 (1940), 445-51.

Concerns Addison and Steele.

1849. [Tuckerman, H.T.] "Joseph Addison." NORTH AMERICAN REVIEW, 79 (1854), 90-109.

1850. Watson, George G. "Contributions to a Dictionary of Critical Terms: IMAGINATION and FANCY." EC, 3 (1953), 201-14.

Includes a discussion of Addison.

1851. Wilkinson, Jean. "Some Aspects of Addison's Philosophy of Art." HLQ, 28 (1964), 31-44.

1852. Winton, Calhoun. "Addison and Steele in the English Enlightenment." TRANSACTIONS OF THE FIRST INTERNATIONAL CONGRESS ON THE ENLIGHTENMENT. Ed. Theodore Besterman. Geneva: Institut et Musée Voltaire, 1963. Pp. 1901-18.

1853. Woolf, Virginia. "Addison." THE COMMON READER. New York: Harcourt, Brace, 1925. Pp. 137-51.

AKENSIDE, MARK

See Nos. 1232 and 1828.

ALLEN, SIR THOMAS

See No. 872.

ALMON, JOHN

See No. 1336.

ANDERSON, AGNES CAMPBELL

1854. Couper, W.J. "Mrs. Anderson and the Royal Prerogative in Printing." PROCEEDINGS OF THE ROYAL PHILOSOPHICAL SOCIETY OF GLASGOW, 48 (1917), 79-102.

Anderson printed Defoe's REVIEW at Edinburgh.

ARBUTHNOT, DR. JOHN

See No. 587.

ARNOLD, MATTHEW

See Nos. 416, 643, 711, 1113, 1304, 1309, 1392, 1474, 1483, 1616, 1624, and 1700.

ASH, DR. EDWARD

See No. 1626.

ASPLAND, ROBERT

See No. 1193.

AUSTEN, JANE

See also Nos. 659, 1031, 1066, 1067, 1164, 1380, 1381, and 1400.

1855. Southam, B.C. "Jane Austen." TLS, 30 November 1962, p. 944.

See also TLS, 14 December 1962, p. 980; S. Graham Brade-Birks in TLS, 21 December 1962, p. 993; and an early obituary (22 July 1817) in the COURIER (no. 7744).

BADCOCK, SAMUEL

See No. 1195.

BAGEHOT, WALTER

See No. 1239.

BAKER, HENRY

1856. Potter, George Reuben. "Henry Baker, F.R.S. (1698-1774)." MP, 39 (1932), 301-21.

See page 305 for information on Baker's personal copy of the UNIVERSAL SPECTATOR in the Hope collection and the numbers that he wrote.

BAKER, THOMAS

See Nos. 819 and 822.

BARNES, THOMAS

See CHAMPION (chapter 3) and No. 1697.

BASIRE, JAMES

See No. 1319.

BATHURST, RICHARD

See Nos. 419 and 420.

BATTEN, BENJAMIN

See No. 872.

BEARDSLEY, AUBREY

See No. 1784.

BEATTIE, JAMES

See Nos. 1107, 1111, and 1163.

BEERBOHM, MAX

See No. 1484.

BELL, JOHN

1857. A CATALOGUE OF BOOKS, NEWSPAPERS, &C. PRINTED BY JOHN BELL, B. 1745 D. 1831, OF 'THE BRITISH LIBRARY,' 'THE MORNING POST,' 'BELL'S WEEKLY MESSENGER,' &C. AND BY JOHN BROWNE BELL, B. 1779 D. 1885, SON OF THE ABOVE: FOUNDER OF 'BELL'S NEW WEEKLY MESSENGER,' 'THE NEWS OF THE WORLD,' ETC. Exhibited at the First Edition Club. London: 1931.

1858. Morison, Stanley. JOHN BELL, 1745-1831, BOOKSELLER, PRINTER, PUBLISHER, TYPEFOUNDER, JOURNALIST, &C. Cambridge: At the University Press, 1930.

BENTLEY, RICHARD

See No. 970.

BERKELEY, GEORGE

See also Nos. 973, 975, 977, 978, 1243, 1406, and 1550.

1859. THE WORKS OF GEORGE BERKELEY, BISHOP OF CLOYNE. London and New York: Nelson, 1955.

Volume VII, edited by A.A. Luce, contains Berkeley's contributions to the GUARDIAN.

BEVERIDGE, WILLIAM

See No. 984.

BEWLEY, WILLIAM

See No. 1199.

BINGLEY, WILLIAM

1860. S.,E. "A Forgotten Journalist." ATHENAEUM, 20 May 1899, p. 626.

William Bingley of the NORTH BRITON, INDEPENDENT CHRONICLE, and BINGLEY'S JOURNAL; OR, THE UNIVERSAL GAZETTE.

BIRKENHEAD, SIR JOHN

See Nos. 1139 and 2131.

BLAKE, WILLIAM

See Nos. 791, 798, and 1319.

BOSWELL, JAMES

See also LONDON MAGAZINE (chapter 3) and Nos. 598, 599, 1296, and 1418.

1861. Brown, Anthony E. "Boswellian Studies: A Bibliography." CAIRO STUDIES IN ENGLISH, 1963-1966, pp. 1-75.

1862. _____. BOSWELLIAN STUDIES. Hamden, Conn.: Archon, 1972.

1863. Brown, J.T.T. "James Boswell as Essayist." SCOTTISH HISTORICAL REVIEW, 18 (1921), 102-16.

The "Hypochondriack" papers in the LONDON MAGAZINE. See also M[argery]. Bailey, "Boswell as Essayist," in JEGP, 22:412-23.

1864. Pottle, Frederick A. "The Incredible Boswell." BLACKWOOD'S MAGAZINE, 218 (1925), 149-65.

On Boswell's personal file of the LONDON CHRONICLE, with his contributions marked in his own hand.

1865. _____. THE LITERARY CAREER OF JAMES BOSWELL, ESQ. BEING THE BIBLIOGRAPHICAL MATERIALS FOR A LIFE OF BOSWELL. Oxford: Clarendon Press, 1929.

Boswell's contributions to periodical publications are listed in Part II, pages 215-66.

1866. Werkmeister, Lucyle. "Jemmie Boswell and the London Daily Press, 1785-1795." BNYPL, 67 (1963), 82-114, 169-85; rpt. New York: New York Public Library, 1963.

BOURNE, NICHOLAS

See Nos. 345 and 1874.

BOWYER, WILLIAM

See No. 303.

BOYER, ABEL

See No. 1990.

BRADLEY, RICHARD

See No. 970.

BRIGHT, MARY DUNNE

See No. 1788.

BRONTË, CHARLOTTE

See also No. 1691.

1867. Brooks, Roger L. "Unrecorded Newspaper Reviews of Charlotte Brontë's SHIRLEY and VILLETTE." PBSA, 53 (1959), 270-71.

BRONTËS, THE

See No. 1043.

BROUGHAM, HENRY, LORD

See Nos. 585, 767, 773, and 774.

BROWN, JOHN

See No. 445.

BROWN, TOM

See also No. 1925.

1868. Boyce, Benjamin. "Two Debits for Tom Brown, with a Credit from Joseph Addison." PQ, 14 (1935), 263-69.

Evidence for the influence of Ned Ward's LONDON SPY on Brown's WALK ROUND LONDON AND WESTMINSTER and of Brown's work on Addison's essay in SPECTATOR, no. 26.

1869. ______. TOM BROWN OF FACETIOUS MEMORY. GRUB STREET IN THE AGE OF DRYDEN. Harvard Studies in English, XXI. Cambridge, Mass.: Harvard University Press, 1939.

For Brown's connection with the LONDON MERCURY, see pages 39-43.

BROWNING, ELIZABETH BARRETT

See Nos. 1005 and 1254.

BROWNING, ROBERT

See Nos. 1307 and 1439.

BUCKLEY, SAMUEL

See Nos. 1511 and 1560.

BUDGELL, EUSTACE

See also No. 505.

1870. Morrison, Lois G. "Eustace Budgell and His Family Background." N&Q, 217 (1972), 178-83, 209-16.

BULWER-LYTTON, EDWARD

See Nos. 490 and 572.

BURKE, EDMUND

See also ANNUAL REGISTER (chapter 3) and No. 1210.

1871. Todd, William B. A BIBLIOGRAPHY OF EDMUND BURKE. London: Rupert Hart-Davis, 1964.

BURNET, THOMAS

See No. 971.

BURNEY, CHARLES

See Nos. 1200, 1203, and 1564.

BURNS, ROBERT

See also Nos. 415, 723, 1490, 1630, and 1631.

1872. Werkmeister, Lucyle. "Robert Burns and the London Daily Press." MP, 63 (1966), 322-35.

Material by and about Burns, 1787-97.

BUTLER, SAMUEL

See No. 1079.

BUTTER, NATHANIEL

See also No. 345.

1873. Arthur, Henry. "Earliest English Newspaper." N&Q, 12 (1903), 29-30.

Also in this issue of N&Q, see the material by J. Eliot Hodgkin (pages 70-71), John B. Wainewright (page 71), Charles L. Lindsay (page 153), and Adrian Wheeler (page 153).

1874. Rostenberg, Leona. "Nathaniel Butter and Nicholas Bourne, First 'Masters of the Staple.'" LIBRARY, 12 (1957), 23-33.

1875. Shaaber, Matthias A. "The History of the First English Newspaper." SP, 29 (1932), 551-87.

BYROM, JOHN

See No. 1571.

BYRON, GEORGE GORDON, LORD

See also Nos. 11, 364, 567, 597, 656, 945, 1050, 1051, 1059, 1083, 1179, 1215, 1773, 1775, 2119, and 2215.

1876. Ward, William S. "Byron's HOURS OF IDLENESS and Other Than Scotch Reviewers." MLN, 59 (1944), 547-50.

CAMBRIDGE, RICHARD OWEN

See also Nos. 1415 and 1781.

1877. Altick, Richard D. RICHARD OWEN CAMBRIDGE: BELATED AUGUSTAN. Diss. University of Pennsylvania, 1941.

CANNING, GEORGE

See also ANTI-JACOBIN (chapter 3).

1878. Marshall, Dorothy. THE RISE OF GEORGE CANNING. London: Longmans, Green, [1938].

1879. Petrie, Sir Charles. GEORGE CANNING. London: Eyre and Spottiswoode, 1930.

1880. Temperley, H.W.V. LIFE OF CANNING. London: James Finch & Co., 1905.

CANNON, GEORGE

See No. 1688.

CARLYLE, THOMAS

See also Nos. 564, 751, 764, 765, 832, 843, 845, and 948.

1881. Seigel, Jules Paul. "Thomas Carlyle and the Periodical Press: A Study in Attitudes." DA, (1966), 186A-87A.

CARROLL, LEWIS

See also No. 1478.

1882. Green, Roger Lancelyn. "Lewis Carroll's Periodical Publications." N&Q, 1 (1954), 118-21.

CARY, HENRY FRANCIS

See No. 1091.

CAVE, EDWARD

See also Nos. 303 and 895.

1883. Carlson, C. Lennart. "Edward Cave's Club, and Its Project for a Literary Review." PQ, 12 (1938), 115-20.

1884. Limouze, A.S. "A Note on Edward Cave's Early London Career." N&Q, 193 (1948), 342-43.

CENTLIVRE, SUSANNA

See also FEMALE TATLER (chapter 3).

1885. Bowyer, John Wilson. THE CELEBRATED MRS. CENTLIVRE. Durham, N.C.: Duke University Press, 1952.

1886. Norton, J.E. "Some Uncollected Authors XIV: Susanna Centlivre." BC, 6 (1957), 172-78, 280-85.

Includes bibliographical description of "Poems Published in Periodicals."

CHAPMAN, DR. JOHN

See No. 1765.

CHATTERTON, THOMAS

See also Nos. 448, 1301, and 1782.

1887. Hyett, Francis Adams, and the Rev. Canon Bazeley, with numerous additions by F.A.H. CHATTERTONIANA. A CLASSIFIED CATALOGUE OF BOOKS, PAMPHLETS, MAGAZINE ARTICLES, AND OTHER PRINTED MATTER, RELATING TO THE LIFE OR WORKS OF CHATTERTON, OR TO THE ROWLEY CONTROVERSY. Reprinted from the BIBLIOGRAPHER'S MANUAL OF GLOUCESTERSHIRE LITERATURE. Gloucester: John Bellows, 1914.

1888. Meyerstein, E.H.W. A LIFE OF THOMAS CHATTERTON. London: Ingpen and Grant, 1930.

1889. Taylor, Donald S., ed., with Benjamin B[eard]. Hoover. THE COMPLETE WORKS OF THOMAS CHATTERTON. 2 vols. Oxford: Clarendon Press, 1971.

Reviewed in PQ, 51:656.

1890. Werkmeister, Lucyle. "Chatterton and the London Daily Press (1792-96)." N&Q, 210 (1965), 27-28.

CHAUCER, GEOFFREY

See Nos. 825, 1557, 1718, and 1729

CHESELDEN, WILLIAM

See No. 970.

CHESTERFIELD, EARL OF. PHILIP DORMER STANHOPE

See Nos. 1739 and 1781.

CHURCHILL, CHARLES

See also Nos. 425, 1070, 1071, 1262, 1267, and 2223.

1891. Weatherly, E.H. "Possible Additions to the Churchill Canon." MLN, 60 (1945), 453-58.

Concerns unsigned poems in THE LIBRARY; OR, MORAL AND CRITICAL MAGAZINE, 1761-62.

CIBBER, COLLEY

See Nos. 666, 896, and 1984.

CLARE, JOHN

See Nos. 1081 and 1488.

COBBETT, WILLIAM

See also No. 1334.

1892. Cole, G.D.H. THE LIFE OF WILLIAM COBBETT. London: W. Collins Sons, 1924.

For other biographies of Cobbett, see Cannon, JOURNALISM (no. 26), p. 63.

1893. Davis, C. Rexford. "William Cobbett: Champion of Freedom." JRUL, 15 (1951), 1-12.

1894. Jensen, Jay. "William Cobbett: John Bull as Journalist." EUQ, 21 (1966), 173-82.

COCKBURN, REV. JOHN

See No. 513.

COCKERELL, SYDNEY

1895. B[riggs], R.C.H. "'I am, Sir, your obedient servant.'" JOURNAL OF THE WILLIAM MORRIS SOCIETY, 1, ii (1962), 18-28.

A list of Cockerell's letters to the press.

COLBURN, HENRY

See No. 1252.

COLERIDGE, SAMUEL TAYLOR

See also FRIEND and WATCHMAN (chapter 3), and Nos. 460, 486, 517, 541, 657, 658, 671, 689, 690, 693, 742, 1177, 1180, 1481, and 1698.

1896. Adams, Maurianne, and Richard Haven. "Coleridge in Victorian Journalism." VPN, no. 2 (June 1968), pp. 20-22.

A report of a bibliography in progress.

1897. Carver, P.L. "The Authorship of a Review of CHRISTABEL Attributed to Hazlitt." JEGP, 29 (1930), 562-78.

1898. D'Itri, Patricia A. "A Study of Samuel Taylor Coleridge's Critical Reception in Five Major Nineteenth Century Periodicals." DAI, 30 (1969), 2479A-80A.

1899. Erdman, David V. "Newspaper Sonnets Put to the Concordance Test: Can They be Attributed to Coleridge?" BNYPL, 61 (1957), 508-16, 611-20; 62 (1958), 46-49.

1900. Haney, John Louis. A BIBLIOGRAPHY OF SAMUEL TAYLOR COLERIDGE. Philadelphia: Printed for private circulation, 1903.

For contributions to periodicals, see pages 44-45.

1901. Patterson, Charles I. "The Authenticity of Coleridge's Reviews of Gothic Romances." JEGP, 50 (1951), 517-21.

1902. Shaaber, Matthias A. "Coleridge as a Journalist." JQ, 7 (1930), 236-50.

1903. Shepherd, Richard Herne. THE BIBLIOGRAPHY OF COLERIDGE. A BIBLIOGRAPHICAL LIST ARRANGED IN CHRONOLOGICAL ORDER OF THE PUBLISHED AND PRIVATELY-PRINTED WRITINGS IN VERSE AND PROSE OF SAMUEL TAYLOR COLERIDGE, INCLUDING HIS CONTRIBUTIONS TO ANNUALS, MAGAZINES, AND PERIODICAL PUBLICATIONS. . . . Rev., corrected and enl. by Colonel W.F. Prideaux. London: Frank Hollings, 1900.

1904. Stuart, Daniel. "Anecdotes of the Poet Coleridge." GENTLEMAN'S MAGAZINE, 9 (1838), 485-92, 557-90; 10 (1838), 22-27, 124-28.

The editor of the MORNING POST attempts to clarify Coleridge's connection with that paper, and to show by his correspondence with the poet and with his nephew H.N. Coleridge the injustice of the claim that Coleridge's writing was a principal agent in the rise of the MORNING POST.

COLLINS, CHURTON

See No. 286.

COLLINS, WILLIAM

1905. Werkmeister, Lucyle. "Collins and the London Daily Press, 1788-1798."

N&Q, 210 (1965), 225-27.

Posthumous references to Collins.

COLMAN, GEORGE, THE ELDER

1906. Page, Eugene R. GEORGE COLMAN THE ELDER, ESSAYIST, DRAMATIST, AND THEATRICAL MANAGER, 1732-1794. Columbia University Studies in English and Comparative Literature, no. 120. New York: Columbia University Press, 1935.

Includes discussion of Colman's relation to the CONNOISSEUR, ST. JAMES'S CHRONICLE, and other journals.

COMBE, WILLIAM

See No. 1696.

CONGREVE, WILLIAM

See No. 1845.

CONINGSBY, GEORGE

See No. 1167.

COOK, E.T.

See No. 1311.

COWPER, WILLIAM

See also Nos. 431, 481, 639, 788, and 1347.

1907. Hartley, Lodwick. WILLIAM COWPER: HUMANITARIAN. Chapel Hill: University of North Carolina Press, 1938.

1908. _____. "'The Stricken Deer' and his Contemporary Reputation." SP, 36 (1939), 637-50.

1909. _____. WILLIAM COWPER: A LIST OF CRITICAL AND BIOGRAPHICAL STUDIES PUBLISHED FROM 1895 TO 1949. STATE COLLEGE RECORD, vol. 49, no. 6. Raleigh: North Carolina State College, 1950.

1910. ______. WILLIAM COWPER: THE CONTINUING REVALUATION. Chapel Hill: University of North Carolina Press, 1960.

1911. Werkmeister, Lucyle. "Two Early Versions of Cowper's 'The Negro's Complaint.'" N&Q, 207 (1962), 26-27.

CRABB, JOHN

See No. 719.

CRABBE, GEORGE

1912. Prichard, M.F. Lloyd. "George Crabbe's First Appearance in Print?" N&Q, 199 (1954), 263-64.

Crabbe contributed a solution to an arithmetic problem to the NORWICH MERCURY, August 1766.

CROKER, JOHN WILSON

See QUARTERLY REVIEW (chapter 3) and Nos. 741 and 1374.

CROLY, GEORGE

See No. 560.

CROSS-GROVE, HENRY

1913. Williams, J.B. "Henry Cross-Grove, Jacobite, Journalist and Printer." LIBRARY, 5 (1914), 206-19.

CUMBERLAND, RICHARD

1914. Williams, Stanley Thomas. RICHARD CUMBERLAND. HIS LIFE AND DRAMATIC WORKS. New Haven, Conn.: Yale University Press, 1917.

CURLL, EDMUND

See also Nos. 240 and 1743.

1915. Straus, Ralph. THE UNSPEAKABLE CURLL. BEING SOME ACCOUNT OF EDMUND CURLL, BOOKSELLER; TO WHICH IS ADDED A FULL LIST OF HIS BOOKS. London: Chapman and Hall, 1927.

CUST, HARRY

See No. 1311.

DALLAS, E.S.

See No. 1287.

DALRYMPLE, SIR DAVID, LORD HAILES

1916. Carnie, Robert Hay. "Lord Hailes's Contributions to Contemporary Magazines." SB, 9 (1957), 233-44.

DEFOE, DANIEL

See also REVIEW (Defoe's; chapter 3) and Nos. 165, 177, 213, 238, 271, 499, 721, 807, 1126, 1127, 1137, 1155, 1167, 1655, 1741, 1745, 1854, and 2189.

1917. Andersen, Hans Holst. "Daniel Defoe: A Study in the Conflict Between Commercialism and Morality in the Early Eighteenth Century." [University of Chicago] ABSTRACTS OF THESES, Humanistic Series, 9 (1930-32), 431-35.

1918. ______. "The Paradox of Trade and Morality in Defoe." MP, 39 (1941), 23-46.

1919. Bateson, Thomas. "The Relations of Defoe and Harley." EHR, 15 (1900), 239-50.

1920. Charlton, J.E. "De Foe--the Journalist." METHODIST REVIEW, 91 (1909), 219-30.

1921. "Daniel Defoe." CORNHILL MAGAZINE, 23 (1871), 310-20.

1922. Dobrée, Bonamy. "Some Aspects of Defoe's Prose." POPE AND HIS CONTEMPORARIES: ESSAYS PRESENTED TO GEORGE SHERBURN. Ed. James L. Clifford and Louis A. Landa. Oxford: Clarendon Press, 1949. Pp. 171-84.

1923. Forster, John. "Daniel De Foe." HISTORICAL AND BIOGRAPHICAL ESSAYS. 2 vols. London: John Murray, 1858. II, 1-103.

From EDINBURGH REVIEW, October 1845, with additions.

1924. Hobman, D.L. "Defoe the Journalist." FORTNIGHTLY, no. 1029 (September 1952), pp. 203-7.

1925. Jackson, Alfred. "Defoe, Ward, Brown and Tutchin, 1700-1703." N&Q, 162 (1932), 418-23.

References to these four men and work they contributed to newspapers.

1926. Lee, William. DANIEL DEFOE: HIS LIFE, AND RECENTLY DISCOVERED WRITINGS: EXTENDING FROM 1716 TO 1729. 3 vols. Vol. I, the LIFE; vols. II-III, the WRITINGS COLLECTED FROM MERCURIUS POLITICUS, MIST'S JOURNAL, WHITEHALL EVENING POST, DAILY POST, APPLEBEE'S JOURNAL, UNIVERSAL SPECTATOR, and FOG'S JOURNAL. London: Hotten, 1869.

Reviewed in BLACKWOOD'S EDINBURGH MAGAZINE, 106: 457-87.

1927. ______. "Daniel Defoe, the News Writer." N&Q, 7 (1865), 244-46.

1928. Moore, John Robert. DEFOE IN THE PILLORY AND OTHER STUDIES. Indiana University Publications, Humanistic Series, no. 1. Bloomington: Indiana University Press, 1939.

1929. ______. "Daniel Defoe, Ambidextrous Mercury." PERIODICAL POST-BOY, 11 (1952), 1-2.

1930. ______. "Daniel Defoe: Star Reporter." BOSTON PUBLIC LIBRARY QUARTERLY, 6 (1954), 195-205.

While Defoe was in Scotland (1706-8) as Harley's agent, he also served as a reporter for Fonvive's London newspaper, THE POST-MAN.

1931. ______. "The Canon of Defoe's Writings." LIBRARY, 11 (1956), 155-69.

Includes comments on Defoe's periodical publications.

1932. ______. DANIEL DEFOE: CITIZEN OF THE MODERN WORLD. Chicago: University of Chicago Press, 1958.

Reviewed in PQ 38:316-19; SAQ 58:495-96; JEGP 58:705-7; JMH 31:361-2.

1933. ______. A CHECKLIST OF THE WRITINGS OF DANIEL DEFOE. Bloomington: Indiana University Press, 1960.

Reviewed in PQ 40:63-64; PBSA 55:164-67; N&Q 207:468-71; LIBRARY 17:323-25.

1934. _____. A CHECKLIST OF THE WRITINGS OF DANIEL DEFOE. 2nd ed. Hamden, Conn.: Archon, 1971.

1935. Murray, John J. "Defoe: News Commentator and Analyst of Northern European Affairs." INDIANA QUARTERLY FOR BOOKMEN, 3 (1947), 39-50.

1936. Payne, William Lytton. MR. REVIEW: DANIEL DEFOE AS AUTHOR OF THE 'REVIEW.' New York: King's Crown Press, 1947.

Reviewed in SAQ 46:584-85; MLN 63:564-65; MLQ 9:363-65.

1937. Roscoe, E.S. "Harley and De Foe, 1703-1714." ROBERT HARLEY, OF OXFORD PRIME MINISTER, 1710-1714; A STUDY OF POLITICS AND LETTERS IN THE AGE OF ANNE. London: Methuen, 1902. Pp. 47-74.

1938. Starr, G.A. DEFOE AND CASUISTRY. Princeton, N.J.: Princeton University Press, 1971.

Includes a discussion of the REVIEW and the influence of the ATHENIAN MERCURY. Reviewed in PQ, 51:664-65.

1939. Sutherland, James. DEFOE. Philadelphia and New York: Lippincott, 1938.

1940. _____. DEFOE. Writers and Their Work, no. 51. London: Longmans, Green for the British Council and The National Book League, 1954.

Includes a very brief discussion of Defoe's journalistic career.

1941. _____. DANIEL DEFOE: A CRITICAL STUDY. Cambridge, Mass.: Harvard University Press, 1971.

Reviewed in PQ, 51:665-66.

1942. Watson, Francis. "Daniel Defoe, Father of Modern Journalism." BOOKMAN (London), 80 (1931), 16-18.

1943. Wilson, Walter. MEMOIRS OF THE LIFE AND TIME OF DANIEL DE FOE. 3 vols. London: Hurst, Chance, 1830.

1944. Wright, Herbert G. "Defoe's Writings on Sweden." RES, 16 (1940), 25-32.

1945. Wright, Thomas. THE LIFE OF DANIEL DEFOE. Bicentenary ed. London: C.J. Farncombe & Sons, 1931.

DE'PRATI, DR.

1946. Haven, Richard. "Dr. De'Prati: A Note and a Query." VPN, 16 (1972), 47-50.

DE QUINCEY, THOMAS

See also Nos. 518, 776, 1027, 1088, 1548, 1768, and 1769.

1947. Jordan, John E. THOMAS DEQUINCEY: LITERARY CRITIC. Berkeley and Los Angeles: University of California Press, 1952.

Some of the criticism discussed appeared in periodicals.

1948. Tave, Stuart M. NEW ESSAYS BY DE QUINCEY: HIS CONTRIBUTIONS TO THE 'EDINBURGH SATURDAY POST' AND THE 'EDINBURGH EVENING POST,' 1827-28. Princeton, N.J.: Princeton University Press, 1966.

DIBDIN, CHARLES

See No. 30.

DICEY, EDWARD

See No. 1283.

DICKENS, CHARLES

See also ALL THE YEAR ROUND, DAILY NEWS, HOUSEHOLD WORDS, and MORNING CHRONICLE (all chapter 3), and Nos. 487, 739, 1030, 1159, 1338, 1565, and 1714.

1949. Carlton, William J. "John Dickens, Journalist." DICKENSIAN 53 (1957), 5-11.

1950. ______. "Charles Dickens, Dramatic Critic." DICKENSIAN, 56 (1960), 11-27.

1951. Collins, Philip Arthur William. DICKENS' PERIODICALS: ARTICLES

ON EDUCATION, AN ANNOTATED BIBLIOGRAPHY. Vaughan College Papers, no. 3. Leicester: University of Leicester, 1957.

1952. Coolidge, Archibald Cary, Jr. "Serialization in the Novels of Charles Dickens." DA, 16 (1956), 2455-56.

1953. Dexter, Walter. "Charles Dickens: Journalist." NC, 115 (1934), 705-16.

1954. Fielding, K.J. "The Monthly Serialisation of Dickens's Novels." DICKENSIAN, 54 (1958), 4-11.

1955. _____. "The Weekly Serialisation of Dickens's Novels." DICKENSIAN, 54 (1958), 134-41.

1956. Grubb, Gerald G. "Charles Dickens: Journalist." Diss. University of North Carolina, 1940.

1957. _____. "Dickens's First Experience as a Parliamentary Reporter." DICKENSIAN, 36 (1941), 211-18.

1958. _____. "Dickens' Pattern of Weekly Serialization." ELH, 9 (1942), 141-56.

1959. _____. "Dickens' Editorial Methods." SP, 40 (1943), 79-100.

1960. _____. "The Editorial Policies of Charles Dickens." PMLA, 58 (1943), 110-24.

1961. Hatton, T., and A.H. Cleaver. A BIBLIOGRAPHY OF THE PERIODICAL WORKS OF CHARLES DICKENS. BIBLIOGRAPHICAL. ANALYTICAL. STATISTICAL. London: Chapman and Hall, 1934.

1962. Levy, Herman Mittle, Jr. "Dickens and the Novel in Parts." DA, 26 (1966), 6024.

1963. "A New Contribution [by Dickens] to the MONTHLY MAGAZINE and an Early Dramatic Criticism in the MORNING CHRONICLE." DICKENSIAN, 30 (1934), 223-25.

1964. Rathburn, Robert Charles. "Dickens' Periodical Essays and Their Relationship to the Novels." DA, 17 (1957), 2002.

1965. Stone, Harry. "Dickens and the Idea of a Periodical: A History of the Triumphant Will." WHR, 21 (1967), 237-65.

1966. Troughton, Marion. "Dickens as Editor." ConR, no. 1094 (1957), pp. 87-91.

D'ISRAELI, ISAAC

See also Nos. 1393 and 1776.

1967. Paston, George. "The Young Disraeli and his Adventures in Journalism." CORNHILL MAGAZINE, 73 (1932), 385-99.

DODGSON, CHARLES LUTWIDGE

See CARROLL, LEWIS (above).

DODSLEY, ROBERT

See also ANNUAL REGISTER (chapter 3) and Nos. 1232, 1340, 1341, and 1986.

1968. Dobson, Austin. "At 'Tully's Head.'" EIGHTEENTH CENTURY VIGNETTES. Second series. New York: Dodd, Mead, 1894. Pp. 28-56.

1969. Straus, Ralph. ROBERT DODSLEY, POET, PUBLISHER & PLAYWRIGHT. London: John Lane, 1910.

Bibliography gives chronological lists of Dodsley's own works and of the works published by him.

DOUCE, FRANCIS

1970. Munby, A.N.L. "The Pains of Authorship: Francis Douce and the Edinburgh Reviewers." EIGHTEENTH-CENTURY STUDIES IN HONOR OF DONALD F. HYDE. Ed. W.H. Bond. New York: Grolier Club, 1970. Pp. 339-45.

DOYLE, RICHARD

See No. 1361.

DRYDEN, JOHN

See also Nos. 276 and 1797.

1971. Sutherland, W.O.S., Jr. "Dryden's Use of Popular Imagery in THE MEDAL." UNIVERSITY OF TEXAS STUDIES IN ENGLISH, 35 (1956), 123-34.

Shows a similarity between Dryden's images and allusions and those in contemporary pamphlets and periodicals.

DUNTON, JOHN

See also ATHENIAN GAZETTE (chapter 3) and Nos. 240, 303, and 1777.

1972. Hatfield, Theodore M. "John Dunton's Periodicals." JQ, 10 (1933), 209-25.

Adds periodicals omitted from TIMES HANDLIST (No. 106), Graham (No. 51), and Crane & Kaye (No. 32), and identifies as Dunton's several others that are listed therein.

1973. _____. "The True Secret History of Mr. John Dunton." HARVARD UNIVERSITY SUMMARIES OF THESES [FOR] 1926, 1930. Pp. 175-77.

1974. McCutcheon, Roger P. "John Dunton's Connection with Book-Reviewing." SP, 25 (1928), 346-61.

1975. Moore, C.A. "John Dunton: Pietist and Imposter." SP, 22 (1925), 467-99.

1976. _____. BACKGROUNDS OF ENGLISH LITERATURE, 1700-1760. Minneapolis: University of Minnesota Press, 1953.

Contains an essay on Dunton as conductor of the ATHENIAN GAZETTE.

DYER, JOHN

See No. 1580.

EGERTON, GEORGE

See BRIGHT, MARY DUNNE (above).

ELIOT, GEORGE

1977. Rust, James Darius. "George Eliot's Periodical Contributions." DA, 27 (1966), 186A.

ELLIOTT, EBENEZER

See No. 1370.

ELLIS, GEORGE

See No. 469.

EVANS, MARY ANN

See ELIOT, GEORGE (above).

FARLEY, FELIX

See BRISTOL JOURNAL (chapter 3).

FIELDING, HENRY

See also CHAMPION and COVENT GARDEN JOURNAL (chapter 3), and Nos. 30, 660, 966, 1526, 1711, 1712, 1746, 1809, and 1996.

1978. Banerji, H.K. HENRY FIELDING: PLAYWRIGHT, JOURNALIST AND MASTER OF THE ART OF FICTION. Oxford: Basil Blackwell, 1929.

Chapter IV is on the CHAMPION; chapter VII is on "politi- TLS, 28 March 1959, p. 170; PQ 38:327-28.

1979. Cleary, Thomas R. "Henry Fielding as a Periodical Essayist." DAI, 31 (1971), 6544A.

1980. Cross, Wilbur L. THE HISTORY OF HENRY FIELDING. 3 vols. New Haven, Conn.: Yale University Press, 1918.

1981. Dudden, F. Homes. HENRY FIELDING: HIS LIFE, WORKS, AND TIMES. 2 vols. Oxford: Clarendon Press, 1952.

Contains discussion of Fielding's journalistic activities, but was very unfavorably reviewed in PQ, 33 (1953), 268.

1982. Leslie-Melville, A.R. "Henry Fielding." TLS, 27 July 1933, p. 512.

On nine letters signed Philanthropos which appeared in the LONDON DAILY ADVERTISER and GENTLEMAN'S MAGAZINE, 1751-53.

1983. MISCELLANIES BY HENRY FIELDING, ESQ; VOLUME ONE. Ed. Henry Knight Miller. The Wesleyan Edition of the Works of Henry Fielding. Oxford: Clarendon Press, 1972.

1984. Nichols, Charles W. "Fielding and the Cibbers." PQ, 1 (1922), 278-89.

In his four satirical plays of 1736-37 Fielding was using jokes against the Cibbers common to the journals of the day.

1985. Rogers, Winfield H. "The Significance of Fielding's TEMPLE BEAU." PMLA, 55 (1940), 440-44.

On the relation of the play to SPECTATOR, no. 105 and GUARDIAN no. 94.

1986. Seymour, Mabel. "Fielding's History of the Forty-Five." PQ, 14 (1935), 105-25.

Deals with the dependence of the HISTORY OF THE PRESENT REBELLION IN SCOTLAND on the LONDON GAZETTE, and the inclusion of Fielding's larger history of the rising (SUCCINCT HISTORY OF THE REBELLION) in Dodsley's MUSEUM (1746).

1987. Steward, Mary Margaret. "Notes on Henry Fielding as a Magistrate." N&Q, 214 (1969), 348-50.

Material from three newspapers, 1748-49.

FLATMAN, THOMAS

See No. 989.

FORSTER, JOHN

See No. 804.

FOX, W.J.

See No. 1193.

FRASER, JAMES

1988. Henderson, James Mercer. "James Fraser, 1645-1731." ABERDEEN UNIVERSITY REVIEW, 25 (1938), 138-46.

The licenser who succeeded Sir Roger L'Estrange.

FROUDE, JAMES ANTHONY

See No. 840.

GARVIN, J.L.

See No. 1311.

GASKELL, ELIZABETH

See also No. 1312.

1989. Carwell, Virginia Alice. "Serialization and the Fiction of Mrs. Gaskell." DA, (1966), 3328.

GAY, JOHN

See also No. 195.

1990. Gay, John. THE PRESENT STATE OF WIT (1711). Intro. Donald F. Bond. And excerpts from THE ENGLISH THEOPHRASTUS: OR THE MANNERS OF THE AGE (1702). With an Introduction by W. Earl Britton. Augustan Reprint Society, Ser. I: Essays on Wit, no. 3. Los Angeles: Clark Memorial Library, 1947.

THE PRESENT STATE OF WIT describes the termination of the TATLER; THE ENGLISH THEOPHRASTUS is attributed to Abel Boyer, editor of the POST BOY from 1705-9.

1991. Irving, William Henry. JOHN GAY, FAVORITE OF THE WITS. Duke University Publications. Durham, N.C.: Duke University Press, 1940.

See chapter 1 for the BRITISH APOLLO.

GAYLARD, DOCTOR

See No. 1125.

GEREE, JOHN

See No. 903.

GIBBON, EDWARD

See No. 898.

GIFFORD, WILLIAM

See also QUARTERLY REVIEW (chapter 3).

1992. Clark, Roy Benjamin. WILLIAM GIFFORD: TORY SATIRIST, CRITIC AND EDITOR. Columbia University Studies in English and Comparative Literature. New York: Columbia University Press, 1930.

Chater III is on the ANTI-JACOBIN.

GILBERT, W.S.

See also No. 865.

1993. Duboise, A.E. "Additions to the Bibliography of W.S. Gilbert's Contributions to Magazines." MLN, 47 (1932), 308-14.

GILLIES, ROBERT PEARSE

See 514 and 829.

GILLRAY, JAMES

See No. 477.

GISSING, GEORGE

See No. 242.

GLADSTONE, WILLIAM EWART

See No. 1396.

GODWIN, WILLIAM

See also Nos. 30, 475, 1241, and 1332.

1994. Godwin, William. UNCOLLECTED WRITINGS (1785-1822): ARTICLES IN PERIODICALS AND SIX PAMPHLETS, ONE WITH COLERIDGE'S MARGINALIA.

Facsims., with intros., by Jack W. Marken and Burton R. Pollin. Gainesville, Fla.: Scholars' Facsimiles & Reprints, 1968.

1995. Pollin, Burton R. GODWIN CRITICISMS, A SYNOPTIC BIBLIOGRAPHY. Toronto: University of Toronto Press, 1967.

Includes materials found in periodicals.

GOLDSMITH, OLIVER

See also BEE, CRITICAL REVIEW, and PUBLIC LEDGER (all chapter 3), and Nos. 453, 595, 635, 673, 674, 781, 1036, 1061, 1064, 1161, 1197, 1719, 1721, 1722, 1748, 1749, and 1809.

1996. Balderston, Katherine C. "Goldsmith's Supposed Attack on Fielding." MLN, 42 (1927), 165-68.

On Letter 83 of the CITIZEN OF THE WORLD.

1997. "The Citizen of the World." BOOKWORM, 2 (1889), 217-20.

1998. Crane, Ronald S. "Goldsmith's 'Essays': Dates of Original Publication." N&Q, 153 (1927), 153.

Considers the journals in which some of the essays first appeared.

1999. Crane, Ronald S., and Hamilton Jewett Smith. "A French Influence on Goldsmith's CITIZEN OF THE WORLD." MP, 19 (1921), 83-92.

2000. Davidson, Levette Jay. "Forerunners of Goldsmith's THE CITIZEN OF THE WORLD." MLN, 36 (1921), 215-20.

2001. Dobson, Austin. "'The Citizen of the World.'" EIGHTEENTH CENTURY VIGNETTES. First Series. New York: Dodd, Mead, 1892. Pp. 115-24.

2002. Friedman, Arthur. "The Immediate Occasion of Goldsmith's CITIZEN

OF THE WORLD, Letter XXXVIII." PQ, 17 (1938), 82-84.

2003. _____. "Goldsmith and Steele's ENGLISHMAN." MLN, 55 (1940), 294-96.

Goldsmith's borrowing from the ENGLISHMAN, no. 40, for his CITIZEN OF THE WORLD, Letter 78.

2004. _____. "Goldsmith and Hanway." MLN, 66 (1951), 553-54.

A source for a portion of CITIZEN OF THE WORLD, Letter 104.

2005. _____, ed. COLLECTED WORKS OF OLIVER GOLDSMITH. 5 vols. Oxford: Clarendon Press, 1966.

Reviewed in PQ 46:349-50; MLR 62:512-14; JEGP 66:459-61.

2006. Goldsmith, Oliver. THE CITIZEN OF THE WORLD. THE BEE. Ed. [Henry] Austin Dobson. Intro. Richard Church. Everyman's Library. London: J.M. Dent & Sons, 1934.

Reviewed in TLS, 1 March 1934, pp. 133-34.

2007. _____. NEW ESSAYS. Coll., ed., intro., notes by Ronald S. Crane. Chicago: University of Chicago Press, 1927.

Eighteen essays contributed anonymously to the BRITISH MAGAZINE, ROYAL MAGAZINE, PUBLIC LEDGER, LADY'S MAGAZINE, and LLOYD'S EVENING POST between 1760-62.

2008. Hawkins, Marion Elizabeth. "Oliver Goldsmith the Essayist: A Study of Themes and Style." DA, 25 (1965), 5904-5.

2009. Hopkins, Robert H. THE TRUE GENIUS OF OLIVER GOLDSMITH. Baltimore: Johns Hopkins University Press, 1969.

Reviewed in PQ 49:353-54; JEGP 69:524-25; MLQ 31:121-23; ELN 8:56-58.

2010. Jones, Claude E. "Goldsmith's 'Natural History'--A Plan." N&Q, 191 (1946), 116-17.

Reprints a plan of Goldsmith's work from the CRITICAL REVIEW (November 1774).

2011. Kirk, Clara M. OLIVER GOLDSMITH. Twayne's English Authors. New York: Twayne, 1967.

2012. Milner-Barry, Alda. "A Note on the Early Literary Relations of Oliver Goldsmith and Thomas Percy." RES, 2 (1926), 51-61.

2013. Quintana, Ricardo. "Oliver Goldsmith As a Critic of the Drama. SEL, 5 (1965), 435-54.

2014. ______. OLIVER GOLDSMITH, A GEORGIAN STUDY. Masters of World Literature Series. New York: Macmillan, 1967.

2015. Reding, Katherine. "A Study of the Influence of Oliver Goldsmith's CITIZEN OF THE WORLD upon the CARTAS MARRUECAS of Jose Cadalso." HISPANIC REVIEW, 2 (1934), 226-34.

The CARTAS MARRUECAS ran in the CORREO DE LOS CIEGOS DE MADRID from 14 February to 25 July 1789.

2016. Seitz, R.W. "GOLDSMITH'S LIVES OF THE FATHERS." MP, 26 (1929), 295-305.

Discusses Goldsmith's connection with the CHRISTIAN'S MAGAZINE and assigns to him two essays in the CRITICAL REVIEW.

2017. Sherwin, Oscar. GOLDY: THE LIFE AND TIMES OF OLIVER GOLDSMITH. New York: Twayne, 1961.

2018. Smith, Hamilton Jewett. OLIVER GOLDSMITH'S THE CITIZEN OF THE WORLD. A STUDY. Yale Studies in English, no. 71. New Haven, Conn.: Yale University Press, 1926.

2019. ______. "Mr. Tatler of Pekin, China. A Venture in Journalism." ESSAYS IN CRITICISM BY MEMBERS OF THE DEPARTMENT OF ENGLISH, UNIVERSITY OF CALIFORNIA. University of California Publications in English, no. I. Berkeley: University of California Press, 1929. Pp. 155-75.

2020. Tupper, Caroline F. "Essays Erroneously Attributed to Goldsmith." PMLA, 39 (1924), 325-42.

Transfers the authorship of seven essays in the BRITISH MAGAZINE (1761-63) from Goldsmith to Smollett.

2021. Wardle, Ralph M. OLIVER GOLDSMITH. Lawrence: University of Kansas Press, 1957.

Reviewed in MLN 73:442-44; COLLEGE ENGLISH 20:151-52; TLS, 28 March 1959, p. 170; PQ 38:327-28.

GORDON, GEORGE

See No. 1237.

GORDON, THOMAS

2022. Anderson, Paul Bunyan. "Thomas Gordon and John Mottley, A TRIP THROUGH LONDON, 1728." PQ, 19 (1940), 244-60.

GOSSE, EDMUND

See No. 286.

GRAY, THOMAS

2023. Jones, W. Powell. "The Contemporary Reception of Gray's ODES." MP, 28 (1930), 61-82.

2024. Solly, E. "Gray's Elegy." BIBLIOGRAPHER, 5 (1884), 57-61.

Mainly on the relation of the poem to the MAGAZINE OF MAGAZINES.

GREENWOOD, FREDERICK

See No. 1310.

GRIFFITHS, RALPH

See also Nos. 1182, 1198, 1201, 1205, and 1206.

2025. Carlson, C. Lennart. "Thomas Godfrey in England." AL, 7 (1935), 302-9.

His reception by Griffiths in the LIBRARY and MONTHLY REVIEW.

2026. ______. "A Further Note on Thomas Godfrey in England." AL, 9 (1937), 73-76.

Publication of poem by Griffiths in the GRAND MAGAZINE OF UNIVERSAL INTELLIGENCE.

2027. Coleman, Everard Home. "R. Griffiths." N&Q, 11 (1885), 275-76.

See additional notes by Ed. Marshall, S. Arnott, W.E. Buckley, and Fred Norgate (page 276).

HALLAM, HENRY

See Nos. 1376 and 1693.

HAMILTON, WILLIAM GERARD

See No. 1210.

HARDY, THOMAS

See also No. 242.

2028. Lerner, Laurence, and John Holmstrom, eds. THOMAS HARDY AND HIS READERS: A SELECTION OF CONTEMPORARY REVIEWS. New York: Barnes & Noble, 1968.

A number of the reviews are from newspapers and periodicals.

2029. "Hardy's Magazine Editors." TLS, 12 July 1941, p. 335.

HARLAND, ALINE AND HENRY

See No. 1784.

HARLEY, ROBERT, EARL OF OXFORD

See Nos. 807, 1919, 1930, 1937, and 2198.

HARRISON, WILLIAM

See No. 1651.

HAWKESWORTH, JOHN

See Nos. 419, 420, 884, and 901.

HAYS, MARY

See No. 1185.

HAYWOOD, MRS. ELIZA

See also FEMALE SPECTATOR (chapter 3).

2030. Whicher, George Frisbie. THE LIFE AND ROMANCES OF MRS. ELIZA HAYWOOD. Columbia University Studies in English and Comparative Literature. New York: Columbia University Press, 1915.

HAZLITT, WILLIAM

See also BLACKWOOD'S MAGAZINE (chapter 3) and Nos. 390, 727, 735, 757, 760, 761, 771, 785, 1099, 1250, 1502, and 1789.

2031. Baker, Herschel. WILLIAM HAZLITT. Cambridge, Mass.: Harvard University Press, 1962.

2032. Brooks, E.L. "Was William Hazlitt a News Reporter?" N&Q, 1 (1954), 355-56.

2033. Howe, P.P., ed. THE COMPLETE WORKS OF WILLIAM HAZLITT. 21 vols. London and Toronto: Dent, 1930-34.

2034. Jones, David L. "Hazlitt and Hunt at the Opera House." SYMPOSIUM, 16 (1962), 5-6.

2035. Klingopulos, G.D. "Hazlitt as Critic." EC, 6 (1956), 386-403.

2036. Neiss, Douglas J. "Hazlitt and the Press: The Periodical Criticism in England and America." DAI, 32 (1972), 6939A.

2037. Patterson, Charles I. "William Hazlitt as a Critic of Prose Fiction." PMLA, 68 (1953), 1001-16.

2038. Schneider, Elisabeth. THE AESTHETICS OF WILLIAM HAZLITT: A STUDY OF THE PHILOSOPHICAL BASIS OF HIS CRITICISM. Philadelphia: University of Pennsylvania Press, 1933; rpt. 1952.

2039. Sikes, Herschel M. WILLIAM HAZLITT'S THEORY OF LITERARY CRITICISM IN ITS CONTEMPORARY APPLICATION. Diss. New York University, 1957.

HESSEY, JAMES

See No. 1094.

HILL, AARON

See also PROMPTER (chapter 3).

2040. Brewster, Dorothy. AARON HILL, POET, DRAMATIST, PROJECTOR. Columbia University Studies in English and Comparative Literature. New York: Columbia University Press, 1913.

Contains analyses of the PLAIN DEALER and PROMPTER.

HILL, JOHN

See No. 1324.

HILLS, HENRY

See No. 1645.

HOGG, ALEXANDER

See No. 50.

HOGG, JAMES

See Nos. 543, 550, 553, 1628, and 1629.

HOLCROFT, THOMAS

See No. 1680.

HOOD, THOMAS

See No. 1699.

HORNE, R.H.

See No. 1193.

HUME, DAVID

See No. 975.

HUNT, JOHN

See No. 1051.

HUNT, LEIGH

See also EXAMINER, LIBERAL, REFLECTOR (all chapter 3), and Nos. 11, 549, 792, 852, 1193, 1251, 1331, and 1713.

2041. Blunden, Edmund. LEIGH HUNT AND HIS CIRCLE. New York: Harper, 1930.

Also published as LEIGH HUNT, A BIOGRAPHY (London: Cobden-Sanderson, 1930).

2042. Fleece, Jeffrey A. "Leigh Hunt's Theatrical Criticism." Diss. University of Iowa, 1952.

2043. _____. "Leigh Hunt's Shakespearean Criticism." ESSAYS IN HONOR OF WALTER CLYDE CURRY. Nashville, Tenn.: Vanderbilt University Press, 1954. Pp. 181-95.

2044. LEIGH HUNT'S DRAMATIC CRITICISM, 1808-1831. Ed. Lawrence H. Houtchens and Carolyn W. Houtchens. New York: Columbia University Press, 1949; London: Oxford University Press, 1950.

2045. LEIGH HUNT'S LITERARY CRITICISM. Ed. Lawrence Huston Houtchens and Carolyn Washburn Houtchens. New York: Columbia University Press, 1956.

2046. LEIGH HUNT'S POLITICAL AND OCCASIONAL ESSAYS. Ed. Lawrence Huston Houtchens and Carolyn Washburn Houtchens. New York: Columbia University Press, 1962.

2047. Mackerness, E.D. "Leigh Hunt's Musical Journalism." MMR, 86 (1956), 212-22.

2048. Strout, George D. "Leigh Hunt on Wordsworth and Coleridge." KSJ, 6 (1957), 59-73.

2049. Trewin, J.C. "Leigh Hunt as a Dramatic Critic." KSMB, 10 (1959), 14-19.

2050. Wheeler, Paul Mowbray. "The Great Quarterlies of the Early Nineteenth Century and Leigh Hunt." SAQ, 29 (1930), 282-303.

HUTCHESON, FRANCIS

See No. 1600.

HUTTON, RICHARD HOLT

See also READER (chapter 3) and Nos. 1025 and 1624.

2051. LeRoy, Gaylord C. "Richard Holt Hutton." PMLA, 56 (1941), 809-40.

Surveys the controversial literary career of this contributor to the SPECTATOR (1828).

2052. Tener, Robert H. "The Writings of Richard Holt Hutton: A Check-list of Identifications." VPN, 17 (1972), 1-79.

Coeditor of the NATIONAL REVIEW and contributor to the READER (1863).

JAMES, HENRY

See No. 301.

JEFFREY, FRANCIS

See also EDINBURGH REVIEW (chapter 3).

2053. Derby, J. Raymond. "The Paradox of Francis Jeffrey: Reason versus Sensibility." MLQ, 7 (1946), 489-500.

JOHNSON, SAMUEL

See also DAILY ADVERTISER, GENTLEMAN'S MAGAZINE, IDLER, LITERARY MAGAZINE, and RAMBLER (all chapter 3), and Nos. 421-24, 598, 893, 1062, 1063, 1065, 1340, 1350, 1352, 1357, 1534, 1539, 1715, 1723, 1725, 1751, 1781, 1809, and 1823.

2054. Bate, Walter Jackson. THE ACHIEVEMENT OF SAMUEL JOHNSON. New York: Oxford University Press, 1955.

2055. Bloom, Edward Alan. SAMUEL JOHNSON AS JOURNALIST. University of Illinois Disseration Abstract. Urbana: University of Illinois, 1947.

2056. ______. "Symbolic Names in Johnson's Periodical Essays." MLQ, 13 (1952), 33-52.

2057. _____. SAMUEL JOHNSON IN GRUB STREET. Brown University Studies, no. 21. Providence, R.I.: Brown University Press, 1957.

Reviewed in PQ 37:337-38.

2058. Bullough, Geoffrey. "Johnson the Essayist." NEW RAMBLER, 5 ser. C (June 1968), 1633.

A general survey, descriptive rather than analytical, of Johnson's periodical writings.

2059. Chapman, R.W. TWO CENTURIES OF JOHNSONIAN SCHOLARSHIP. David Murray Foundation Lecture. Glasgow: Jackson, Son & Co., 1945.

Reviewed in RES 22:241-42; MLR 41:211-12.

2060. Chapman, R.W., with the collaboration of Allen T. Hazen. "Johnson Bibliography: A Supplement to Courtney." OXFORD BIBLIOGRAPHICAL SOCIETY PROCEEDINGS & PAPERS, 5, iii, for 1938 (1939), 119-66.

See also No. 2065.

2061. Christie, O.F. JOHNSON THE ESSAYIST. HIS OPINIONS ON MEN, MORALS AND MANNERS. A STUDY. London: Grant Richards, 1924.

2062. Clifford, James L. JOHNSONIAN STUDIES, 1887-1950: A SURVEY AND BIBLIOGRAPHY. Minneapolis: University of Minnesota Press; London: Cumberlege, 1951.

An important collection of precise data on 1,753 items with a significant introductory essay.

2063. Clifford, James L., and Donald J. Greene. SAMUEL JOHNSON: A SURVEY AND BIBLIOGRAPHY OF CRITICAL STUDIES. Minneapolis: University of Minnesota Press, 1970.

Reviewed in PQ 50:445-46.

2064. Congleton, J.E. THEORIES OF PASTORAL POETRY IN ENGLAND, 1684-1798. Gainesville: University of Florida Press, 1952.

Includes discussion of Johnson's RAMBLER, nos. 36 and 37.

2065. Courtney, William Prideaux. A BIBLIOGRAPHY OF SAMUEL JOHNSON. REVISED AND SEEN THROUGH THE PRESS BY DAVID NICHOL SMITH. Oxford Historical and Literary Studies, vol. 4. Oxford: Clarendon Press, 1915.

2066. Cyples, William. "Johnson Without Boswell." ConR, 32 (1878), 707-27.

On the RAMBLER, IDLER, ADVENTURER.

2067. Fleeman, J.D. A PRELIMINARY HANDLIST OF DOCUMENTS AND MANUSCRIPTS OF SAMUEL JOHNSON. Oxford: Oxford Bibliographical Society, 1967.

2068. Greene, D.J. "The Johnsonian Canon: A Neglected Attribution." PMLA, 65 (1950), 427-34.

Prints text of "Observations" appended to "A Letter from a French Refugee in America to his Friend a Gentleman in Ireland," which appeared in the LITERARY MAGAZINE (June 1756), and argues that it is by Johnson.

2069. ______. THE POLITICS OF SAMUEL JOHNSON. New Haven, Conn.: Yale University Press, 1960.

Reviewed in PQ 40:81-82; MLR 56:630-31.

2070. ______. SAMUEL JOHNSON. New York: Twayne, 1970.

Reviewed in PQ 50:446-47.

2071. Hagstrum, Jean. SAMUEL JOHNSON'S LITERARY CRITICISM. Minneapolis: University of Minnesota Press; London: Cumberlege, 1952.

2072. Hazen, Allen T. SAMUEL JOHNSON'S PREFACES & DEDICATIONS. New Haven, Conn.: Yale University Press, 1937.

Johnson contributed preliminary matter to the LITERARY MAGAZINE (1756), LONDON CHRONICLE (1757), UNIVERSAL CHRONICLE (1758), and possibly MONTHLY MELODY (1760).

2073. Hutton, Arthur Wollaston. "Dr. Johnson and the 'Gentleman's Magazine.'" ENGLISH ILLUSTRATED MAGAZINE, 17 (1897); rpt. JOHNSON CLUB PAPERS. By various hands. London: T. Fisher Unwin, 1899. Pp. 95-113.

2074. 'THE IDLER' AND 'THE ADVENTURER.' Ed. W[alter]. J[ackson]. Bate, John M. Bullitt, and L.F. Powell. The Yale Edition of the Works of Samuel Johnson, vol. II. New Haven, Conn.: Yale University Press, 1963.

Reviewed in PQ 43:438-39; MLR 59:275-76; MP 61:298-309.

2075. Krutch, Joseph Wood. SAMUEL JOHNSON. New York: Henry Holt, 1944.

2076. Lang, Daniel Robert. DR. SAMUEL JOHNSON IN AMERICA. A STUDY OF HIS REPUTATION: 1750-1812. University of Illinois Thesis Abstract. Urbana: University of Illinois Press, 1939.

2077. McAdam, E.L., Jr. "New Essays by Dr. Johnson." RES, 18 (1942), 197-207.

A series of three essays called "The Weekly Correspondent" which appeared in the PUBLIC LEDGER on 2, 9, and 16 December 1760.

2078. Macray, J. "Dr. Johnson's Early Contributions to a Birmingham Newspaper." N&Q, 2 (1868), 130.

2079. Monk, Samuel H. "Samuel Johnson Quotes Addison." N&Q, 202 (1957), 154.

2080. Reade, Aleyn Lyell. THE DOCTOR'S LIFE, 1735-1740. JOHNSONIAN GLEANINGS. Part VI. London: Privately printed for the author, 1933.

Chapter VIII: "Early Journalistic Writing."

2081. Riely, John Cabell. "The Pattern of Imagery in Johnson's Periodical Essays." ECS, 3 (1970), 384-97.

2082. Rypins, Stanley. "Johnson's Dictionary Reviewed by his Contemporaries." PQ, 4 (1925), 281-86.

2083. Sherbo, Arthur. "Two Additions to the Johnson Canon." JEGP, 52 (1953), 543-48.

The additions are a letter to the DAILY ADVERTISER for 13 April 1739 in defense of the GENTLEMAN'S MAGAZINE, and the "Abridgement of Foreign History" in the GENTLEMAN'S MAGAZINE for November 1747.

2084. Taylor, Warner. "The Prose Style of Johnson." STUDIES BY MEMBERS OF THE DEPARTMENT OF ENGLISH. University of Wisconsin Studies in Language and Literature, no. 2. Madison: University of Wisconsin Press, 1918. Pp. 22-56.

Analysis of stylistic elements; includes study of RAMBLER and IDLER.

2085. Wahba, Magdi, ed. JOHNSONIAN STUDIES, INCLUDING A BIBLIOGRAPHY OF JOHNSONIAN STUDIES, 1950-1960, COMPILED BY JAMES L. CLIFFORD & DONALD J. GREENE. Cairo: Distributed by Oxford University Press, 1962.

This volume includes Arthur Sherbo, "Samuel Johnson and the GENTLEMAN'S MAGAZINE, 1750-1755," pp. 133-59, and "A Bibliography . . .," pp. 263-350. Reviewed in TLS 16 November 1962, p. 874; N&Q 208:394-59.

2086. Wimsatt, W.K., Jr. THE PROSE STYLE OF SAMUEL JOHNSON. Yale Studies in English, vol. XCIV. New Haven, Conn.: Yale University Press, 1941.

Includes discussion of Johnson's style in his contributions to periodicals, especially the RAMBLER.

JONES, ERNEST

2089. Jones, Ernest. 'NOTES TO THE PEOPLE': MAY 1851-MAY 1852. 2 vols. New York: Barnes & Noble, 1968.

A reprint of Jones's journal.

KAMES, HENRY HOME

See No. 2301.

KEATS, JOHN

See also Nos. 11, 434, 608, 610, 1402, and 1546.

2088. Harwell, Thomas Meade. "Keats and the Critics, 1848-1900." DA, 26 (1966), 4628-29.

Much of the criticism was published in periodicals.

2089. Jack, Ian. KEATS AND THE MIRROR OF ART. Oxford: Oxford University Press, 1967.

Chapter 3 discusses ANNALS OF THE FINE ARTS and the EXAMINER.

2090. Marsh, George L., and Newman I. White. "Keats and the Periodicals of His Time." MP, 32 (1934), 37-53.

2091. Schwartz, Lewis M. KEATS REVIEWED BY HIS CONTEMPORARIES: A COLLECTION OF NOTICES FOR THE YEARS 1816-1821. Metuchen, N.J.: Scarecrow, 1973.

KIMBER, ISAAC AND EDWARD

See No. 1090.

KINGSLEY, HENRY

See also No. 891.

2092. Scheuerle, William H. "Periodicals in the Novels of Henry Kingsley." VPN, 12 (1971), 11-14.

KIPLING, RUDYARD

2093. Dua, M.R. "Rudyard Kipling as a Journalist: An Indian Evaluation." JQ, 45 (1968), 113-16.

2094. Rouse, John Junior. "The Literary Reputation of Rudyard Kipling: A Study of the Criticism of Kipling's Works in British Periodicals from 1886-1960." DA, 25 (1964), 1199.

KNAPTON, JAMES

See No. 165.

KNIGHT, CHARLES

See No. 1774.

LAMARTINE, ALPHONSE MARIE DE

2095. Lonbard, C. "Portrait of Lamartine in the English Periodical (1820-70)." MLR, 56 (1961), 335-38.

LAMB, CHARLES

See also Nos. 390, 805, 1022, 1091, 1096, 1192, and 1698.

2096. Baker, Harry Torsey. "Lamb and the Periodical Essay." NORTH AMERICAN REVIEW, 215 (1922), 519-28.

2097. Hutchinson, Thomas, ed. THE WORKS OF CHARLES LAMB. London: Oxford University Press, 1924.

Includes Lamb's contributions to periodicals.

2098. Lamb, Charles. THE COMPLETE WORKS AND LETTERS OF CHARLES LAMB. New York: Modern Library, 1935.

Includes Lamb's contributions to periodicals.

2099. Lucas, E.V. "Charles Lamb as a Journalist." N&Q, 8 (1901), 60-61.

His connection with the ALBION and the MORNING POST (1800-1803). Also in this issue of N&Q, see Alfred Ringer (pages 85-86) and Myops (pages 125-26, 166-68).

LANDOR, WALTER SAVAGE

2100. Proudfit, Charles L. "More Unrecorded Periodical Contributions of Walter Savage Landor." N&Q, 18 (1971), 90-91.

2101. Super, R.H. "Landor's Unrecorded Contributions to Periodicals." N&Q, 197 (1952), 497-98.

LANG, ANDREW

See also No. 286.

2102. Salmond, J.B. ANDREW LANG AND JOURNALISM. Andrew Lang Lecture for 1949. Edinburgh: Nelson, 1950.

LECKY, W.E.H.

See No. 449.

LEMON, MARK

See PUNCH (chapter 3).

LENNOX, CHARLOTTE RAMSAY

2103. Small, Miriam Rossiter. CHARLOTTE RAMSAY LENNOX, AN EIGHTEENTH CENTURY LADY OF LETTERS. Yale Studies in English, vol. LXXXV. New Haven, Conn.: Yale University Press, 1935.

L'ESTRANGE, SIR ROGER

See also OBSERVATOR (chapter 3) and No. 2131.

2104. Allen, C.G. "Roger L'Estrange." TLS, 11 April 1958, p. 195.

Bibliography of L'ESTRANGE HIS APOLOGY.

2105. Kitchin, George. SIR ROGER L'ESTRANGE. A CONTRIBUTION TO THE HISTORY OF THE PRESS IN THE SEVENTEENTH CENTURY. London: Kegan Paul, Trench, Trubner, 1913.

2106. Sensabaugh, George F. "Adaptations of AREOPAGITICA." HLQ, 13 (1950), 201-5.

LEWES, GEORGE HENRY

See No. 523.

LEWIS, JOHN

2107. Jenkins, R.T. "John Lewis, the Printer, and His Family." PROCEEDINGS OF THE WESLEY HISTORICAL SOCIETY, 21 (1938), 128-30.

Lewis printed the WEEKLY HISTORY and the CHRISTIAN'S AMUSEMENT.

LEWIS, RICHARD

See No. 179.

LINTOT, BERNARD

See Nos. 5 and 1173.

LOCKE, JOHN

See No. 1805.

LOCKHART, JOHN GIBSON

See BLACKWOOD'S MAGAZINE and QUARTERLY REVIEW (chapter 3).

2108. Hildyard, Margaret Clive. LOCKHART'S LITERARY CRITICISM, WITH INTRODUCTION AND BIBLIOGRAPHY. Oxford: Oxford University Press, 1931.

LUCAS, SAMUEL

See No. 1285.

LYTTELTON, GEORGE, LORD

2109. Davis, Rose Mary. THE GOOD LORD LYTTELTON. A STUDY IN EIGHTEENTH CENTURY POLITICS AND CULTURE. Bethlehem, Pa.: Times Publishing Co., 1939.

MACAULAY, THOMAS BABINGTON

See Nos. 741, 763, and 765.

MACKENZIE, HENRY

See also Nos. 425 and 1163.

2110. C.,W.A. "'The Scottish Addison.'" N&Q, 2 (1874), 325-26.

2111. Parker, W.M. "'Our Scottish Addison.'" QR, 291 (1953), 248-60.

2112. Thompson, Harold William. A SCOTTISH MAN OF FEELING. SOME ACCOUNT OF HENRY MACKENZIE, ESQ. OF EDINBURGH AND OF THE GOLDEN AGE OF BURNS AND SCOTT. London and New York: Oxford University Press, 1931.

Chapter VIII, "The Scottish Addison," deals with the MIRROR and LOUNGER.

MAGINN, WILLIAM

See No. 845.

MALEBRANCHE, NICHOLAS

See No. 1523.

MANDEVILLE, BERNARD

See Nos. 815 and 823.

MANLEY, MRS. MARY DE LA RIVIÈRE

See also FEMALE TATLER (chapter 3).

2113. Anderson, Paul Bunyan. "Mary de la Rivière Manley, A Cavalier's Daughter in Grub Street." HARVARD UNIVERSITY SUMMARIES OF THESES [FOR] 1931, 1932, pp. 194-97.

2114. ______. "Mistress Delarivière Manley's Biography." MP, 33 (1936), 216-78.

2115. Duff, Dolores Diane Clarke. "Materials toward a Biography of Mary Delarivière Manley." DA, 26 (1965), 6695.

2116. Needham, Gwendolyn B. "Mrs. Manley: An Eighteenth-Century Wife of Bath." HLQ, 15 (1951), 259-84.

The career of one of the presumed authors of the FEMALE TATLER.

MARLOWE, CHRISTOPHER

See Nos. 143 and 448.

MARRYAT, THOMAS

See No. 1195.

MARTYN, JOHN

See No. 970.

MARVELL, ANDREW

See No. 1562.

MASEFIELD, JOHN

See No. 1134.

MATHER, INCREASE

See No. 1281.

MATILDA, ROSA

See No. 1215.

MAXSE, LEO

See No. 1238.

MAYNWARING, ARTHUR

See No. 1445.

MAZZINI, GIUSEPPE

See No. 1758.

MEREDITH, GEORGE

See Nos. 839, 1306, and 1761.

MILL, JOHN STUART

See Nos. 796 and 1757.

MILMAN, HENRY HART

See No. 1395.

MILTON, JOHN

See also Nos. 324, 325, 679, 1152, 1460, 1503, 1540, 1590, 1604, and 2106.

2117. McCarthey, B. Eugene. "Milton Criticism in the First Half of the Eighteenth Century." DA, 28 (1968), 3150A.

2118. Williams, J.B. "John Milton Journalist." OXFORD AND CAMBRIDGE REVIEW, no. 18 (1912), pp. 73-88.

MIST, NATHANIEL

See WEEKLY JOURNAL (chapter 3).

MITFORD, MARY RUSSELL

2119. Coles, William A. "Magazine and Other Contributions by Mary Russell Mitford and Thomas Noon Talfourd." SB, 12 (1959), 218-26.

Identifies reviews of Byron and of the LIBERAL in the LADY'S MAGAZINE and in the LONDON MAGAZINE.

MOIR, DAVID MACBETH

See No. 536.

MOLL, HERMAN

See No. 165.

MONTAGU, EDWARD WORTLEY

See No. 1646.

MOORE, EDWARD

2120. Caskey, John Homer. THE LIFE AND WORKS OF EDWARD MOORE. Yale Studies in English, no. 75. New Haven, Conn.: Yale University Press, 1927.

Chapter X is on the WORLD.

MOORE, GEORGE

See No. 242.

MOORE, THOMAS

See Nos. 742, 761, 770, 771, and 772.

MORGAN, RICHARD COPE

2121. Scott, P.G. "Richard Cope Morgan, Religious Periodicals, and the Pontifex Factor." VPN, 16 (1972), 1-17.

MORLEY, JOHN

See No. 1311.

MORRIS, WILLIAM

See No. 1290.

MOTTEUX, PETER

See also GENTLEMAN'S JOURNAL (chapter 3).

2122. Cunningham, R.N. "A Bibliography of the Writings of Peter Anthony Motteux." OXFORD BIBLIOGRAPHICAL SOCIETY PROCEEDINGS & PAPERS, 3 (1931-33), 317-37.

2123. ______. PETER ANTHONY MOTTEUX, 1663-1718. A BIOGRAPHICAL AND CRITICAL STUDY. Oxford: Blackwell, 1933.

MOTTLEY, JOHN

See No. 2022.

MUDDIMAN, HENRY

2124. Cooper, C.H., and Thompson Cooper. "Henry Muddiman, the News-writer." N&Q, 2 (1862), 147-48.

See also M.A. Everett Green (pages 195-96).

2125. Muddiman, J.G. THE KING'S JOURNALIST, 1659-1689. STUDIES IN THE REIGN OF CHARLES II. London: John Lane, 1923.

2126. T.,W.J. "Henry Muddiman." N&Q, 11 (1861), 328.

See also W.D. Macray (page 459).

MUDIE, GEORGE

2127. Armytage, W.H.G. "George Mudie: Journalist and Utopian." N&Q, 4 (1957), 214-16.

MURPHY, ARTHUR

See also GRAY'S INN JOURNAL (chapter 3) and Nos. 180, 962, 1069, and 2159.

2128. Caskey, J. Homer. "Arthur Murphy and the War on Sentimental Comedy." JEGP, 30 (1931), 563-77.

Uses Murphy's criticism in GRAY'S INN JOURNAL and MONTHLY REVIEW.

2129. Emery, John Pike. "The Life and Works of Arthur Murphy." HARVARD UNIVERSITY SUMMARIES OF THESES [FOR] 1936, 1938, pp. 316-18.

2130. White, Milton Christian. "Arthur Murphy: His Life and Work with Especial Reference to the Contemporary Stage." SUMMARIES OF DOCTORAL DISSERTATIONS, UNIVERSITY OF WISCONSIN, 1 (1935-36), 297-300.

Chapter II is on Murphy's connection with the GRAY'S INN JOURNAL.

MURRAY, JOHN

See Nos. 1373, 1375, 1383, and 1393.

NEALE, JOHN

See No. 1762.

NEEDHAM, MARCHAMONT

See also No. 1152.

2131. Elmes, James. "The Three Patriarchs of Newspapers." N&Q, 6 (1858), 369-71.

On Needham, Sir John Birkenhead, and Sir Roger L'Estrange.

NEWBERRY, JOHN

See Nos. 1161 and 1716.

NEWMAN, JOHN HENRY

See Nos. 1437, 1438, and 1441.

NEWTON, ISAAC

See No. 1504.

NICHOLS, JOHN

See also Nos. 912 and 914.

2132. Dobson, Austin. "A Literary Printer." NATIONAL REVIEW, 61 (1913), 1086-104.

2133. Smith, Albert H. "John Nichols, Printer and Publisher." LIBRARY, 18 (1965), 169-90.

OLDISWORTH, WILLIAM

See No. 806.

OLDMIXON, JOHN

See No. 663.

PACKINGTON, SIR JOHN

See No. 1816.

PATER, WALTER

See No. 1384.

PEACOCK, THOMAS LOVE

2134. Young, A.B. "T.L. Peacock: Contributions to Periodicals." N&Q, 8 (1907), 2-3.

Also in this issue of N&Q, see page 157.

PEELE, GEORGE

See No. 448.

PEPYS, SAMUEL

2135. McCutcheon, Roger P. "Pepys in the Newspapers of 1676-1680." AHR, 32 (1926), 61-64.

PERCY, THOMAS

See No. 2012.

PERKS, JOHN

See No. 1323.

PHILIPS, AMBROSE

See also FREE-THINKER (chapter 3) and No. 971.

2136. Bryan, Adophus Jerome. "The Life and Works of Ambrose Philips." HARVARD UNIVERSITY SUMMARIES OF THESES [FOR] 1936, 1938, pp. 313-16.

PHILLIPS, SIR RICHARD

See also No. 1186.

2137. Herne, Frank S. "An Old Leicester Bookseller (Sir Richard Phillips)." TRANSACTIONS OF THE LEICESTER LITERARY & PHILOSOPHICAL SOCIETY, 3 (1893), 65-73.

Phillips edited the LEICESTER HERALD and the MUSEUM, and published the MONTHLY MAGAZINE.

PITTIS, WILLIAM

2138. Newton, Theodore F.M. "William Pittis and Queen Anne Journalism." MP, 33 (1935-36), 169-86, 279-302.

PLACE, FRANCIS

See Nos. 1756 and 1763.

POPE, ALEXANDER

See also Nos. 679, 972, 1479, 1480, 1510, 1551, 1649, 1797, and 1846.

2139. Griffith, Reginald Harvey. ALEXANDER POPE: A BIBLIOGRAPHY. 2 vols. POPE'S OWN WRITINGS. Vol. I: 1709-34; vol. II: 1735-51. London: Holland Press, 1962.

2140. Lopez, Cecilia A. ALEXANDER POPE: AN ANNOTATED BIBLIOGRAPHY, 1945-1967. Gainesville: University of Florida Press, 1970.

2141. THE PROSE WORKS OF ALEXANDER POPE. Ed. Norman Ault. Vol. I: THE EARLIER WORKS, 1711-1720. Oxford: Blackwell, 1936.

Includes Pope's contributions to the SPECTATOR and GUARDIAN, "acknowledged by Pope himself, previously attributed to him, and now ascribed to him for the first time." Reviewed in RES, 13:488-93.

2142. Sherburn, George. THE EARLY CAREER OF ALEXANDER POPE. Oxford: Clarendon Press, 1934.

Uses considerable evidence from contemporary journals.

2143. Tobin, James Edward. ALEXANDER POPE: A LIST OF CRITICAL STUDIES PUBLISHED FROM 1895 TO 1944. New York: Cosmopolitan Science and Art Service Co., 1945.

Includes studies of Pope's periodical contributions.

POPPLE, WILLIAM

See Nos. 1343 and 1344.

RAWLINS, EDWARD

See No. 989.

REYNOLDS, JOHN HAMILTON

See No. 610.

RHODES, HENRY

See No. 1188.

RICHARDSON, SAMUEL

See Nos. 30, 704, and 705.

2144. McKillop, Alan Dugald. SAMUEL RICHARDSON, PRINTER AND NOVELIST. Chapel Hill: University of North Carolina Press, 1936.

For Richardson's connection with journals (PLAIN DEALER,

PROMPTER, WEEKLY MISCELLANY, DAILY JOURNAL, DAILY GAZETTEER, and CITIZEN) see especially pages 299-308.

RIDPATH, GEORGE

See No. 2145.

RIGBY, ELIZABETH

See No. 1389.

ROBE, REV. JAMES

See Nos. 950-52.

ROBINSON, HENRY CRABB

See No. 1692.

ROLT, RICHARD

See Nos. 1726 and 1727.

ROPER, ABEL

2145. Yeowell, J. "Abel Roper and George Ridpath." N&Q, 8 (1859), 182.

ROSSETTI, DANTE GABRIEL

See GERM (chapter 3).

ROU, LEWIS

See No. 668.

ROWE, NICHOLAS

See No. 422.

RUDDIMAN, THOMAS

2146. Chalmers, George. THE LIFE OF THOMAS RUDDIMAN. London: 1794.

Appendix 6: A chronological list of newspapers, from the epoch of the civil wars.

RUSKIN, JOHN

See No. 524.

RUSSELL, WILLIAM HOWARD

See No. 1694.

SAINTSBURY, GEORGE

See No. 286.

SAULT, RICHARD

See No. 493.

SAVAGE, JOHN

See No. 1488.

SCOTT, JOHN

See also Nos. 551, 554, 556, and 1084.

2147. Hughes, T. Rowland. "John Scott: Editor, Author, and Critic." LONDON MERCURY, 21 (1930), 518-28.

2148. Strout, Alan Lang. "John Scott and Maga." TLS, 29 August 1936, p. 697.

SCOTT, SIR WALTER

See also QUARTERLY REVIEW (chapter 3) and Nos. 533, 552, 1328, 1373, 1379, 1380, 1387, 1400, and 1403.

2149. Ball, Margaret. SIR WALTER SCOTT AS A CRITIC OF LITERATURE. Columbia University Studies in English, ser. II, vol. II, no. 1. New York: Columbia University Press, 1907.

2150. Cline, C.L. "The Fate of Cassandra: The Newspaper War of 1821-22 and Sir Walter Scott." TQ, 14, iv (1971), 6-60.

2151. Corson, James C. A BIBLIOGRAPHY OF SIR WALTER SCOTT. London: Oliver and Boyd, 1943.

2152. Gordon, Robert C. "A Victorian Anticipation of Recent Scott Criticism." PQ, 36 (1957), 272-75.

Concerns reviews of Scott by Carlyle and Wedgwood in Victorian critical journals.

2153. Kern, John D. "An Unidentified Review, Possibly by Scott." MLQ, 6 (1945), 327-28.

2154. Lauber, John. "Scott on the Art of Fiction." SEL, 3 (1963), 543-54.

Includes a discussion of reviews in the QUARTERLY REVIEW, the EDINBURGH REVIEW, and BLACKWOOD'S MAGAZINE.

SHAFTESBURY, ANTHONY ASHLEY COOPER, EARL OF

See No. 783.

SHAKESPEARE, WILLIAM

See Nos. 361, 786, 963, 1345, 1529, 1530, 1548, and 1662.

SHAW, BERNARD

See No. 1484.

SHEBBEARE, JOHN

See No. 672.

SHELLEY, MARY

See No. 533.

SHELLEY, PERCY BYSSHE

See also Nos. 11, 540, 567, 790, 794, 800, 841, 860, 1050, 1216, 1444, 1688, and 1774.

2155. Ward, William S. "Shelley and the Reviewers Once More." MLN, 59 (1944), 539-42.

2156. White, Newman I. THE UNEXTINGUISHED HEARTH: SHELLEY AND HIS CONTEMPORARY CRITICS. Durham, N.C.: Duke University Press, 1938.

SHENSTONE, WILLIAM

See No. 1110.

SHERIDAN, RICHARD BRINSLEY

See Nos. 502 and 1219.

SIMPSON, RICHARD

See Nos. 1440 and 1441.

SMART, CHRISTOPHER

See also GENTLEMAN'S MAGAZINE, LILLIPUTIAN MAGAZINE, MIDWIFE, and UNIVERSAL VISTER (all chapter 3), and Nos. 632 and 928.

2157. Ainsworth, Edward G., and Charles E. Noyes. CHRISTOPHER SMART: A BIOGRAPHICAL AND CRITICAL STUDY. University of Missouri Studies, vol. XVIII, no. 4. Columbia: University of Missouri, 1943.

2158. Botting, Roland B. "Christopher Smart in London." RESEARCH STUDIES OF THE STATE COLLEGE OF WASHINGTON, 7 (1939), 3-54.

2159. ______. "Christopher Smart's Association with Arthur Murphy." JEGP, 43 (1944), 49-56.

2160. Brittain, Robert E. "Christopher Smart in the Magazines." LIBRARY, 21 (1941), 320-36.

2161. Devlin, Christopher. POOR KIT SMART. London: Hart-Davis, 1961.

Reviewed in TLS, 29 December 1961, pp. 921-22.

2162. Gray, G.J. "A Bibliography of the Writings of Christopher Smart, with Biographical References." TRANSACTIONS OF THE BIBLIOGRAPHICAL SOCIETY, 6 (1901), 269-303.

See pages 277-79 and 287-88 for contributions to the MIDWIFE and the UNIVERSAL VISITER.

2163. Grigson, Geoffrey. CHRISTOPHER SMART. Writers and Their Work, no. 136. London: Longmans, Green for the British Council and The National Book League, 1961.

2164. Sherbo, Arthur. "Christopher Smart, Reader of Obituaries." MLN, 71 (1956), 177-82.

Suggests a connection between names in JUBILATE AGNO and in contemporary obituary notices, especially in the GENTLEMAN'S MAGAZINE.

2165. ______. CHRISTOPHER SMART, SCHOLAR OF THE UNIVERSITY. East Lansing: Michigan State University, 1967.

2166. Swann, John H. "Christopher Smart." PAPERS OF THE MANCHESTER LITERARY CLUB, 21 (1902), 18-92.

Touches briefly on Smart's connection with the UNIVERSAL VISITER and that of his wife with the READING MERCURY.

SMELLIE, WILLIAM

See Nos. 686 and 729.

SMITH, ADAM

See No. 510.

SMITH, GEORGE MURRAY

See No. 1310.

SMITH, HORACE

See No. 1252.

SMOLLETT, TOBIAS

See also CRITICAL REVIEW (chapter 3) and Nos. 30 and 2020.

2167. Foster, James R. "Smollett's Pamphleteering Foe Shebbeare." PMLA, 57 (1942), 1053-100.

2168. Knapp, Lewis M. "Smollett and the Elder Pitt." MLN, 59 (1944), 250-57.

2169. Korte, Donald M. AN ANNOTATED BIBLIOGRAPHY OF SMOLLETT SCHOLARSHIP: 1946-1968. Toronto: University of Toronto Press, 1969.

2170. Martz, Louis L. THE LATER CAREER OF TOBIAS SMOLLETT. New Haven, Conn.: Yale University Press, 1942.

2171. Whitridge, Arnold. TOBIAS SMOLLETT: A STUDY OF HIS MISCELLANEOUS WORKS. Diss. Columbia University; [Brooklyn]: Published by the author, [1925].

Chapters on Smollett as journalist and as political pamphleteer.

SOUTHEY, ROBERT

See also Nos. 656, 701, 753, 834, 1197, 1218, 1229, 1370, 1376, and 1378.

2172. Carnall, Geoffrey. ROBERT SOUTHEY AND HIS AGE. Oxford: Clarendon Press, 1960.

Makes extended use of numerous periodicals and newspapers.

2173. Fahey, David M. "Southey's Review of Hallam." N&Q, 211 (1966), 178-79.

2174. Graham, Walter. "Robert Southey as Tory Reviewer." PQ, 2 (1923), 97-111.

SPENSER, EDMUND

See Nos. 679 and 1729.

STEAD, W.T.

See Nos. 580 and 1311.

STEELE, RICHARD

See also ADDISON, JOSEPH (above), HONEST GENTLEMAN, GUARDIAN, SPECTATOR, and TATLER (all chapter 3), and Nos. 390, 1124, 1445, and 2206.

2175. Aitken, George A. THE LIFE OF RICHARD STEELE. 2 vols. London: William Isbister, 1889.

See also the review by [Henry] Austin Dobson in ConR, 56 (1889), 503-15.

2176. Blanchard, Rae. "Richard Steele and the Status of Women." SP, 26 (1929), 325-55.

2177. _____. "Richard Steele's Maryland Story." AQ, 10 (1958), 78-82.

2178. _____, ed. RICHARD STEELE'S PERIODICAL JOURNALISM, 1714-16. THE LOVER, THE READER, TOWN-TALK IN A LETTER TO A LADY IN THE COUNTRY, CHIT-CHAT IN A LETTER TO A LADY IN THE COUNTRY. Oxford: Clarendon Press, 1959.

Reviewed in TLS, 30 October 1959, page 626; PQ, 39:360; MP, 58:60-62; MLR, 56:107-8; RES, 12:299-300; and N&Q, 206:276-77.

2179. _____, ed. TRACTS AND PAMPHLETS BY RICHARD STEELE. Baltimore: Johns Hopkins Press, 1944.

2180. Blunden, Edmund. "Richard Steele." VOTIVE TABLETS: STUDIES CHIEFLY APPRECIATIVE OF ENGLISH AUTHORS AND BOOKS. London: Cobden-Sanderson, 1931. Pp. 107-12.

2181. Connely, Willard. SIR RICHARD STEELE. New York: Scribner, 1934.

2182. Dobson, [Henry] Austin. RICHARD STEELE. English Worthies. New York: D. Appleton, 1886.

2183. Dust, Alvin I. "An Aspect of the Addison-Steele Relationship." ELN, 1 (1964), 196-200.

Financial details after 1707.

2184. Forster, John. "Sir Richard Steele." HISTORICAL AND BIOGRAPHICAL ESSAYS. 2 vols. London: Murray, 1858. II, 105-207.

From QUARTERLY REVIEW (March 1855) with additions. On Macaulay's ON THE LIFE AND WRITINGS OF ADDISON, 1852.

2185. Horne, Colin J. "Notes on Steele and the Beef-Steak Club." RES, 21 (1945), 239-44.

2186. Humphries, A.R. STEELE, ADDISON AND THEIR PERIODICAL ESSAYS. Writers and Their Work, no. 109. London: Longmans, Green for the British Council and The National Book League, 1959.

2187. Kenny, Shirley S. "Recent Scholarship on Richard Steele." BRITISH STUDIES MONITOR, 4 (1973), 12-24.

Includes a bibliography of forty-five items, most dated between 1950-72.

2188. Loftis, John. "The Blenheim Papers and Steele's Journalism, 1715-1718." PMLA, 66 (1951), 197-210.

Finds matters related to TOWN-TALK, CHIT-CHAT, a projected periodical to be entitled the WHIG, and Ambrose Philips's FREE-THINKER in the Steele MSS and memoranda preserved at Blenheim Palace.

2189. Moore, John Robert. "Defoe, Steele, and the Demolition of Dunkirk." HLQ, 13 (1950), 279-302.

Uses these two writers as representative of two opposing views of one of the provisions of the Treaty of Utrecht.

2190. "Richard Steele." TLS, 31 October 1902, p. 321.

2191. "Richard Steele." TLS, 29 August 1929, pp. 657-58.

2192. Routh, Harold. "Steele and Addison." See No. 177.

2193. SELECTIONS FROM THE WORKS OF SIR RICHARD STEELE. Ed., notes, intro. by George Rice Carpenter. Athenaeum Press Series. Boston: Ginn, 1897.

2194. "Sir Richard Steele." QR, 96 (1855), 509-68.

A refutation of Macaulay's "contemptuous depreciation of Steele" in his LIFE AND WRITINGS OF ADDISON.

2195. Thackeray, William Makepeace. "Steele." THE ENGLISH HUMORISTS OF THE EIGHTEENTH CENTURY. The Complete Works, vol. XXIII. New York: Crowell, [1904]. Pp. 83-123.

2196. Tullo, J.K. "Dick Steele." GENTLEMAN'S MAGAZINE, 294 (1903), 457-74.

2197. Waugh, Arthur. "Richard Steele." FR, 132 (1929), 388-96.

2198. Winton, Calhoun. "Steele and the Fall of Harley in 1714." PQ, 37 (1958), 440-47.

Concerns Steele's political journalism.

2199. _____. CAPTAIN STEELE: THE EARLY CAREER OF RICHARD STEELE. Baltimore: Johns Hopkins Press, 1964.

Reviewed in PQ 44:370-71; MP 62:259-60; RES 16:431-32.

2200. _____. SIR RICHARD STEELE, M.P.: THE LATER CAREER. Baltimore: Johns Hopkins Press, 1970.

Reviewed in PQ 50:482-83.

STEPHEN, LESLIE

See also Nos. 650 and 653.

2201. Vogeler, Martha S. "Leslie Stephen's 'Dryasdust.'" VPN, 14 (1972), 23-26.

STEPHENS, HENRY

See FREE-THINKER (chapter 3).

STERNE, LAURENCE

See also Nos. 30, 918, and 1588.

2202. Curtis, Lewis Perry. THE POLITICKS OF LAURENCE STERNE. London: Oxford University Press, 1929.

Includes discussion of the YORK COURANT and YORK GAZETTEER.

2203. Hartley, Lodwick. THIS IS LORENCE: A NARRATIVE OF THE REVER-

END LAURENCE STERNE. Chapel Hill: University of North Carolina Press, 1943.

2204. ______. LAURENCE STERNE IN THE TWENTIETH CENTURY. Chapel Hill: University of North Carolina Press, 1966.

STEVENSON, ROBERT LOUIS

See No. 530.

STRAHAN, ALEXANDER

See No. 1198.

SWIFT, JONATHAN

See also EXAMINER (chapter 3) and Nos. 854, 856, 940, 976, 1011, 1322, 1326, 1471, 1535, 1636, 1651, 1740, and 1793.

2205. Ewald, William Bragg, Jr. THE MASKS OF JONATHAN SWIFT. Oxford: Blackwell; Cambridge, Mass.: Harvard University Press, 1954.

The persona of THE EXAMINER is discussed in chapter vii.

2206. Goldgar, Bertrand A. THE CURSE OF PARTY: SWIFT'S RELATIONS WITH ADDISON AND STEELE. Lincoln: University of Nebraska Press, 1961.

Reviewed in PQ 41:233-34; COLLEGE ENGLISH 23:513; JEGP 41:648-50.

2207. Landa, Louis A., and James Edward Tobin. JONATHAN SWIFT: A LIST OF CRITICAL STUDIES PUBLISHED FROM 1895 TO 1945. New York: Cosmopolitan Science and Art Service Co., 1945.

2208. Paul, Herbert. "The Prince of Journalists." NC, 47 (1900), 73-87.

2209. Quintana, Ricardo. SWIFT: AN INTRODUCTION. London: Oxford University Press, 1955.

2210. Stathis, James J. A BIBLIOGRAPHY OF SWIFT STUDIES, 1945-1965. Nashville, Tenn.: Vanderbilt University Press, 1967.

Reviewed in PQ 47:436-38.

2211. Swift, Jonathan. BICKERSTAFF PAPERS AND PAMPHLETS ON THE CHURCH. Ed. Herbert Davis. Prose Works, vol. II. Oxford: Blackwell, 1939.

Contains the contributions to the TATLER, SPECTATOR, and Harrison's TATLER, attributed to him, or containing hints furnished by him.

2212. Teerink, H. A BIBLIOGRAPHY OF THE WRITINGS OF JONATHAN SWIFT. 2nd ed., rev. and corr. Ed. Arthur H. Scouten. Philadelphia: University of Pennsylvania Press, 1963.

Reviewed in PQ 43:394-96; COLLEGE ENGLISH 25:477; BOOK COLLECTOR 13:379-80.

2213. Voigt, Milton. SWIFT AND THE TWENTIETH CENTURY. Detroit: Wayne State University Press, 1964.

A summary of twentieth-century scholarship. Reviewed in ELN 1:302-3; N&Q 209:314-17; PQ 44:373-75; RES 16:208-10.

2214. Wilson, T.G. "Swift: The Prince of Journalists." DUBLIN MAGAZINE, 6, no. 3 (1967), 46-73.

SWINBURNE, ALGERNON C.

See Nos. 1293, 1305, 1618, and 1622.

TALFOURD, THOMAS NOON

See also Nos. 1255 and 2119.

2215. Coles, William A. "Thomas Noon Talfourd on Byron and the Imagination." KSJ, (1960), 99-113.

2216. Ward, William S. "An Early Champion of Wordsworth: Thomas Noon Talfourd." PMLA, 68 (1953), 992-1000.

TAYLOR, JOHN

See No. 1094.

TEMPLE, SIR WILLIAM

See No. 903.

TENNYSON, ALFRED

See also Nos. 538, 1239, 1374, and 1521.

2217. Paden, W.D. "Tennyson and the Reviewers (1829-1835)." STUDIES IN ENGLISH IN HONOR OF RAPHAEL DORMAN O'LEARY AND SELDEN LINCOLN WITCOMB. Bulletin of the University of Kansas, Humanistic Studies, no. 4. Lawrence: University of Kansas Press, 1940. Pp. 15-39.

2218. Shannon, Edgar F., Jr. "Tennyson and the Reviewers, 1830-1842." PMLA, 58 (1943), 181-94.

2219. ______. TENNYSON AND THE REVIEWERS: A STUDY OF HIS LITERARY REPUTATION AND THE INFLUENCE OF THE CRITICS UPON HIS POETRY, 1827-1851. Cambridge, Mass.: Harvard University Press, 1952.

2220. Vent, Maryanne C. "Tennyson's IDYLLS OF THE KING and the Victorian Periodical Press." DAI, 32 (1971), 2071A.

THACKERAY, WILLIAM MAKEPEACE

See also Nos. 844, 845, 846, 1212, 1220, and 1366.

2221. Cohen, J.A.W. "Thackeray's Reviewers." TLS, 22 March 1947, p. 127.

THEOBALD, LEWIS

See Nos. 600 and 601.

THOMPSON, JAMES

See also No. 1330.

2222. Werkmeister, Lucyle. "Thompson and the London Daily Press 1789-97." MP, 62 (1965), 237-40.

Quotes references during this period.

THOMS, W.J.

See also No. 1276.

THORNTON, BONNELL

See also No. 420.

2223. Liebert, Herman W. "Whose Book? An Exercise in Detection." YALE UNIVERSITY LIBRARY GAZETTE, 28 (1953), 71-74.

Identifies Thornton as the author of three reviews published in the PUBLIC ADVERTISER, 1764, of Charles Churchill's poems.

TICKELL, THOMAS

See also No. 1549.

2224. Tickell, Richard Eustace. THOMAS TICKELL AND THE EIGHTEENTH CENTURY POETS (1685-1740). CONTAINING NUMEROUS LETTERS AND POEMS HITHERTO UNPUBLISHED. London: Constable, 1931.

TILLOTSON, REV. JOHN

See No. 984.

TONSON, JACOB

See also No. 1511.

2225. Geduld, Harry M. PRINCE OF PUBLISHERS: A STUDY OF THE WORK AND CAREER OF JACOB TONSON. Indiana University Publications, Humanities Series, no. 66. Bloomington: Indiana University Press, 1969.

Reviewed briefly in PQ, 49:293.

2226. Lynch, Kathleen M. JACOB TONSON: KIT-CAT PUBLISHER. Knoxville: University of Tennessee Press, 1971.

Reviewed in PQ 51:513; JQ 48:778.

2227. Papali, G.F. JACOB TONSON, PUBLISHER: HIS LIFE AND WORK (1656-1736). Auckland: Tonson Publishing House, 1968.

Reviewed briefly in PQ 49:293.

TOPHAM, EDWARD

2228. Morison, Stanley. "Captain Edward Topham." COLOPHON, pt. vi, 1931.

TOPLADY, AUGUSTUS M.

2229. Wright, Thomas. AUGUSTUS M. TOPLADY AND CONTEMPORARY HYMN-WRITERS. The Lives of the British Hymn Writers: Being Personal Memoirs Derived Largely from Unpublished Materials, vol. II. London: Farncombe & Son, 1911.

TROLLOPE, ANTHONY

See Nos. 487, 797, 1308, 1619, and 1695.

TUTCHIN, JOHN

See No. 1925.

VANSOMMER, JOHN

See No. 583.

VERSCHOYLE, JOHN

See No. 836.

WALFORD, EDWARD

See No. 1286.

WALPOLE, ROBERT

See also Nos. 238, 311, and 1074.

2230. Largmann, Malcolm Gerard. "The Political Image of Sir Robert Walpole Created by Satire in the Opposition Press, 1731-1742." DA, 27 (1966), 181A-82A.

WALSH, WILLIAM

See No. 1816.

WALSINGHAM, F.

See No. 847.

WARD, EDWARD [NED]

See also LONDON SPY (chapter 3) and Nos. 1023, 1740, 1868, and 1925.

2231. Allen, Robert. "Ned Ward and THE WEEKLY COMEDY." HARVARD STUDIES AND NOTES IN PHILOLOGY AND LITERATURE, 17 (1935), 1-13.

Analyzes the two journals called the WEEKLY COMEDY (1699 and 1707-8) and THE HUMOURS OF A COFFEE-HOUSE (1707).

2232. Bourne, Ruth. "The Wooden World Dissected." PACIFIC HISTORICAL RECORD, 14 (1945), 326-34.

2233. Cameron, W.J. "Bibliography of Ned Ward (1667-1731)." N&Q, 198 (1953), 284-86.

2234. Jones, Claude E. "Short-Title Checklist of Works Attributed to Edward Ward (1667-1731)." N&Q, 190 (1946), 135-39.

2235. Troyer, Howard William. "No Mean Talent: A Study of the Life and Writings of Edward Ward (1667-1731)." SUMMARIES OF DOCTORAL DISSERTATIONS, UNIVERSITY OF WISCONSIN, 4 (1938-39), 243-44.

2236. _____. NED WARD OF GRUBSTREET: A STUDY OF SUB-LITERARY LONDON IN THE EIGHTEENTH CENTURY. Cambridge, Mass.: Harvard University Press, 1946.

Reviewed in QUEEN'S QUARTERLY 53:127-28; PQ 26:142-43.

2237. Ward, S.H. "The Works of Edward Ward." N&Q, 198 (1953), 436-38.

WARD, WILLIAM G.

See No. 717.

WARTON, JOSEPH

See No. 783.

WATSON, JAMES

2238. Couper, W.J. "James Watson, King's Printer." SCOTTISH HISTORI-

CAL REVIEW, 7 (1910), 244-62.

2239. ______. WATSON'S PREFACE TO THE 'HISTORY OF PRINTING,' 1713. Edinburgh: Darien Press, 1913.

2240. Cowan, William. "The Holyrood Press, 1686-1688." PUBLICATIONS OF THE EDINBURGH BIBLIOGRAPHICAL SOCIETY, 6 (1902), 83-100.

2241. Gibb, John S. "James Watson, Printer: Notes of his Life and Work." PUBLICATIONS OF THE EDINBURGH BIBLIOGRAPHICAL SOCIETY, 1, ii (1890), 1-8.

2242. Tawse, George. "James Watson--the Edinburgh Printer." BIBLIOGRAPHER, 2 (1882), 124-30.

WEAVER, JOHN

See No. 1564.

WESLEY, JOHN

See also ARMINIAN MAGAZINE and CHRISTIAN'S AMUSEMENT (chapter 3).

2243. Herbert, Thomas Walter. JOHN WESLEY AS EDITOR AND AUTHOR. Princeton Studies in English, no. 17. Princeton, N.J.: Princeton University Press, 1940.

WHARTON, PHILIP

See No. 1709.

WHATELEY, RICHARD, ARCHBISHOP

See No. 1400.

WILKES, JOHN

See also NORTH BRITON (chapter 3) and No. 271.

2244. Bredvold, Louis I. THE CONTRIBUTIONS OF JOHN WILKES TO THE 'GAZETTE LITTERAIRE DE L'EUROPE.' University of Michigan Contributions in Modern Philology, no. 15. [Ann Arbor]: University of

Michigan Press, 1950.

Identifies Wilkes's critical contributions, including two articles long attributed to Voltaire, and disposes of Wilkes's pretensions as a critic.

2245. Cordasco, Francesco. "Did John Wilkes Correct the MS. of Junius's Letters? A Note on John Almon's Edition (1806)." N&Q, 196 (1951), 300-301.

2246. [Dilke, Charles Wentworth]. "John Wilkes." ATHENAEUM, 3 January 1852, pp. 7-10; 10 January 1852, pp. 46-49.

Reprinted in Dilke's PAPERS OF A CRITIC (1875), II, 229-64.

2247. Lucas, Reginald. "Wilkes." LORD NORTH, SECOND EARL OF GUILFORD, K.G., 1732. 2 vols. London: Arthur L. Humphreys, 1913. I, 76-109.

2248. Quennell, Peter. "John Wilkes." THE PROFANE VIRTUES: FOUR STUDIES OF THE EIGHTEENTH CENTURY. New York: Viking Press, 1945. Pp. 173-218.

Published in England under the title FOUR PORTRAITS.

2249. Rhodon. "Anonymous Works Relating to John Wilkes " N&Q 164 (1933), 208-9.

2250. ______. "Two Letters of John Wilkes." N&Q, 166 (1934), 272-73.

2251. Sherrard, O.A. A LIFE OF JOHN WILKES. London: George Allen & Unwin, 1930.

See pages 72-106 for a summary of Wilkes' connection with the NORTH BRITON and of the action of the government against him.

2252. Thomas, Peter D.G. "John Wilkes and the Freedom of the Press (1771)." BIHR 33 (1960), 86-89.

WILLIS, W.H.

See No. 1000.

WILSON, JOHN FORBES

See BLACKWOOD'S MAGAZINE (chapter 3) and No. 209.

WINSTON, JAMES

See THEATRIC TOURIST (chapter 3).

WOLLSTONECRAFT, MARY

See Nos. 430, 432, 433, and 784.

WORDSWORTH, WILLIAM

See also Nos. 386, 542, 860, 863, 1228, 1229, 1527, 1769, and 2216.

2253. Ames, Alfred C. "Contemporary Defense of Wordsworth's 'Pedlar.'" MLN, 63 (1948), 543-45.

2254. Barry, Joseph A.A. "The First Review of Wordsworth's Poetry." MLN, 44 (1929), 299-302.

2255. McGillivray, James R. "A Possible First Review of Wordsworth's Poetry." MLN, 45 (1930), 387-88.

2256. Poole, W.F. "Bibliography of Review and Magazine Articles in Criticism of Wordsworth." TRANSACTIONS OF THE WORDSWORTH SOCIETY, no. 5 (1883?), pp. 95-100.

2257. Woof, R.S., "Wordsworth's Poetry and Stuart's Newspapers: 1797-1803." SB, 15 (1962), 149-89.

An annotated check-list of poems by Wordsworth which appeared in the MORNING POST or the COURIER.

WORTLEY, EDWARD

See No. 1646.

YONGE, SIR WILLIAM

See No. 966.

Chapter 5
PLACES

ABERDEEN

2258. Bulloch, J. Malcolm. "A Bibliography of Local Periodical Literature." SN&Q, 1 (1887-88), 3-5, 131, 147-50.

ARBROATH

See No. 480.

CAMBRIDGE

See also No. 1634.

2259. Fenton, W.A. "Cambridge Periodicals, 1750-1931." CAMBRIDGE PUBLIC LIBRARY RECORD, 3 (1931), 50-60, 85-89, 115-27.

CORK

2260. Dix, E.R. McC. "Printing in Cork in the First Quarter of the Eighteenth Century (1701-1725)." PROCEEDINGS OF THE ROYAL IRISH ACADEMY, 36, sec. C, 10-14.

DUBLIN

2261. Dix, E.R. McC. "The Earliest Periodical Journals Published in Dublin." PROCEEDINGS OF THE ROYAL IRISH ACADEMY, 6 (1900), 33-35.

2262. ______. "Rare Ephemeral Magazines of the Eighteenth Century." IRISH BOOK LOVER, 1 (1910), 71-73.

2263. ______. "Some Rare Dublin Magazines of the Eighteenth Century."

IRISH BOOK LOVER, 8 (1917), 1-3, 25-28.

2264. Lawrence, W.J. "Some Old Dublin Theatrical Journals." IRISH BOOK LOVER, 14 (1924), 115-16, 130-32.

2265. "Some Rare Dublin Periodicals." IRISH BOOK LOVER, 12 (1921), 104-6.

Notes on the British Museum collection of eighteenth-century Irish periodicals.

DUNDEE

2266. Bushnell, George H. "The Dundee Book Trade in the 18th Century." SN&Q, 6 (1928), 136-37.

Accounts of printers and booksellers who were connected with editing and publishing periodicals and newspapers.

2267. C.,W.J. "The Earliest Dundee Periodical." SN&Q, 7 (1906), 186.

Discusses the evidence for the claim of the existence of the DUNDEE MAGAZINE and the DUNDEE WEEKLY INTELLIGENCER in the 1750s.

2268. Lamb, Alexander C. "Bibliography of Dundee Periodical Literature." SN&Q, 3 (1889), 97-100.

See also W.J.C. in SN&Q, 7 (1906), 134.

EDINBURGH

2269. Anderson, P.J. "Bibliography of Edinburgh University Periodicals." SN&Q, 2 (1900), 89.

2270. Couper, W.J. "A Bibliography of Edinburgh Periodical Literature." SN&Q, 2 (1900-1901), 25-27, 39, 56-58, 71, 168; 5 (1904), 167-68, 181-83; 6 (1904), 5-6, 21-23, 36-38, 52-53, 70-72, 85; 7 (1905-6), 87-89, 101-2, 123-24, 130-32, 165-66, 178-80; 8 (1906-7), 10-11, 35-39, 72-74, 107-9, 121-22, 150-51, 166-68, 179-81; 8 (1930), 190-93, 207-9, 229-32; 9 (1931), 3-6, 30-32, 47-50, 65.

This bibliography continues the work started by Scott (No. 2273). The two series form the basis of Couper's EDINBURGH PERIODICAL PRESS (No. 2271). The notes which he published in the third series of SN&Q (1930-31) supplement this book.

2271. ______. THE EDINBURGH PERIODICAL PRESS. BEING A BIBLIO-

GRAPHICAL ACCOUNT OF THE NEWSPAPERS, JOURNALS AND MAGAZINES ISSUED IN EDINBURGH FROM THE EARLIEST TIMES TO 1800. 2 vols. Stirling: Eneas Mackay, 1908.

Volume I contains a long introduction and a critical bibliography for 1642-1711; volume II continues the bibliography to 1800.

2272. Norrie, William. EDINBURGH NEWSPAPERS PAST AND PRESENT. Earlston: Waverly Press, 1891.

Long notes on each paper listed.

2273. Scott, James W. "A Bibliography of Edinburgh Periodical Literature." SN&Q, 5 (1891-92), 20-21, 33-35, 51-53, 71-73, 84-87, 102-6, 117-20, 132; 6 (1892-93), 70, 167-68.

The bibliography was continued by W.J. Couper (see No. 2270).

2274. _____. "Newspapers." N&Q, 6 (1888), 47.

For replies, see pages 112, 195-96.

ESSEX

See No. 1717.

GALWAY

2275. Dix, E.R. McC. "Printing in Galway, 1754-1820." IRISH BOOK LOVER, 2 (1910), 50-54.

GLASGOW

2276. Couper, W.J. "The Glasgow Periodical Press in the Eighteenth Century." RECORDS OF THE GLASGOW BIBLIOGRAPHICAL SOCIETY, 8 (1930), 99-135.

2277. Dale, Cragsley. "The Glasgow Periodical Press in the Eighteenth Century." SN&Q, 13 (1935), 165-68.

2278. [Duncan, W.J.] NOTICES AND DOCUMENTS ILLUSTRATIVE OF THE LITERARY HISTORY OF GLASGOW, DURING THE GREATER PART OF LAST CENTURY. Glasgow: Maitland Club, 1831.

See pages 5-9 for GLASGOW COURANT and GLASGOW JOURNAL.

2279. Tierney, J.H. EARLY GLASGOW NEWSPAPERS, PERIODICALS AND DIRECTORIES. [Glasgow: James Hedderwick & Sons, 1934].

"Read in an abridged form as a lecture to the Old Glasgow Club, on February 8th, 1934."

IRELAND

2280. "The First Irish Papers." IRISH BOOK LOVER, 4 (1912), 61.

Reprinted from the TIMES, no. 40,000. See also E.R. McC. Dix in this issue of IRISH BOOK LOVER (pages 97-98).

2281. Lang, W.J. "Irish Newspapers Wanted." N&Q, 166 (1934), 281.

2282. McDowell, R.B. "The Irish Government and the Provincial Press." HERMATHENA, no. 53 (1939), pp. 138-47.

Deals with the BELFAST NEWS-LETTER, NORTHERN STAR, CORK GAZETTE, and other journals at the end of the eighteenth century.

2283. Madden, Richard Robert. THE HISTORY OF IRISH PERIODICAL LITERATURE, FROM THE END OF THE 17TH TO THE MIDDLE OF THE 19TH CENTURY. 2 vols. London: 1867.

2284. Munter, R.L. A HAND-LIST OF IRISH NEWSPAPERS, 1685-1750. Cambridge Bibliographical Society Monographs, no. 4. London: Bowes & Bowes, 1960.

2285. ______. THE HISTORY OF THE IRISH NEWSPAPER, 1685-1760. Cambridge: At the University Press, 1967.

2286. Power, John. LIST OF IRISH PERIODICAL PUBLICATIONS (CHIEFLY LITERARY) FROM 1729 TO THE PRESENT TIME. London: Printed for Private Distribution Only, 1866.

Reprinted with additions and corrections from N&Q, 3, 24 March 1866 and 21, 28 April 1866, and IRISH LITERARY INQUIRER, No. iv, 1866.

LEEDS

See No. 320.

LONDON

2287. Bourne, H.R. Fox. "Some Newspaper Pioneers." GENTLEMAN'S MAGAZINE, 263 (1887), 224-44.

London papers and their editors in the last quarter of the eighteenth century.

2288. L.,P. "London Newspapers." N&Q, 5 (1906), 10.

A bibliography of information on eighteenth-century London newspapers. Also in this issue of N&Q, see J. Holden MacMichael (pages 10-11), Ralph Thomas (pages 70-71), J.H. and G.L. Apperson (page 71).

2289. "The London Daily Press." WESTMINSTER REVIEW, 64 (1955), 258-73.

Review-article on Hunt's THE FOURTH ESTATE and THE TIMES, 1788-1855.

2290. Savage, James. AN ACCOUNT OF THE LONDON DAILY NEWSPAPERS, AND THE MANNER IN WHICH THEY ARE CONDUCTED. London: Printed for the author by B.R. Howlett, [1811].

The "account" deals with those papers in existence at the date of writing, but the information about the way news is collected, the typographical make-up of the papers, and the editorial policies and political affiliations of the various newspapers may well apply to the late eighteenth century. An appendix gives specimen pages from a model advertisement account book.

2291. Sper, Felix. THE PERIODICAL PRESS OF LONDON THEATRICAL AND LITERARY (EXCLUDING THE DAILY NEWSPAPER) 1800-1830. Useful Reference Series, no. 60. Boston: F.W. Faxon, 1937.

Titles grouped under five divisions: theatrical, literary-theatrical, literary-domestic, literary-miscellaneous, literary.

MANCHESTER

See Nos. 320 and 1256.

NORWICH

2292. Fawcett, Trevor. "Early Norwich Newspapers." N&Q, 19 (1972), 63-65.

OXFORD

See also Nos. 284 and 913.

2293. Hudson, Derek. "Three Hundred Years of University Journalism." OXFORD, 7 (1940), 54-64.

Includes brief comment on MERCURIUS AULICUS, MERCURIUS ACADEMICUS, MERCURIUS RUSTICUS, MERCURIUS AQUATICUS, OXFORD GAZETTE, MERCURIUS OXONIENSIS, TERRAE FILIUS, STUDENT, OXFORD MAGAZINE, OLLA PODRIDA, LOITERER, and BIRCH.

2294. Madan, Falconer. "Periodicals, 1641-50"; "Oxford Periodicals, 1651-80." OXFORD BOOKS, A BIBLIOGRAPHY OF PRINTED WORKS RELATING TO THE UNIVERSITY AND CITY OF OXFORD. 3 vols. Oxford: Clarendon Press, 1912-31. II, 491-99; II, 391-94.

Valuable bibliographic notes on the MERCURIUS AULICUS and the OXFORD GAZETTE.

2295. Symon, J.D. "The Earlier Oxford Magazines." OXFORD AND CAMBRIDGE REVIEW, no. 13 (1911), pp. 39-57.

SCOTLAND

See also No. 929.

2296. A.,R. "First Newspaper in Scotland; ABERDEEN JOURNAL." N&Q, 1 (1908), 139.

See also J.B.T. (page 144).

2297. Cockburn, J.D. "Beginnings of the Scottish Newspaper Press." SCOTTISH REVIEW, 18 (1891), 366-77; 21 (1893), 399-419.

Bibliography (pages 415-19) includes a chronological list of periodicals, 1652-1799.

2298. Craig, Mary Elizabeth. THE SCOTTISH PERIODICAL PRESS, 1750-1789. Edinburgh: Oliver and Boyd, 1931.

2299. "The Newspaper Press of Scotland: The Edinburgh Newspapers; The Provincial Papers." FRASER'S MAGAZINE, 17 (1838), 559-71; 18 (1838), 75-85, 201-9.

2300. Sinclair, G.A. "Periodical Literature of the Eighteenth Century."

SCOTTISH HISTORICAL REVIEW, 2 (1905), 136-49.

2301. Woodhouselee, Alexander Fraser Tytler. MEMOIRS OF THE LIFE AND WRITINGS OF THE HONOURABLE HENRY HOME OF KAMES. 2 vols. Edinburgh: W. Creech, 1807. I, 226-42.

Notes on Scottish periodicals, particularly the TATLER (1711) and the EDINBURGH REVIEW (1755).

SHEFFIELD

See No. 320.

STRATFORD

See No. 1633.

INDEX OF AUTHORS

This index is alphabetized letter-by-letter and numbers refer to entry numbers. It includes authors, editors, compilers, illustrators of importance, and the contributors of introductions and forewords.

A

Index of Authors

B

C

D

G

H

N

O

P

Q

R

S

INDEX OF PERIODICALS

This index is alphabetized letter-by-letter and numbers refer to page numbers. In each case, the reader is referred to the main entry in chapter 3. Cross-references in chapter 3 will lead to secondary entries.

A

B

M

N

O

P

Q

R

S

Index of Periodicals

INDEX OF PERSONS

This index is alphabetized letter-by-letter and numbers refer to page numbers. In each case, the reader is referred to the main entry for the person in chapter 4. Cross-references in chapter 4 will lead to secondary entries.

A

B

Index of Persons

V

W

Y

INDEX OF PLACES

This index is alphabetized letter-by-letter and numbers refer to page numbers. In each case, the reader is referred to the main entry in chapter 5. Cross-references in chapter 5 will lead to secondary entries.